HOSPITALITY FRONT OFFICE AND REVENUE MANAGEMENT

Jay Prakash Kant

AMAN PUBLICATIONS
NEW DELHI

Published by
Rajiv Jain for Aman Publications
LG-4A, Ganpati Bhawan,
4675-B/21, Ansari Road,
Darya Ganj, Delhi-110002
E-mail: sshjbs@yahoo.com

First Edition 2018

Hospitality Front Office and Revenue Management

ISBN–978-81-8204-099-1

SOLE DISTRIBUTOR
JINDAL BOOK SERVICES
LG-4A, Ganpati Bhawan,
4675-B/21, Ansari Road,
Darya Ganj, Delhi-110002

Jacket Designed by :
S.M. Graphics

Typesetting by :
J.K. Graphics (India)
97177-82194, 93125-57182

Printed by:
Balaji Offest, Shahdara, Delhi-32 (India)
92127-19107

HOSPITALITY FRONT OFFICE AND REVENUE MANAGEMENT

CONTENTS

SECTION 3

PREFACE

"The Secret of business is to know something that nobody else knows"
Aristotle Onassis

"A business that makes nothing but Money is a poor business"
Henry Ford

"Sales are contingent upon the attitude of the salesman, not the attitude of prospect"
W. Clement Stone

Incomes, Profit, Business and Management are some of the terms which are easier said than done. Every aspect of a good business and life now depends upon the Profits and losses, earned and degraded by responsible personnel.

An important theory and fact quoted by **W. Edwards Deming** quoted as "Profit in business comes from repeat customers, customers that boast about your project or service, and that bring friends with them." Stresses upon the importance of methods about planned operations and department management for the expansion and promotion of a business which I have tried to speak and implement through this book. I wish and hope with this book student may learn study and become better managers of their life and Job. Through this book I have endeavored the prime of my efforts to inkling and acknowledge the reader to the notions and concepts of department and business management easily and effectively, this book has been compiled after a thorough research of hospitality and hotel industry.

This book complies studies according to the syllabus of 'Front Office Operations' & 'Front Office Department Management' provided by **National Council of Hotel Management and Catering Technology (NCHMCT)**, with the study material strictly foot held upon **NCHMCT** curriculum I hope to find it's appointment in many other professional courses too.

This book covers wide aspects and pro et contra of the concerned subjects, and probably falls on the plot rightly. And finally through the columns of this book I, Jay Prakash Kant would dote on to educate and empower the students and future professionals with generality of **Business & Management**.

ACKNOWLEDGMENT

I would like to mention certain people and organizations who have either directly or indirectly contributed towards this book.

First and foremost, I would like to mention **Mr. T.K. Razdan** honorable Principal **Chandigarh Institute Of Hotel Management and Catering Technology, CIHMCT, Chandigarh** for having his fidelity in me and constantly providing me with his guidance and support in writing this book.

Also heartiest thanks to **Mr. L.K. Gangully** honorable Director(A&F) & Member Secretary And **Mr. Satvir Singh** honorable Director Studies , **National Council of Hotel Management & Catering Technology, Noida** both are my guide and an able mentor; with their constant blessings and support, they continues to inspire me with their benign presence.

I would like to thank my learning and educating institution of **IHM, Meerut**, from where I have learnt and went on to grow as a professional.

I am grateful to professionals in the industry and academics who have in some ways influenced the development of this book.

Last but not the least; I would like to thank my parents **Shri A.P. Kant** and **Smt. Rajwati Kant** for their unconditional support to make me empowered and given me education and made me worthwhile to write a book which would benefit many, my wife **Saroj Prakash Kant** who has given her fullest support in this venture of mine and shown immense patience while I sat late nights to compile this work and my children **Pihu & Priyan,** the fortune of my life who have been a great support and cheered me up on every instance and added humor in moments of fragile stress.

My sincere thanks to **Aman Publications** who have given me their valuable time and have considered my capable efforts to help me provide the platform for my book to publish and distribute under their esteemed and famed label.

I would also like to thank my students at **CIHMCT,** Chandigarh specially **Bhavya Sharma** with a great sense of gratitude for being the primary inspiration in compilation of this book, and for their valuable inputs at various stages of my learning and development.

Jay Prakash Kant

SECTION 1

1

INTRODUCTION TO TOURISM

- SIGNIFICANCE OF TOURISM
- GROWTH OF TOURISM INDUSTRY
- HIGHLIGHTS OF INDIAN TOURISM
- TYPES OF TOURISM
- QUESTIONNAIRE

Tourism is travel for recreational, leisure, or purposes, usually of a limited duration. Tourism is commonly associated business with transnational travel, but may also refer to travel to another location within the same country.

The World Tourism Organization defines tourists as people "traveling to and staying in places outside their usual environment for not more than one consecutive year for leisure, business and other purposes".

Tourism has become a popular global leisure activity. Tourism can be domestic or international, and international tourism has both incoming and outgoing implications on a country's balance of payments. Today, tourism is major source of income for many countries, and affects the economy of both the source and host countries, in some cases it is of vital importance.

SIGNIFICANCE OF TOURISM

Tourism is an important, even vital, source of income for many countries. Its importance was recognized in the *Manila Declaration on World Tourism of 1980* as "an activity essential to the life of nations because of its direct effects on the social, cultural, educational, and economic sectors of national societies and on their international relations."

Tourism brings in large amounts of income into a local economy in the form of payment for goods and services needed by tourists, accounting for 30% of the world's trade of services, and 6% of overall exports of goods and services.[5] It also creates opportunities for employment in the service sector of the economy associated with tourism.

The service industries which benefit from tourism include transportation services, such as airlines, cruise ships, and taxicabs; hospitality services, such as accommodations, including hotels and resorts; and entertainment venues, such as amusement parks, casinos, shopping malls, music venues, and theatres. This is in addition to goods bought by tourists, including souvenirs, clothing and other supplies.

GROWTH OF TOURISM IN INDIA AND FUTURE OF INDIAN TOURISM INDUSTRY

Tourism in India is expanding every year. According to the estimates of Ministry of Tourism, Government of India, the projected figures for the foreign tourist visiting India during the year 2010 will increase to 10 millions. India is one of the most prospective markets for tourism in the world. There are so many India travel packages offered by India Tourism for foreigners all over India. In addition many private operators also offer many package deals. Tourists can travel to the places of historical and religious importance, explore cultural heritage, natural beauty and enjoy many outdoor sports activities like skiing in snow or mountaineering etc., in natural settings. The local state departments of tourism in India and many private organizations also offer several India travel packages package to places worth visiting.

India is a charming place for its various destinations with numerous captivating natural scenes and culture. Latest trends of tourism in India show India as fast emerging and highly ranked tourist place of South East Asia.

There has been a tremendous growth in tourism in India because of the policies of the government and support from all levels. There are recently many events that have taken place or coming up in the futures, which are a big catalyst for prompting tourism in India. The international sports events like 20/20 IPL Cricket matches, upcoming Commonwealth Games are also helping the tourism industry in India and it will prosper to great heights and standards in the near future.

The remarkable growth in Indian Tourism market, which has identically benefited many support industries like aviation, transport, medical tourism, hotel and sports. The year 2008 had witnessed an enormous increase in the eco tourism in India In addition the government has come up with a new idea of India tourism named as "Rural Tourism", which is very successful in promoting tourism by offering exclusive India travel packages for rural tourism.

India had hosted Asian Games long back that had brought many developments in India and, upgraded the quality of tourism in India and attracted many tourists to India from all over the world. Common Wealth Games 2010, being organized in Delhi, capital of India, will give a pioneer opportunity to tourism in India. The industry can gain a lot of business by coming up with various travel packages for attraction and benefit of tourists. In 2010, it a estimated that over 3.5 million tourist will be visiting India to witness the Common wealth Games scheduled in Oct 2010 at Delhi. It is the very important event and Indian tourism industry has to plan, organize and cater to the needs of such a big rush of foreign tourists that will depend on the fights, transport, hotel bookings and for their travel itineraries, visas and other facilities. Many agencies are preparing to handle this tourist rush so that visitors and players feel it homely, comfortably and safe.

There are indications that the growth of tourism in India will be very steep in the next couple of years. The Indian share of tourist will augment about 1.5 % in 2010. India tourism industry is going to earn maximum business from tourist visiting Agra, Andhra Pradesh, Kerala, Tamil Nadu and Rajasthan where maximum numbers of tourists are expected.

India's tourism industry is experiencing a strong period of growth, driven by the burgeoning Indian middle class, growth in high spending foreign tourists, and coordinated government campaigns to promote 'Incredible India'.

The tourism industry in India is substantial and vibrant, and the country is fast becoming a major global destination. India's travel and tourism industry is one of them most profitable industries in the country, and also credited with contributing a substantial amount of foreign exchange. This is illustrated by the fact that during 2006, four million tourists visited India and spent US $8.9 billion.

Several reasons are cited for the growth and prosperity of India's travel and tourism industry. Economic growth has added millions annually to the ranks of India's middle class, a group that is driving domestic tourism growth. Disposable income in India has grown by 10.11% annually from 2001-2006, and much of that is being spent on travel.

Thanks in part to its booming IT and outsourcing industry a growing number of business trips are made by foreigners to India, who will often add a weekend break or longer holiday to their trip. Foreign tourists spend more in India than almost any other country worldwide. Tourist arrivals are projected to increase by over 22% per year through till 2010, with a 33% increase in foreign exchange earnings recorded in 2004.

The Tourism Ministry has also played an important role in the development of the industry, initiating advertising campaigns such as the 'Incredible India' campaign, which promoted India's culture and tourist attractions in a fresh and memorable way. The campaign helped create a colorful image of India in the minds of consumers all over the world, and has directly led to an increase in the interest among tourists.

The tourism industry has helped growth in other sectors as diverse as horticulture, handicrafts, agriculture, construction and even poultry.

Both directly and indirectly, increased tourism in India has created jobs in a variety of related sectors. The numbers tell the story: almost 20 million people are now working in the India's tourism industry.

India's governmental bodies have also made a significant impact in tourism by requiring that each and every state of India have a corporation to administer support issues related to tourism.

HIGHLIGHTS OF INDIAN TOURISM.

The following are the scope and highlights of Indian tourism:

- Increase in GDPC making the tourism industry a unifying force
- Helping to preserve, retain and enrich our cultural heritages
- Increase in international trade
- Giving more in health care management
- Offering more tourism education
- Growth in healthcare management
- Progress in health care industries
- Multi-socio cultural activities
- Growth in hotel industry
- Expansion in transport[both urban and rural], Air Travel and shipping
- Focus on rural tourism
- Motivating private sectors top attract more tourists

TYPES OF TOURISM

Ecotourism

Ecotourism, also known as ecological tourism, is responsible travel to fragile, pristine, and usually protected areas that strives to be low impact and (often) small scale. It helps educate the traveler; provides funds for conservation; directly benefits the economic development and political empowerment of local communities; and fosters respect for different cultures and for human rights.

Take only memories and leave only footprints are a very common slogan in protected areas. Tourist destinations are shifting to low carbon emissions following the trend of visitors more focused in being environmental responsible adopting a sustainable behavior.

Medical Tourism

When there is a significant price difference between countries for a given medical procedure, particularly in Southeast Asia, India, Eastern Europe and where there are different regulatory regimes, in relation to particular medical procedures (e.g. dentistry), traveling to take advantage of the price or regulatory differences is often referred to as "medical tourism".

Educational Tourism

Educational tourism developed, because of the growing popularity of teaching and learning of knowledge and the enhancing of technical competency outside of the classroom environment. In educational tourism, the main focus of the tour or leisure activity includes visiting another country to learn about the culture Study Tours, or to work and apply skills learned inside the classroom in a different environment, such as in the International Practicum Training Program.

Creative Tourism

Creative tourism has existed as a form of cultural tourism, since the early beginnings of tourism itself. Its European roots date back to the time of the Grand Tour, which saw the sons of aristocratic families traveling for the purpose of mostly interactive, educational experiences.

They have defined "creative tourism" as tourism related to the active participation of travelers in the culture of the host community, through interactive workshops and informal learning experiences.

Meanwhile, the concept of creative tourism has been picked up by high-profile organizations such as UNESCO, who through the Creative Cities Network, have endorsed creative tourism as an engaged, authentic experience that promotes an active understanding of the specific cultural features of a place.

More recently, creative tourism has gained popularity as a form of cultural tourism, drawing on active participation by travelers in the culture of the host communities they visit. Several countries offer examples of this type of tourism development, including the United Kingdom, Austria, France, the Bahamas, Jamaica, Spain, Italy and New Zealand.

The growing interest of tourists in this new way to discover a culture regards particularly the operators and branding managers, attentive to the possibility of attracting a quality tourism, highlighting the intangible heritage (craft workshops, cooking classes, etc.) and optimizing the use of existing infrastructure (for example, through the rent of halls and auditorium).

Dark Tourism

One emerging area of special interest has been identified by Lennon and Foley (2000) as "dark" tourism. This type of tourism involves visits to "dark" sites, such as battlegrounds, scenes of horrific crimes or acts of genocide, for example: concentration camps. Dark tourism remains a small niche market, driven by varied motivations, such as mourning, remembrance, education, macabre curiosity or even entertainment. Its early origins are rooted in fairgrounds and medieval fairs.

Doom Tourism

Also known as "Tourism of Doom," or "Last Chance Tourism" this emerging trend involves traveling to places that are environmentally or otherwise threatened (such as the ice caps of Mount Kilimanjaro, the melting glaciers of Patagonia, or the coral of the Great Barrier Reef) before it is too late. Identified by travel trade magazine Travel Age West editor-in-chief Kenneth Shapiro in 2007 and later explored in The New York Times, this type of tourism is believed to be on the rise. Some see the trend as related to sustainable tourism or ecotourism due to the fact that a number of these tourist destinations are considered threatened by environmental factors such as global warming, overpopulation or climate change. Others worry that travel to many of these threatened locations increases an individual's carbon footprint and only hastens problems threatened locations are already facing.

Amelia Glacier, South Patagonia, Chile

Sports Tourism

Since the late 1980s, sports tourism has become increasingly popular. Events such as rugby, Olympics, Commonwealth games, Asian Games and football World Cups have enabled specialist travel companies to gain official ticket allocation and then sell them in packages that include flights, hotels and excursions.

The focus on sport and spreading knowledge on the subject, especially more so recently, lead to the increase in the sport tourism. Most notably, the international event such as the Olympics caused a shift in focus in the audience who now realize the variety of sports that exist in the world. In the United States, one of the most popular sports that usually are focused on was Football. This popularity was increased through major events like the World Cups. In Asian countries, the numerous football events also increased the popularity of football. But, it was the Olympics that brought together the different sports that lead to the increase in sport tourism. The drastic interest increase in sports in general and not just one sport caught the attention of travel companies, who then began to sell flights in packages. Due to the low number of people who actually purchase these packages than predicted, the cost of these packages plummeted initially. As the number start to rise slightly the packages increased to regain the lost profits. With the certain economic state, the number of purchases decreased once again. The fluctuation in the

number of packages sold was solely dependent on the economic situation, therefore, most travel companies were forced to set aside the plan to execute the marketing of any new package features.

Growth of Tourism

The World Tourism Organization (UNWTO) forecasts that international tourism will continue growing at the average annual rate of 4%. With the advent of e-commerce, tourism products have become one of the most traded items on the internet. Tourism products and services have been made available through intermediaries, although tourism providers (hotels, airlines, etc.), including small-scale operators, can sell their services directly. This has put pressure on intermediaries from both on-line and traditional shops.

It has been suggested there is a strong correlation between tourism expenditure per capita and the degree to which countries play in the global context. Not only as a result of the important economic contribution of the tourism industry, but also as an indicator of the degree of confidence with which global citizens leverage the resources of the globe for the benefit of their local economies. This is why any projections of growth in tourism may serve as an indication of the relative influence that each country will exercise in the future.

There has been a limited amount of orbital space tourism, with only the Russian Space Agency providing transport to date. A 2010 report into space tourism anticipated that it could become a billion dollar market by 2030.

Role of Hotels in Promotion of Tourism

Hotels are an important component of the tourism product. They contribute in the overall tourism experience through the standards of facilities and services offered by them. With the aim of providing contemporary standards of facilities and services available in the hotels, the Ministry of Tourism has formulated a voluntary scheme for classification of operational hotels which will be applicable to the following categories:

Star Category Hotels: 5 Star Deluxe, 5 Star, 4 Star, 3 Star, 2 Star & 1 Star

Heritage Category Hotels: Heritage Grand, Heritage Classic & Heritage Basic

With now services and experiences becoming wide and vivid there are many activities and plans proposed and provided by the hotels under the same roof and brand name. Some famous hotels brands operate under a **parent company** some of them are mentioned as follows:

1. **EIH Limited**, under the aegis of The **Oberoi Group**, operates hotels and cruisers in five countries under the luxury 'Oberoi' and five-star 'Trident' brands. The Group is also engaged in flight catering, airport restaurants, travel and tour services, car rentals, project management and corporate air charters.

2. **ITC** was incorporated on August 24, 1910 under the name Imperial Tobacco Company of India Limited. As the Company's ownership progressively Indianised, the name of the Company was changed from Imperial Tobacco Company of India Limited to India Tobacco Company Limited in 1970 and then to I.T.C. Limited in 1974. In recognition of the Company's multi-business portfolio encompassing a wide range of businesses - Fast Moving Consumer Goods comprising Foods, Personal Care, Cigarettes and Cigars, Branded Apparel, Education and Stationery Products, Incense Sticks and Safety Matches, Hotels, Paperboards & Specialty Papers, Packaging, Agri-Business and Information Technology - the full stops in the Company's name were removed effective September 18, 2001. The Company now stands rechristened 'ITC Limited,'where 'ITC' is today no longer an acronym or an initialised form

   The Seventies witnessed the beginnings of a corporate transformation that would usher in momentous changes in the life of the Company. In 1975, the Company launched its Hotels business with the acquisition of a hotel in Chennai which was rechristened 'ITC-Welcome group Hotel Chola' (now renamed My Fortune, Chennai). The objective of ITC's entry into the hotels business was rooted in the concept of creating value for the nation. ITC chose the Hotels business for its potential to earn high levels of foreign exchange, create tourism infrastructure and generate large scale direct and indirect employment. Since then ITC's Hotels business has grown to occupy a position of leadership, with over 100 owned and managed properties spread across India under four brands namely **ITC Hotels - Luxury Collection, Welcome Hotels, Fortune Hotels and Welcome Heritage.**

   ITC Hotels recently took its first step toward international expansion with an upcoming super premium luxury hotel in Colombo, Sri Lanka. In addition, ITC Hotels also recently tied up with RP Group Hotels & Resorts to manage 5 hotels in Dubai and India under ITC Hotels' 5-star 'WelcomHotel' brand and the mid-market to upscale 'Fortune' brand.

3. **InterContinental Hotels Group** (**IHG**) was created in 2003 after Six Continents split into two daughter companies: Mitchells & Butlers PLC

to handle restaurant assets, and **IHG** to focus on soft drinks and hotels, including the Holiday Inn brand.

4. **Radisson Blu**, the brand name for **Radisson hotels** outside the United States, including those in Europe, Africa and Asia. These are operated by **Carlson Rezidor** Hotel Group which **Carlson** is the main stakeholder. **Park Plaza** and Country **Inn** share the same concern with Carlson Rezidor.
5. **Hyatt Hotels Corporation** is the parent entity of companies that own, operate, manage and franchise hotel, resort, residential and **vacation ownership properties** under the brand names Hyatt®, Park Hyatt®, Andaz™, Grand Hyatt®, Hyatt Regency®, Hyatt Place®, Hyatt Summerfield Suites™ and Hyatt Vacation Club®
6. The current company was founded in 1983, when the brand was bought from the previous owners to start **The Ritz-Carlton Hotel Company**, L.L.C., based in Boston, Massachusetts, which began expansion of the brand to other locations. The hotel company is today a subsidiary of **Marriott International.**
7. Canadian businessman Isadore **Sharp** founded Four Seasons in 1960. While a young architect working for his father, **Sharp** designed a motel for a family friend that succeeded and inspired him to try creating his own hotel in Toronto.
8. **Ramada International** is the company that owns, operates, and franchises hotels using the Ramada name outside of the United States and Canada. Ramada International was formerly owned by Marriott International, a competitor of Cendant, which owned Ramada in the United States and Canada. In 2004, however, Cendant purchased Ramada International from Marriott, which gives Cendant worldwide rights to the Ramada name. Despite now being under the same ownership, Ramada and Ramada International remained separate entities. In 2006, the hotels and hospitality divisions of Cendant were spun off into Wyndham Worldwide.
9. **Starwood Hotels and Resorts** was originally formed by the real estate investment firm Starwood Capital to take advantage of a tax break; at the time the company was known as Starwood Lodging. Initially, Starwood Lodging owned a number of hotels throughout North America, all under different brand names. The Westin Hotel Company was purchased in 1994 from **Aoki Corporation of Japan**. Starwood acquired the Sheraton, Four Points by Sheraton, and The Luxury Collection brands from ITT Sheraton in 1998.

Starwood Hotels & Resorts offers a unique range of brands-Sheraton, **Westin**, **Four Points by Sheraton**, **W Hotels**, **St. Regis**, The Luxury Collection, Le Méridien, and element and aloft-with a presence in the world's most exciting destinations.

10. **The Indian Hotels Company (IHCL)** and its subsidiaries, collectively known as **Taj Group**, is one of Asia's largest and finest groups of hotels. Incorporated by the founder of the **Tata group, Jamsetji Tata**, the company opened its first property, the Taj Mahal Palace, in Bombay in 1903.

    The Taj, a symbol of Indian hospitality, completed its centenary year in 2003.

    The Company was incorporated in 1902 and it opened its first hotel,

    The Taj Mahal Palace & Tower, Mumbai, in 1903. The Company then undertook major expansion of The Taj Mahal Palace & Tower, Mumbai by constructing an adjacent tower block and increasing the number of rooms from 225 to 565 rooms. With the completion of its initial public offering in the early 1970s, the Company began a long term programme of geographic expansion and development of new tourist destinations in India which led to its emergence as a leading hotel chain in India. From the 1970s to the present day, the Taj Group has played an important role in launching several of India's key tourist destinations, working in close association with the Indian Government.

QUESTIONNAIRE

1. What is tourism, explain its significance?
2. Enumerate the growth of tourism in Indian economy.
3. Name various types of tourism, explain any 3.
4. What is doom tourism?
5. Explain briefly about sports tourism.
6. What is WTO, explain its forecast.
7. What is dark tourism?
8. What are highlights and scope of Indian tourism?

2

CLASSIFICATION OF HOTELS

- ON THE BASIS OF STAR CATEGORY
- ON THE BASIS OF OWNERSHIP
- ON THE BASIS OF SIZE
- VARIOUS TYPES OF HOTELS
- GENERAL FEATURES
- QUESTIONNAIRE

INTRODUCTION

A **hotel** is an establishment that provides lodging paid on a short-term basis. The provision of basic accommodation, in times past, consisting only of a room with a bed, a cupboard, a small table and a washstand has largely been replaced by rooms with modern facilities, including en-suite bathrooms and air conditioning or climate control. Additional common features found in hotel rooms are a telephone, an alarm clock, a television, a safe, a mini-bar with snack foods and drinks, and facilities for making tea and coffee. Luxury features include bathrobes and slippers, a pillow menu, twin-sink vanities, and Jacuzzi bathtubs. Larger hotels may provide additional guest facilities such as a swimming pool, fitness center, business center, childcare, conference facilities and social function services.

Hotel rooms are usually numbered (or named in some smaller hotels and B&Bs) to allow guests to identify their room. Some hotels offer meals as part of a room and board arrangement. In the United Kingdom, a hotel is required by law to serve food and drinks to all guests within certain stated hours. In Japan, capsule hotels provide a minimized amount of room space and shared facilities

CLASSIFICATION OF HOTEL

A hotel provides many services and facilities to its guests, yet hotels may have different characteristics and assets. Most of the hotels do not fit into a single category because of the services provided by them.

Hotels are classified into several distinct categories to help a guest in selecting the right type of hotel matching his standard and requirement. Hotels are classified into SIZE, TARGET MARKETS, LEVEL OF SERVICE, & OWNERSHIP & AFFILIATION.

SIZE

Hotels are grouped in four categories i.e.

- Under 150 rooms
- 150 to 299 rooms,
- 300 to 600 rooms,
- More than 600 rooms,

TARGET MARKET

With the help of marketing research, tools, and strategies hotels seek to identify TARGET MARKET, these are defined as group of people that the hotel hopes to retain or attracts as guest. A hotel may targets many markets and can be classified according to the market they attempt to attract and serve. The most common types of properties based on target market include are:

- Commercial
- Airport
- Residential
- Resort
- Time share
- Bed and breakfast
- Casino
- Conference center
- Convention hotels
- Condominium.

COMMERCIAL HOTEL

Commercial hotels are situated in the heart of the city. Mostly the businessmen or commercial executives patronize these hotels. Guest facilities at these hotels are – complimentary newspaper, color TV with cable, E-mail, fax connection, car rental, airport pick up, coffee shop, bar, specialty restaurant, swimming pool, health club, room service, concierge, business center, conference room etc., length of stay in these hotels are from one day to few days.

AIRPORT HOTELS

These hotels are situated near the airport and are frequented by businessmen, airline passengers, layover passengers, crew members etc. facilities provided are similar to that of a commercial hotels but the only difference is that airport pick up is provided from hotel to airport and vice versa. Length of stay in these hotels is from few hours to few days.

RESIDENTIAL HOTELS

These hotels provide long term or permanent accommodation. Advance rent is collected while other charges are billed weekly. There may be a restaurant serving all types of cuisine and there will be laundry service. These hotels normally work on European plan. Recently these types of hotels are converted into cooperative hotels or condominiums. Length of stay is from a week to one or more months.

RESORT HOTEL

A resort may be located in the mountains, on an island, or in some other location away from crowded area. Most of the resort hotels provide extensive food and beverage, valet and room service for the vacationers. These hotels also provide special activities such as golf, tennis, horseback riding, nature hikes, sailing, skiing, swimming and dancing etc. resorts also try to be destination within a destination by providing wide range of services, facilities and activities giving a guests with many choices.

CASINO HOTELS

Hotels with gambling facilities are casino hotels. Although the guest rooms and F&B operations may be quite luxurious, but there function is secondary and supportive of casino operations. Similar to resort hotels these hotels also cater to leisure and vacation travelers. These hotels attract guests by promoting gambling. A recent trend in casino hotels now days are to provide a broad range of entertainment opportunities, spas, golf, tennis court. These hotels also have specialty restaurant. Length of stay is one week or more.

CONFERENCE CENTERS & CONVENTION CENTERS

Most of the hotels provides meeting space & they also offer overnight accommodations and because meetings are their focal point these centers place great emphasis on providing all services and equipment necessary to ensure a meetings success- technical production assistance, high quality audiovisual equipment, business center, flipchart, display chart and so forth. These centers also provides extensive leisure facilities like golf course, swimming pool, tennis court, fitness center, jogging track etc. Guest amenities may not be plentiful at conferences centers since these centers concentrate more on fulfilling the needs of meeting planners and organizers then on meeting the needs of program attendees.

Convention hotels are another segment of the lodging industry that has grown significantly in recent years. These hotels have 50,000 sq; feet or more of exhibit hall space plus ballroom and assortment of meeting rooms. These hotels also have sufficient no. of guestrooms to accommodate all the attendees of most conventions. These hotels are primarily directed towards business travelers and offer business services such as secretarial assistance, language translator, fax machines, computer room, tele-conference etc. convention hotels usually attract the convention market from state, national and international association and other corporate houses. (PG)

TIME SHARE AND CONDOMINIUM HOTELS

Time-share hotels are referred to as the vacation ownership hotels. The concept is that for a set period which may be one week or more in a year the person gets the right to enjoy stay and other facilities and services in an apartment are any other type of lodging in a tourist complex. It is like advance purchase of time in holiday accommodation. Here the purchaser has to pay a onetime capital sum and then annual contribution towards the maintenance of the property.

The fee usually covers services such as cleaning and maintenance of apartment and public areas, electricity, gas, water, etc. Avelon resorts. Sterling resorts, Mahindra holding etc. are the few time-share hotels in India.

Condominiums involve a joint ownership of a complex. Each owner has the full benefit of a unit and shares the cost that is common to the entire complex such as taxes, maintenance; upkeep of building etc. each owner can occupy or sell his unit independently but is obliged under the terms of contract to contribute towards the pool of common facilities and services. The owner can enjoy recreational exclusive to the complex and the management looks after the unit in the absence of the owner and if permitted by the owner let it out to provide income to him.

BED AND BREAKFAST HOTELS

These hotels are houses with a few rooms converted to overnight facilities to small building having 20 to 30 rooms. The owner lives in the premises and is responsible for looking after the guest, in these hotels only breakfast is served and meeting rooms, laundry, lunch and dinner and recreational facilities are offered in these hotels, however some hotels do offer limited food service.

SUPPLEMENTRY ACCOMMODATION

It consists of all types of accommodations other then the convention type; it may be described as a premise that provides accommodation but not the other services which is provided by the hotels. The main distinguish features of supplementary accommodations are:

- Standard of comfort is modest as compared to that of a hotel,
- They can sell accommodation at a very low price,
- There is an informal atmosphere and freedom regarding dress code.

Supplementary accommodation plays a very important role in the total available tourist accommodation in a country; it caters to both the international and domestic tourist traffic.

Types of supplementary accommodations are:

- Dharamsalas or sarae,
- Dak bungalows,
- Youth hostel,
- Dormitories,
- Sanatoria,
- Paying guest accommodation,

LEVELS OF SERVICE

Another way to classify hotels is by way of guest service and it is the benefits provided by the hotel to its guests, which varies with the type of the hotels size. This level of service is reflected in the guest room

THE INTANGIBILITY OF SERVICE

Hotels are not in the business of selling tangible services such as beds and food, infect it is the intangible services, which a hotel provides to its guests. These services are not just the physical things but actions, deeds, performances or efforts. Services cannot be touched, tasted, or tried on for size and are virtually impossible to return.

A guest leaves the hotel with only the memories of his stay therefore a hotel try to create an image of their services that is powerful, clear, and precise which becomes a recognizable standard or the trade mark of that hotel- almost like a tangible product.

QUALITY ASSURANCE

The intangible services that a hotel delivers tends to be less standardized than the tangible objects and one of the greatest challenges facing the hotel industries is controlling service variability, the consistent delivery is quality assurance. In hotels some quality control techniques are: rooms are inspected after they are cleaned, registration is a service that is produced, delivered and consumed simultaneously in the presence of the guest.

Consistency is the key to quality service and only the staff can make this a reality, which often creates or sustains guest's loyalty and preferences as well as a unique market niche.

WORLD CLASS SERVICE

These hotels are also called as luxury service hotels. These hotels targets top business executives, entertainment celebrities, high-ranking political figures and wealthy clienteles. These have upscale restaurant, exquisite decor, concierge service, oversized guest rooms and housekeeping service is provided twice in a day, and magazines and newspaper in each room. These hotels also have different restaurant for different cuisines, and they stress on personalized services and maintains high ratio of staff to guest.

MID RANGE SERVICE

These hotels appeal to the large section of people, mid range service is often modest but sufficient. These hotels have a specialty restaurant, coffee shop, room service, and lounge service, which may have entertainment in the evening. Guest likely to stay in these hotels is businessmen, individual travelers and families. Room rates are lower the world class hotels since meeting rooms are usually available in these hotels people planning small conference, group meeting and conventions may find these hotels attractive.

ECONOMY/ LIMITED SERVICE

These hotels provide clean, comfortable, inexpensive rooms and meet the basic needs of a guest. These hotels are frequented by budget minded guests who wants rooms with minimal amenities. These hotels have a very large market because large portion of the population travels on limited funds. The clientele of these hotels include families, groups, vacationers etc. Now a day these hotels offer cable television in the room, limited F&B service.

OWNERSHIP AND AFFILIATION

This provides another means by which to classify hotels i.e. independent hotel and chain hotels.

INDEPENDENT HOTEL

These are family owned and operated hotels that is not required to confirm to any policy or procedure's, they also do not need to adhere to a particular image and can offer a level of service geared towards attracting a specific target market and can quickly adapt to changing market condition. However these hotels do not enjoy the advantage of volume purchase, advertising exposure or management insight and consultancy power of a chain hotel.

CHAIN HOTEL

Chain hotel ownership can take a number of forms. Depending on the association that the chain organization has with each property. These hotels usually impose certain minimum standards, rules, policies, and procedures, which is to be followed by other properties of the same chain. These hotels are usually classified as operating a management contract or as a franchise or referral group.

MANAGEMENT CONTRACT HOTEL

These hotels are the properties owned by other entities. Under this type of contract, the owner or developer usually retains the financial and legal responsibility for the property, the management company pays its expenses and in turn receives an agreed upon fee from the owner or developer and the remaining cash goes to the owner who also pays for debts, insurance, taxes.

FRANCHISE AND REFERRAL GROUP

Franchising is simply a method of distribution whereby one entity that has developed a particular pattern or format for doing business. The franchiser usually provides a strong brand name, national and international central reservation system, management training programs, advanced technology, and central purchasing services.

Referral groups consist of independent hotels, which have joined together for some common purpose. While each property in the referral system is same but there is no similarity in the quality of service and guest expectations. Hotels within this group refer their guests to other affiliated hotels. With this kind of an approach a hotel may gain a much greater level of exposure.

STAR CLASSIFICATION

Hotel star		Excerpt of the catalogue of criteria
★	*Tourist*	• 100% of the rooms with shower/WC or bath tub/ WC • Daily room cleaning • 100% of the rooms with colour-TV together with remote control • Table and chair • Soap or body wash • Reception service • Facsimile at the reception • Publicly available telephone for guests • Extended breakfast • Beverage offer in the hotel • Deposit possibility
★S	*Superior Tourist*	The Superior flag is provided when the additional service and accommodation provisions are not sufficient for the next Hotel star. The bathroom facilities are usually at the same level as for two stars hotels but built from cheaper materials. The cost for regular inspection by independent associations is waived as well.
★★	*Standard*	In addition to the single star (*) hotels: • Breakfast buffet • Reading light next to the bed • Bath essence or shower gel • Bath towels • Linen shelves • Offer of sanitary products (e.g. toothbrush, toothpaste, shaving kit) • Credit Cards
★★S	*Superior Standard*	The Superior flag is provided when the additional service and accommodation provisions are not sufficient for the next Hotel star. The Standard-Superior does usually offer the same service level as three-star hotels but the interiors of the hotel are smaller and cheaper so that the three stars were not to be awarded by the inspection body. A two-star superior does not require mystery guesting.

★★★	*Comfort*	In addition to the standard star (**) hotels: • Reception opened 14 hours, accessible by phone 24 hours from inside and outside, bilingual staff (e.g. German/English) • Three piece suite at the reception, luggage service • Beverage offer in the room • Telephone in the room • Internet access in the room or in the public area • Heating facility in the bathroom, hair-dryer, cleansing tissue • Dressing mirror, place to put the luggage/ suitcase • Sewing kit, shoe polish utensils, laundry and ironing service • Additional pillow and additional blanket on demand • Systematic complaint management system
★★★S	*Superior Comfort*	The Superior flag is provided when the additional service and accommodation provisions are not sufficient for the next Hotel star. The accommodation facilities for a superior hotel need to be on a modern level and fully renovated which is checked regularly.
★★★★	*First Class*	In addition to the comfort star (***) hotels: • Reception opened 18 hours, accessible by phone 24 hours from inside and outside • Lobby with seats and beverage service • Breakfast buffet or breakfast menu card via room service • Minibar or 24 hours beverages via room service • Upholstered chair/couch with side table • Bath robe and slippers on demand • Cosmetic products (e.g. shower cap, nail file, cotton swabs), vanity mirror, tray of a large scale in the bathroom • Internet access and internet terminal • "À la carte"-restaurant
★★★★S	*First Class Superior*	The Superior flag is provided when the first class hotel has a proven high quality not only in the rooms. The superior hotels provide for additional facilities in the hotel like a sauna or a workout room. The quality is checked regularly by mystery guesting of an external inspection service.

★★★★★	*Luxury*	In addition to the first class (****) hotels: • Reception opened 24 hours, multilingual staff • Doorman-service or valet parking • Concierge, page boy • Spacious reception hall with several seats and beverage service • Personalized greeting for each guest with fresh flowers or a present in the room • Minibar and food and beverage offer via room service during 24 hours • Personal care products in flacons • Internet-PC in the room • Safe in the room • Ironing service (return within 1 hour), shoe polish service • Turndown service in the evening • Mystery guesting
★★★★★S	*Superior Luxury*	The Luxury star hotels need to attain high expectations of an international guest service. The Superior Luxury star is only awarded with a system of intensive guest care.

Department of Tourism, Government of India classifies hotels under star system in our country. There is a committee known as hotel and restaurant approval and classification committee (HRACC). Which comprises of representatives from the Ministry, Industry & the Institute?

In the * Rating, 1 * is the min Rating and 5 * deluxe is the max. Rating.

5 * deluxe is considered to be equivalent of 1st Class hotel by international standard. In America hotels are

- Classified according to plans they offer.

In Europe they have

- Deluxe Hotel
- 1st Class Hotel
- Economic Hotel
- Budgeted Hotel

Once the hotel gets standard classification from HRACC they become eligible for various benefits and reliefs from Government of India.

- Foreign Exchange

To get a star classification a hotel has to apply on a prescribed form to the Ministry of Tourism and pay a nominal fee which is as follow:

	Rs.
Restaurant	4000.00
1 Star	6000.00
2 Star	8000.00
3 Star	10000.00
4 Star	15000.00
5 Star	2000.00
5 Star Deluxe	25000.00

This is reduced to 50% if hotel applies for reclassification)

To be eligible to apply for classification the hotel must fulfill following basic requirements.

Must have at least 10 lettable rooms which can be rented.

Carpet area of respective rooms and area of bathroom should adhere to the following units –

5 Star Deluxe & 5 Star hotels

Single Room – 180 Sq. Ft.

Double Room – 200 Sq. Ft.

Bathroom – 45 Sq. Ft.

4 Star Hotel & 3 Star Hotel

Single A.C. & Non A.C. – 120 Sq. Ft.

Double A.C. & Non A.C. – 140 Sq. Ft.

Extra area may be provided if twin beds are provided in the room

Bathroom – 36 Sq. Ft.

2 Star and 1 Star Hotel

Single A.C. & Single Non A.C. – 100 Sq. Ft.

Double A.C. & Double non A.C. – 120 Sq. Ft.

Bathroom – 30 Sq. Ft. (or subject to local by laws)

All rooms should be provided with proper vitalization & ceiling fans. (2 Star and 1 Star hotel's case)

GENERAL FEATURES

5 Star Categories

- It must have at least 25 lettable rooms with attached bathrooms having along bath and with most modern shower chambers.
- Construction, locality and architect of hotel should have a distinct quality of a 5 Star hotel.
- All public & private areas should be centrally air conditioned, carpeted and equipped with high quality furniture.
- There should be a well designed and properly equipped swimming pool having life guards in attendance.
- There should be adequate member of guest elevator & service elevator functioning 24 hrs. By laws if more than 4 floors definitely lift should be there. Escalator also.
- There should be well equipped ladies and gents cloak rooms and well designed and well lit lobby area.
- There should be a reception, information and cash counter functioning 24 hrs and attended by highly qualified experienced staff members. Also at the cash counter 24 hrs money changing facility available.
- There should be a shopping arcade having Flower shop, Beauty Parlor, Barber shop, Book shop, Antique shop and a recognized travel agency.
- Each room should be providing with telephone having STD & ISD facility. Also in the lobby there should be pay telephones and house telephones
- Should be a provision of channel music in public and private rooms. Each room is provided with colour T.V. and refrigerator.
- There should be well equipped specialty restaurants serving different cuisines.
- There should be at least one bar or at least a permit room (whichever by law)
- Pantry & Cold storage facility should be professionally designed.
- Hotels should offer both national & international cuisines and F&B Service should be of highest quality.

- There should be professionally qualified, experienced trained staff members who are smart & courteous having good communication skills.
- 24 hrs room service & coffee shop service.
- 24 hrs service for telephone
- 24 hrs service for hot and cold running H 2 O.
- Provision for laundry and any cleaning services.
- There should be adequate parking facilities for guest cars.
- Each room is provided with a vacuum thermos flask with iced cold drinking water.
- H/k in the hotel should be of the highest studs. With plentiful supply of clean linen, towels and blankets which is of the highest quality.
- There should be a dancing facility in the restaurant of hotel having light music, ghazals etc.
- There should be a business centre in the hotel.

4 Star Categories

- Services provided in a 4 Star hotel are same as in a 5 Star hotel except there is no provision for swimming, pool and also 50% guest rooms do not have guest baths.

3 Star Categories

- Hotel must have at least 20 lettable room with atleast 50% rooms AC and rest of the rooms are well ventilated having a ceiling fan or air coolers.
- Facilities provided are similar to that of 4 Star hotel.

2 Star Category

- At least 10 lettable rooms out of which 75% rooms must have attached bathroom having a modern shower chamber and rest of the rooms will have a bathroom for every four of the remaining rooms with modern sanitation and running cold water.
- There should be an adequate supply of hot H 2 O, soap and toilet paper.
- 25% of rooms should be air conditioned & all the rooms should be ventilated clean and comfortable. There should be a reception counter with a telephone and this is maintained by trained staff members.

- If all rooms are not provided with a telephone then each room should have a call bell and a telephone on each floor corridor.

1 Star Category

- Minimum 10 lettable rooms out of which 25% with attached bathroom and a bathroom for every 4 of the remaining rooms.
- At least 25% of the bathroom should have a W.C. with adequate supply of hot and cold water.
- All the rooms should be properly ventilated & all rooms are provided with ceiling fan.
- Should be reception counter manned by trained staff members and a telephone for guest use.

S. No.		Essential	Necessary	Desirable
1	Construction		10	
2	Maintenance		20	
3	Parking			5
4	Swimming Pool		10	
5	Bathrooms	30		
6	Reception		15	
7	Lobby Area		10	
8	Conference Facility		10	
9	Shopping Facility		20	
10	Lift		10	
11	Bedroom Furnishing	25		
12	Lighting		10	
13	Telephones		10	
14	Radio			5
15	Vacuum Jugs & Flasks		5	
16	Restaurants	15		
17	Carpeting and Wooden Flooring			15
18	Linen, Blankets and towels		10	
19	Crockery	10		
20	Bar		10	
21	Entertainment			10
22	Cuisine		30	

23	Restaurant Services		25	
24	Room Services		20	
25	Beverage Services		15	
26	Hygiene	20		
27	24 hrs Reception, Telephone and information	10		
28	Laundry & Dry cleaning		10	
29	Staffing		10	
30	Executive Staff		10	
31	Other Staff		20	
32	Smart Clean Staff		10	
33	Staff contact with guest and atleast supervisory or senior in each shift		10	
34	Housekeeping	25		
35	Fire Fighting		10	

QUESTIONNAIRE

1. What is a hotel?
2. Briefly classify hotel by their type.
3. Classify and explain hotels by size
4. What is a target market?
5. Explain the following terms:
    - Commercial hotel
    - Airport hotel
    - Residential hotel
    - Casino hotel
    - Conference centres
    - Convention centres & hotels
6. What is a time share?
7. Explain the concept of condominium
8. Differentiate between timeshares and condominium
9. What are supplementary accommodation, explain its types

10. What is a world class service?
11. Classify hotels on the basis of ownership and affiliation
12. Classify hctels on the basis of star classification.
13. Give general features of a five star hotel.

3

TYPES OF ROOMS

- HOTEL ROOMS
- TYPES OF HOTEL ROOMS
- QUESTIONNAIRE

HOTEL ROOMS

It is quite strange, that so far in the hotel industry has not appeared a unified classification system for the hotel rooms. Of course, today almost any modern hotel has at its disposal standard rooms and suites. But often the same category of rooms in different hotels may imply different living conditions.

There are basic classification systems, which are used in some counties mort than one decade. It basically concerns the hotel sector in Western Europe, USA, **hotels in Australia**, Brazil, Japan and some countries of the Asian region. During recent years, the system of hotel room classification was adopted by numerous residence buildings and hotels in Russia.

The class of the room in the hotel mostly depends on the structure of the hotel itself. The classification of the hotel rooms is often used not so much for the indication of comfort, as for the reflection of the number of beds. You can safely say that the general standard for the international hotel business today is a single room. Tourist, staying in it, can count on the separate bathroom, wardrobe, TV set. WI-FI connection to the Internet is a default option practically in all the rooms of new hotels.

Depending on the host country and the status of the hotel a standard room can have additional functions and features. For example, in many **hotels in Britain** washstands with the separate faucet for cold and hot water can be found. In Chine the standard set for the bathroom includes a hairbrush, a toothbrush and paste. Thereby the standard set for the bathroom in the world hotel industry includes soap, towels for body and hands and, of late, a shower gel.

In addition to the standard room, the world classification distinguishes more than 30 different types of rooms. The type of the hotel room can depend on the view from the window, the number and the size of rooms, the quality of furniture, the content of mini-bar and the availability of office equipment. In addition to the classification of rooms there is a classification of accommodation. There are also a lot of options: from a double room, where three or more people can stay, to accommodation with children or in the separate cabin on the territory of the hotel. Both the room types and the accommodation types have alphabetic acronyms, primarily in English. For example, BO stands for bed only and means that meals are not included. An abbreviation SV (sea view) in the description of the room means that you will be able to observe the sea through your window.

In this column we will try to tell you about the most common types of rooms and accommodation, adopted in many countries around the world.

TYPES OF ROOM CATEGORIES

- SINGLE ROOM
- DOUBLE ROOM
- TWIN ROOM
- INTERCONNECTING ROOM
- ADJOINING ROOM
- HOLLYWOOD TWIN ROOM
- DUPLEX ROOM
- CABANA ROOM
- STUDIO ROOM
- PARLOR ROOM
- LANAI ROOM
- EFFICIENCY ROOM
- HOSPITALITY ROOM
- SUITE

Single Room

A room which has single bed facility

Double Room

A room which as double bed facility.

Interconnecting Room

Two rooms which shares a common door, mostly used by families.

Adjoining Room

Two rooms which share a common wall, mostly preferred by group.

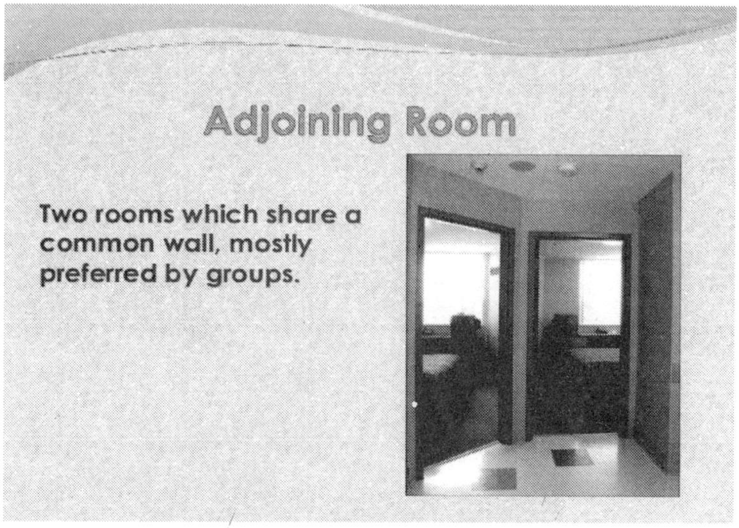

Adjacent rooms

Rooms close to each other, but not necessarily adjoining perhaps across the hall or corridor from each other .

Hollywood Twin Room

A room which has two single bed but shares a common head board.

Duplex Room

A room which has been spread on two floors connected by an internal staircase.

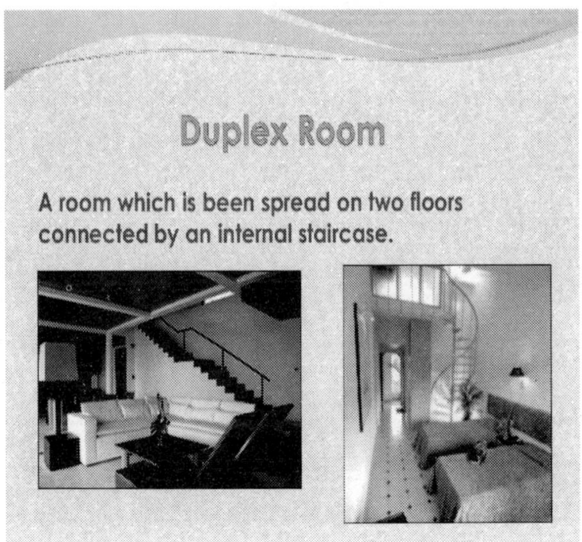

Cabana

A room which is near a water body or beside swimming pool.

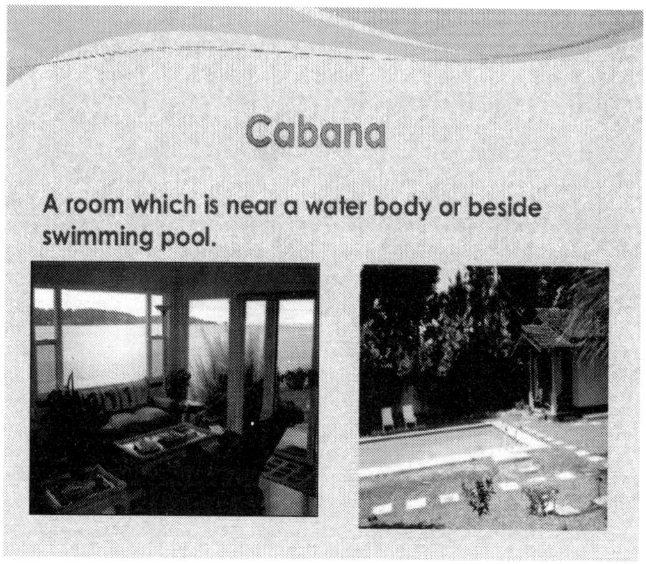

Studio Room

A room with a sofa-cum-bed facility

Parlor

A room which is used for sitting and cannot be used for sleeping purpose.

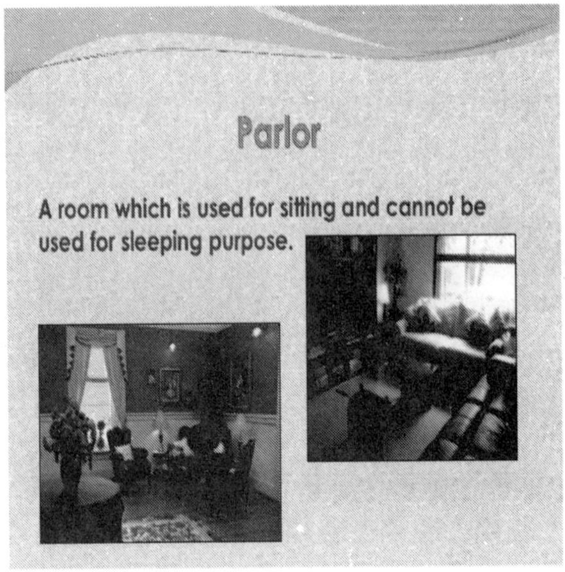

Lanai

A room which oversees a scenic beauty e.g. Garden, landscape or water fall.

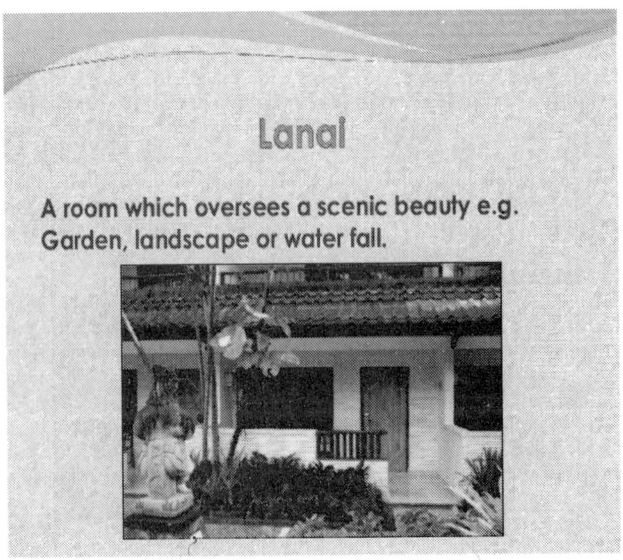

Efficiency Room

A room with a kitchen facility

Hospitality Room

A room where hotel staff would entertain their guests.

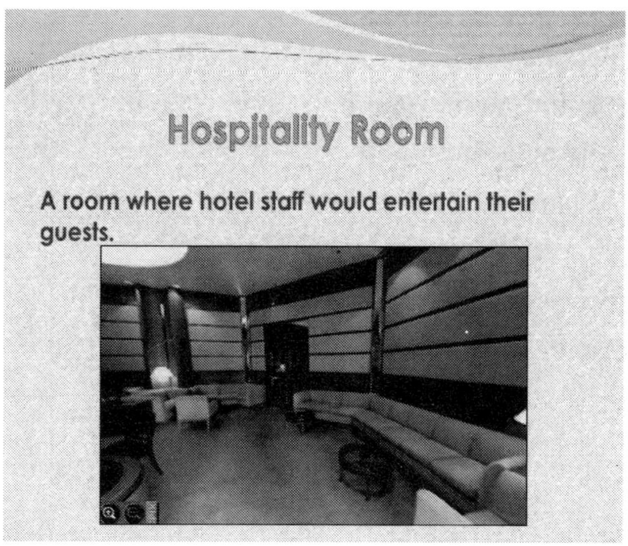

Suite

A room comprises of two or more bedroom, a living room and a dining area.

QUESTIONNAIRE

1. What is a hotel room?
2. Name types of room?
3. Differentiate between;
    - Double room and twin room
    - Adjoining and adjacent room
    - Cabana and lanai
4. What is a studio room?
5. What is an efficiency room?
6. Give salient features of a suite of a five star hotel?

4

TIMESHARE AND VACATION OWNERSHIP

- INTRODUCTION
- USES OF TIMESHARE

INTRODUCTION

A timeshare is a property with a particular form of ownership or use rights. These properties are typically resort condominium units, in which multiple parties hold rights to use the property, and each sharer is allotted a period of time (typically one week and almost always the same time every year) in which they may use the property. Units may be on a partial ownership, lease, or "right to use" basis, in which the sharer holds no claim to ownership of the property. A timeshare is a property or the right to use a property, typically a resort condominium unit, in which multiple parties have rights, such as the right-to-use. The notion of a timeshare was originally created in Europe in the 1960s. A ski resort developer in the French Alps marketed his resort by encouraging guests to "stop renting a room" and instead "buy the hotel". The timeshare concept was quickly embraced by developers' worldwide, boosting sales of surplus condominium units at a time when the resort industry was depressed. Due to the promise of timeshares for exchange, timeshares or "vacation ownership" often sell regardless of their deeded resort (most timeshares are deeded into a certain resort site). What is not often disclosed is that all timeshares differ in trading power. If a timeshare is in Hawaii or Southern California it will exchange extremely well, however, those areas are some of the most expensive in the world. The vast majority of timeshares trade through two international exchange companies; Interval international and RCI. Critics contend timeshares are often overpriced, especially in places such as Mexico and Florida where almost every resort offers timeshare. As such, timeshares are unique among real estate assets in that buyers are almost certain to save significant money if the owners travel annually.

The timeshare concept has in recent years been embraced by many lodging companies, including category leaders Starwood, Hyatt, Hilton, Marriott, and Disney. Timeshares are an extremely profitable segment for such companies. The timeshare segment is expected to provide continued revenue and profit growth through 2030, despite an expected slowdown in traditional hotel operations. Being once known as the travel vehicle of the future timeshares will now only become more expensive as they enter the American mainstream.

The first hotel timeshare in the US was the Hilton Hale Kaanapali on the Island of Maui in Hawaii. Time share ownership is not the same as real estate ownership, and real estate brokers do not typically handle timeshares. There are many companies and websites which specialize in reselling time-shares. Be sure to research the company to be sure they can do the job.

USES OF TIMESHARE

Timeshare is business model whereby a company owning property, typically resort condominiums, sells small time slices of property to customers. Timeshare buyers:

- Use their usage time,
- Rent out their owned usage,
- Give it as a gift,
- Exchange internally within the same resort or resort group,
- Exchange externally into thousands of other timeshare resorts,
- Assign their usage time to the point system to be exchanged for airline tickets, hotels, travel packages, cruises, amusement park tickets,
- Instead of renting all their actual usage time, rent part of their points without actually getting any usage time and use the rest of the points,
- Rent more points from either the internal exchange entity or another owner to get a larger unit or more vacation time or at a better location,
- Save or move points from one year to another.

Some developers, however, may limit which of these options are available at their properties.

Timeshare owners can elect to stay at their resort during the prescribed period, which varies depending on the nature of their ownership. In many resorts, they can rent out their week or give it as a gift to friends and family.

Timeshares offer owners the possibility of exchanging their week, either independently or through several exchange agencies, to stay at one of the thousands of other resorts worldwide. There are many exchange agencies, of which the two largest are Resort Condominiums International and Interval International. They have resort affiliate programs and members can only exchange to affiliate resorts. It is most common for a resort to be affiliated with only one of the larger exchange agencies, but it isn't rare to find a dual affiliate resort. Together they have over 7,000 resorts. The timeshare resort one purchases determines which of the major exchange companies can be used to make exchanges. RCI and II charge a yearly membership fee and fees for when they find an exchange. They also bar members from renting weeks for which they already have exchanged.

Timeshare owners can also exchange their timeshare through independent timeshare exchange companies. Dial an Exchange, Trading Places, Hawaii Timeshare Exchange; Platinum Interchange, The San Francisco Exchange, Timex and Redweek.com are the main independent exchange companies. Owners can exchange with these independent exchange without needing the resort to have a formal affiliation agreement with the companies.

Timeshare owners may also arrange a direct exchange. This requires locating a timeshare owner with the location and weeks both mutually desire. This form of exchange is rare but since it can save in exchange fees it is often sought after. Several bulletin boards have been created to help timeshare owners meet others and swap.

Timeshares take different forms depending on the seller. The vast majority consist of one week of ownership, i.e. 1/52 year, but some developers sell point based systems that are a different form of vacation currency that allow hotel stays, car rentals, and stays at large networks of resorts.

TYPES OF TIMESHARE

There are three basic types of Timeshare Programs: Fee simple, Leasehold Right-to-Use ('RTU'). Also included in the mix are Points systems, which are essentially a type of RTU, and fractional/private residence clubs.

Fee Simple: In this system you purchase an actual deeded interest in real estate, which is recorded with the land court or other proper authorities and for which you receive a title in perpetuity.

Leasehold: This ownership option provides the same basic ownership rights, protections, obligations and interests, etc. as the Fee Simple system with the primary exception being that Leasehold, unlike Fee Simple, is not in perpetuity and has a specified expiration date (which may include a first right to renew the ownership interest prior to the expiration of the leasehold). This type of ownership has been common in Hawaii for many years, though it is becoming less common as resort companies purchase full ownership rights to the land underlying the resorts.

Right-to-Use ('RTU'): In this system you purchase the right to use a particular unit or unit size each year, but you do not have an ownership interest in the real estate. Traditionally, your right to use that property will expire after a stated number of years (usually 20-30), and the property will revert to the developer or the owner of the leasehold property. Legal ownership is typically vested in a trust company. This is the prevailing type of timeshare ownership in the UK and Mexico and many other countries outside of the USA, where it is illegal to sell timeshare as a deeded entity.

Within those types of timeshare, there are a few sub-types:

Fixed week: Where you own rights to a specific week, often in a specific condo/villa (this is called fixed week/fixed unit). This is your "home resort", which you can either return to every year (same week every year) or trade through an exchange system for something similar in another part of the world, though not necessarily in the same week that you own. The advantage to fixed week/fixed unit ownership is the assurance that your specific timeshare unit will be waiting for you faithfully at the same time each year.

- An example of fixed unit/fixed week would be that you purchase Christmas week in Unit 152B– every year you automatically have *that week in that unit* assigned to you.
- An example of a fixed week that is *not* in a fixed unit would be that every year during Christmas week you get the size of unit you purchased (i.e. a 2-bedroom ocean view), but not necessarily Unit 152B.

Floating (or Flex) time: Instead of owning a specific week, you own a week (or a time period which may be longer than a week) within a specific range of time. Usually you will not purchase a specific unit (i.e. Unit 152B) but instead will purchase a unit size (i.e. a 2-bdrm 2-bath). It is then your responsibility to contact your resort each year to book the week you want to use. This works on a first-come-first-served basis, subject to availability, so the most desirable weeks are taken up quickly and it behooves you to make your plans as early as your resort allows. Also, if you intend to exchange your week through one of the exchange companies, you must first reserve your time at your resort before the exchange companies will accept it for deposit in the "exchange bank".

- An example of floating time would be that you choose a 2-bedroom villa (not necessarily a specific unit) that is available to you any time between, say, June 1 and September 1.

Points/Club Membership: Under a traditional points system, each unit/week of time is appointed a specific number of points based on its location, size, desirability, time of year, etc. These points are then "spent" like money to reserve a unit for your next vacation. Owners can use, for instance, 3 days here and 4 days over there rather than spending an entire week at the same resort. The number of points you own determines what, where and when you can go.

Originally points were tied to a deed (and most still are), with the underlying deeds being held in common either by the resort developer or by the timeshare owners themselves, collectively. This meant that only a set number of points could be sold, corresponding to the number of units in a timeshare development.

When buying into that kind of points system, a buyer should make sure they know what they are getting. Developers often maintain sales rooms at sold-out resorts, selling the entire resort system to potential owners.

You may think you are getting a deeded interest at a specific resort, which is what you want, only to find out later that your deeded interest is for another resort in the system entirely. Most of the time this really should make no difference, but occasionally it can be a problem for the owner.

Popular Timeshare Brands :

- Disney Vacation Club.
- Starwood Vacation Ownership.
- Marriott Vacation Club.
- Hilton Grand Vacations Club.
- Westgate Resorts.

Role of RCI

RCI is a timeshare exchange broker, it does not develop or sell timeshares (this falls within the province of RCI's sister Wyndham Worldwide subsidiary Wyndham Vacation Club). A customer who buys a timeshare with an RCI-affiliated developer (whether Wyndham or another entity) has the option to become a member of RCI. Such membership entitles the individual to exchange their timeshare with other members; RCI facilitates and fulfils the exchange. Alternatively, a timeshare owner with an RCI-affiliated developer under a points-based system can book reservations through RCI with another RCI affiliate.

RCI is a timeshare exchange broker. It does not develop or sell timeshares (this falls within the province of RCI's sister Wyndham Worldwide subsidiary Wyndham Vacation Ownership). A customer who buys a timeshare with an RCI-affiliated developer (whether Wyndham or another entity) has the option to become a member of RCI. Such membership entitles the individual to exchange their timeshare with other members; RCI facilitates and fulfils the exchange. Alternatively, a timeshare owner with an RCI-affiliated developer under a points-based system can book reservations through RCI with another RCI affiliate.

AIRD – All India resort association

Although, Government does not have any direct role in running the **timeshare industry** in India but it's their duty to provide the right environment for growth of this Industry. This creates an atmosphere which will inspire investors to focus only on running their business instead of focusing on other infrastructural issues.

Following are the issues in which Government plays an important role:

1. Security: Safety and Security is an important concern for tourism industry. A tourist always wants to roam free in the tourist place without fear of safety of himself and his belongings. It is government's duty to take good care of security arrangements. At some places government has started a concept of Tourist Police who takes responsibility of extra care of these tourist places.
2. Infrastructure: Timeshare industry is totally dependent upon infrastructure provided by Timeshare companies. And government monitors this Infrastructure. Government takes care of proper roads, electricity, drinking water, sewage lines, garbage disposal facility, street lights etc. in these tourist places
3. Capital: Timeshare industry is cannot be run without proper investments. It requires huge initial investment. Government provides financial assistance by providing loans to these timeshare companies. Government can also promote this industry by generating money from import duty, excise duty etc.
4. Regulatory Commission: Timeshare industry had lost it's credibility because of freelance operators before. Government now is helping the industry by acting as a regulatory commission which keeps an eye on all the players in this business and controls the financial transactions between holiday homes and timeshare companies.
5. Taxation: Government collects taxes and dues from timeshare companies and this money is later used to improvise infrastructure of these tourist places.

AIRDA: In 1998, a visionary group of resort developers and RCI inked a blueprint for an independent body – an association with a purpose and an agenda – keeping in mind the nascent profile of timeshare in the country and the constructive role that could be played by developers to grow the industry. Importantly, to work hand-in-hand with both promoters and consumers. This was how the foundation was laid for the All India Resort Development Association (AIRDA).

5

FRONT OFFICE ORGANISATION

- INTRODUCTION
- OVERVIEW OF FRONT OFFICE DEPARTMENT
- HIERARCHY OF FRONT OFFICE
- DUTIES & RESPONSIBILITIES OF FRONT OFFICE STAFF
- QUESTIONNAIRE

INTRODUCTION

As the title suggest hotel front office department is the first place where hotel and guest interact with each other. This department holds a foremost importance in hotel, due to its nature of work profile and profound contribution in revenue generation. Generally revenue collected from the sale of room's contributed more than 50 percent of total hotel sales. At here, the term "sale of room" means the use of hotel room at a given price for a particular night. A room is termed as sold for the day when a guest leases the room for stay in the hotel. There are different grades of rooms which sold at different rates, these different rates are collectively called as "Room Tariff". Room tariff is computed for a 'Revenue Day' which begins at room of a participation day and ends after 12 hrs. On next day.

Front office has also complimentary role of image building because it is the first and the last point of contact of every guest. The term front office is used in large organisation whereas small establishment call it as a reception. The basic work profile of both is completely alike – to reserve, receive, register, assign rooms to guest and act as continuous source of information to guest during guest stay at the hotel. The difference between both comes in-size, sections, expenses and number of employees. There are various sections of front office department like reservation, reception, concierge, etc.

OVERVIEW OF FRONT OFFICE DEPARTMENT

As we have already learned, front office department is responsible for the room sale through systematic way of reservation, followed by registration and assigning room to the guest. Nowadays, majority of hotel uses room division word instead of front office. The organisation structure of room division varying from hotel to hotel. These variations can be caused by difference in size of hotels, the types and levels of services and finally the preference of management. Room division manager is responsible for supervision of front office, reservation, housekeeping, concierge, guest services, security, and communications. The major department in room division are- front office, housekeeping & uniformed service department. These departments come under direct control of the Room Division Manager or Directors of rooms.

LAYOUT OF A FRONT OFFICE

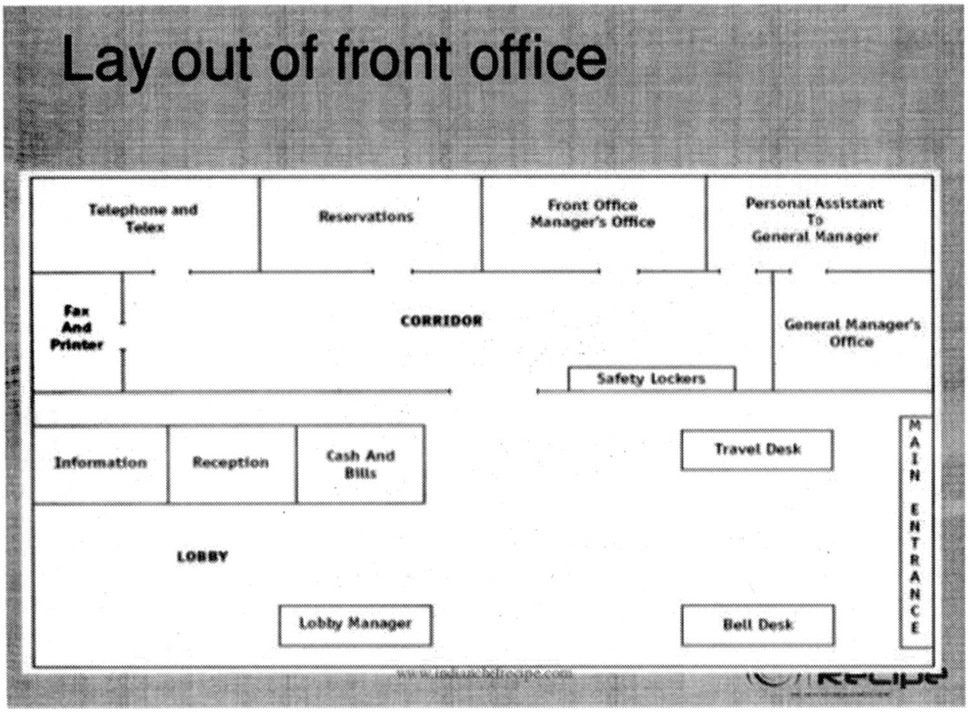

FRONT OFFICE

Front office is the nerve centre of a hotel. The front office is to act as the public face of the hotel, primarily by greetings hotel patrons & checking in guest. Members of the front office staff welcomes the guests carry their luggage, help them register, give them their room keys and mail, answer questions about the activities in the hotel and surroundings areas, and finally check out them. In fact, the only direct contact most guests have with hotel employees, other than in the restaurants, is with members of the front-office staff. Front office also provides assistance to guests during their stay and lastly collects charges. Thus, the front office functions can be divided into five general areas:

- Reception
- Bell service
- Business centre
- Mail and information
- Cashier and night auditors

UNIFORMED SERVICE

Uniformed service or guest service department is usually responsible for the take care of guests and their needs. The department is usually provides most personalized services to the hotel guests. Some of them are as follows:

- Bell attendants
- Door attendants
- Valet parking attendants
- Transportation personnel
- Concierges/ Information

The two major departments are represented in the above list. The employees staffing in the first four areas are in the rooms departments. The fifth is the financial areas, where guest charges are accumulated and posted to the bills or guests accounts, and all cash transactions are consummated. These are all accounting department functions, so the cashier and night auditors may also consider as an account department's part.

ORGANISATION CHART OF FIVE STAR HOTEL

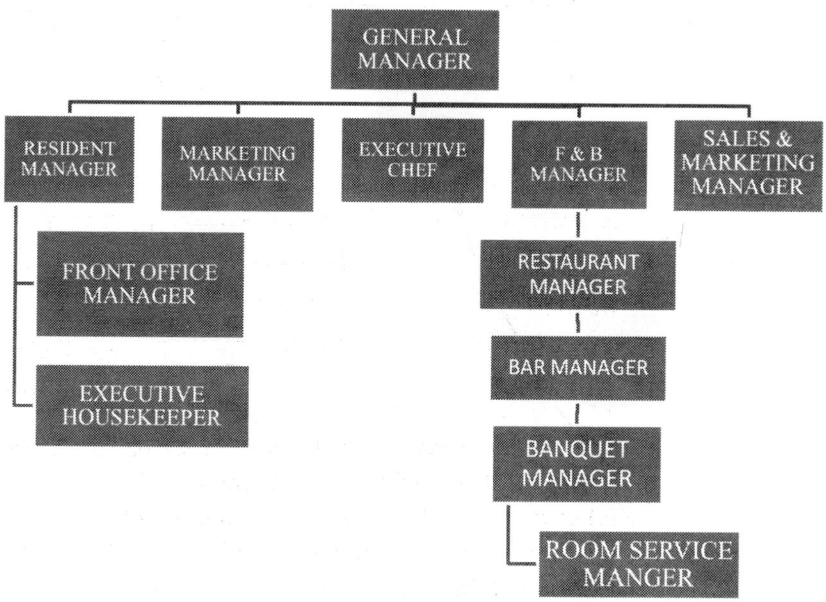

ORGANISATION CHART OF THREE STAR HOTEL

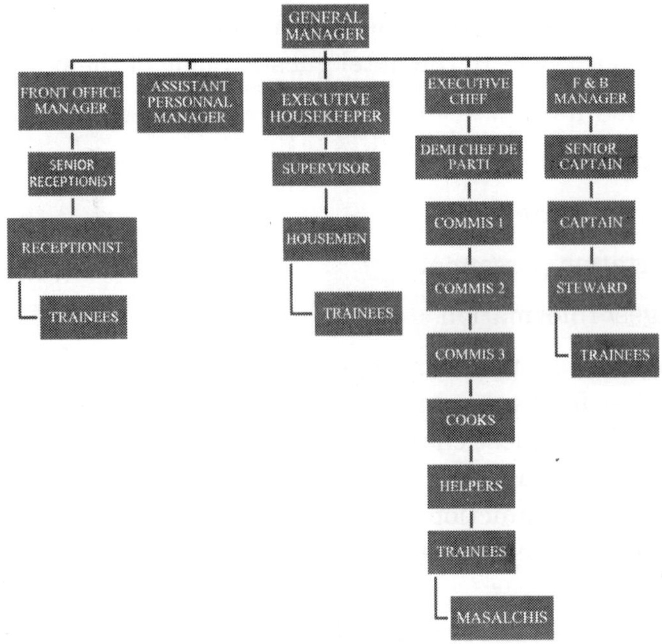

ORGANISATION CHART OF FRONT OFFICE FIVE STAR HOTEL

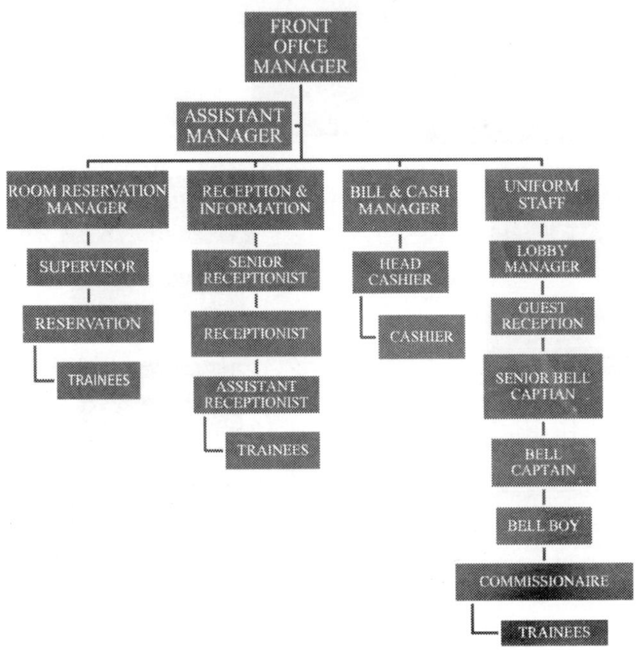

ORGANISATION CHART OF FRONT OFFICE THREE STAR HOTEL

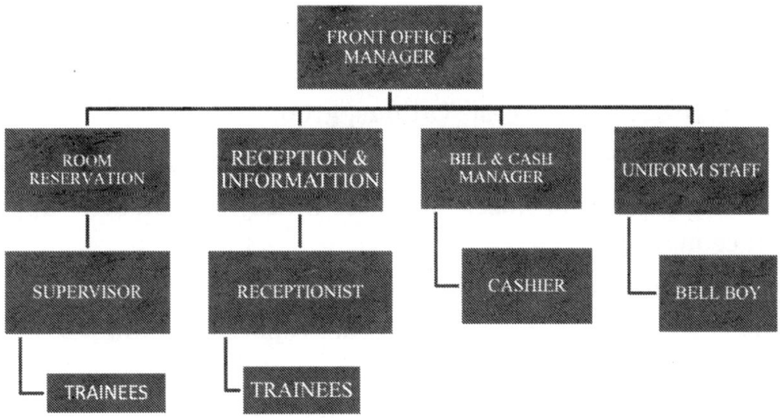

DUTIES AND RESPONSIBILITIES OF FRONT OFFICE STAFF

FRONT OFFICE MANAGER

1. He directs and coordinates the activities of the front office department, which includes dept. like, front desk, lobby, reservation, bell desk, telephones,
2. He is responsible to ensure the proper upkeep, staff cleanness, punctuality and efficiency by his staff in his department,
3. Ensures that each and every guest is provided with smooth, efficient, courteous and personalized service by his staff,
4. He prepares the duty chart for his staff and also sanctions weekly offs, an leaves to his subordinates,
5. He deals with front office correspondences on reservation, enquires, room booking, discount to company etc., and inter departmental communication,
6. He checks the functioning of various records, racks, intimations, arrival list, room position,
7. He deals with complaints against his staff and other complaints of his guest,
8. He is responsible for making decisions at times of unusual events such as death, fire, theft,
9. Prepares report to the management about the anticipated rooms occupancy, reservation patterns, expected check-in and check-out,

10. Responsible along with the personal department, for the employment and training of staff,

ASSISTANT MANAGER RESERVATION

1. To keep trace of all room reservations, groups, crew, FIT, and others,
2. He prepares monthly reports, ten day forecast and materialization reports,
3. Sets booking levels and closes out dates if fully booked after approval from front office manager,
4. Updates the perpetual year planner according to room position,
5. Prepares the room status report, forecast report and mail it to all the hotels and reservation offices to the chain,
6. Liaises with asst. manager group, for all group details,
7. Process all reservations in the normal way,
8. Provides on the job training and prepares training schedules of all new recruits,
9. Assign responsibilities to his staff and monitors their performance,
10. Prepares replies to all incoming mails,,
11. Keep control on all suites and their availability,
12. Keep a record of various sources of business and monitors booking received from the world wide sales office and hotels,
13. Ensures that his staff answers phones promptly and use the laid down procedures,
14. Handles all bookings for hotels worldwide,
15. Ensures that reservation staff make every effort to up sell suites,
16. Updates all special screens on the computer and creates new ones if necessary,
17. Ensures cleanliness and orderliness of the area,
18. Any other assignment as directed by the front office manager.

FRONT OFFICE SUPERVISOR

1. Checks statistical data on day's proceedings as regards to room revenue and reports,
2. Prepares budgets/three monthly outlook report,
3. Ensure that all the staff reports on time with proper uniform and are properly groomed,

4. Brief staff to ensure maximum efficiency,
5. Check if any repeat guest/ VIP has checked in as walk-in see that proper status is given to him to ensure personalized services are provided to that guest,
6. Check that proper room position is calculated and give the "pick up" room figures to reservation in charge,
7. Check and sign the log book and take follow up action,
8. Check the arrival rack for the day and leave instructions on the reservation slip,
9. Ensure that no room keys are missing to prevent security risk,
10. Meet and greet all guest s on arrival and ensures proper rooming,
11. Train staff on existing/new policies and procedures laid down by the management,
12. Ensures that all gadgets in the front office are in working order to ensures smooth operation in the department,
13. Check if mail, messages, packets, special requests of guests are being looked after and dealt with properly as appropriate,
14. Check correctness of:
    a) House count,
    b) Sales recapitulation
    c) VIP list/ list of complimentary,
    d) Room reports

FRONT OFFICE ASSISTANT

1. Courteously and promptly handle all reservations on phone, fax, E-mail,
2. Up-date the reservation registers/ records in order to have update inventory
3. Type out advance reservation slips and maintain reservation racks,
4. Carry out amendments and cancellations accurately,
5. Keep availability status chart updated,
6. Display reservation position on the flash board,
7. Check on reservation stationery and keep a satisfactory par,

LOBBY MANAGER

1. Prepares the duty chart for the staff working under him,
2. Co- ordinates with various department for effective guest handling,
3. Co-ordinates with front office (reception & information) to facilitate rooming and departure of guest and front office cash (to allow credits),
4. Takes constant round at night of all operation areas to ensure smooth functioning during his shift,
5. Passes credit bills in the absences of front office/ asst. front office manager,
6. Trains all staff under him,
7. Co-ordinates with security and ensures that no unwanted happening takes place in the hotel.

RECEPTIONIST

1. The receptionists primary duty is to receive and welcome the guest, enquire his requirements and room him,
2. Registering the guest,
3. Allocate the room to a guest,
4. Room the guest by handing over the room key to the bell boy who will accompany the guest,
5. In smaller hotels the receptionist is required to do other duties in the front office such as:
   a) Reservation and reservation enquires,
   b) Recording the guest bills and posting of all vouchers,
   c) Receive the money in settlements of the bills,
   d) Handling the telephones and messages,

   At times the receptionist has to acts as a manager in small hotel

RESERVATIONS CLERK

1. Prepares the room status for several days ahead,
2. Books the room in advance,
3. Fill in the reservation slip, Whitney slip, or feed into the computer and keep a proper record,

4. Attends to the reservation enquiries, personal letter, fax telephones, e-mail and gives proper information,
5. Confirm the booking and arrange the Whitney rack,
6. Prepares the arrival list and informs the receptionist,

TELEPHONE OPERATOR

1. Extend a warm and courteous telephone service to guest/management and employees of the hotel,
2. Handle wakeup call and ensure prompt and timely service followed by reminder wake call service,
3. Be familiar with all operational procedures within the department,
4. Ensure proper use/care, upkeep and maintenance of equipment installed,
5. Keep the guest information rack, VIP, group, crew list updated at all times,
6. Responsible for proper and accurate accounting of trunk calls made by hotel officials/guests and promptly transmit telephone vouchers to front office cashier in case of a guest,
7. Use proper and distinct pronunciation in order to make one selves audible and easily understood. Be expressive than impressive,
8. Maintain speed and accuracy when connecting all incoming and outgoing calls,
9. Avoid interruptions,
10. Brief the next shift operator regarding all pending works to be done,
11. Avoid transferring calls too many times,
12. Sense mood of the caller when dealing with him.

CONCIERGE

1. Concierge can be called as a ' man- about- town' or ' mister- know- it- all', usually resourceful and knowledgeable about hotel and the surrounding,
2. Should be equipped with the brochures, travel facilities information, sightseeing, shopping, and other such things for providing assistance to the guest,
3. He/she is required to make airlines booking, taxi booking and planning of itineraries for guest

4. Serves as guests liaison with hotel and non hotel services,
5. Provides personal approach to guest services.
6. To ensure a proper use of the telephone etiquette standards.
7. To oversee the concierge operations, doormen, bellmen, valet parking and to supervise the area ensuring that all standards and procedures are fully known and followed.
8. To ensure that all necessary equipment are maintained properly with sufficient stock for day to day operations.
9. To ensure that guest luggage records are accurately maintained and all special requests are met.
10. Stay current and up to date with all hotel services as well as daily VIP requests and special events.

FRONT OFFICE CASHIER

1. He is to receive payment from the guest in settlement of their bills,
2. Posting of vouchers into the individual bills,
3. Looking after the safe deposit vault,
4. Checking the petty cash float, operating and maintaining cash registers and billing machines,
5. Maintain the visitor tabular ledger, and post guest vouchers into the VTL,
6. Check the correctness the bills.
7. Operates front office posting software.
8. Obtains the house bank and keeps it balanced.
9. Completes cashier pre-shift supply checklist.
10. Completes guest check-in procedures.
11. Clarifies customers question or concerns about the charges on their bills.
12. Maintains adequate supplies of outlet stationery for cashiers.
13. Assists with distribution of month end reports as directed by accounts or front office manager.
14. Maintains a track of all high balance guests.
15. Check the billing instructions are correct for all expected departure guest and setup required auto routing or auto transfer on the PMS / Guest folio.

QUESTIONNAIRE

1. Write in brief about Front Office Organisation.
2. Draw the organisation chart of a Five-star hotel with 500 rooms and three star hotels with 150 rooms.
3. Draw the organisation chart of front office of a Five-star hotel with 500 rooms.
4. Draw the organisation chart of front office of a Three-star hotel with 500 rooms.
5. Write in detail the Qualities and Duties of a good Receptionist.
6. Explain the duties of front Office Manager and Reservation Manager.
7. What are the duties and responsibilities of Lobby Manager and Concierge?

6

HOTEL ENTRANCE, LOBBY AND ITS VARIOUS EQUIPMENTS

- INTRODUCTION
- LOBBY
- TYPES OF FRONT DESKS
- EQUIPMENT USED IN FRONT DESK
- TELEPHONE EQUIPMENT
- QUESTIONER

INTRODUCTION

The atmosphere, décor and the staff are suggestive of what guest is going to get on his visit to the hotel. Many times in addition to the building ambience, the main entrance and approach play a very important role in the selection of Hotel for a guest. The main entrance should be identifiable and directly lead to reception area that is the lobby of the Hotel. Lobby should be spacious but not wasteful. The natural flow of guest should be toward reception/ information counter on his arrival in the Hotel. Sufficient space should be in the lobby before either sending to room or to the car during the guest's departure.

Lobby of the Hotel includes general circulation and waiting area which leads to check in, information and cashier counter and also the desk such as concierge, bell desk, travel counter and elevator, etc. Front office is situated in front of the Hotel. The area is headed by the senior Lobby manager whose counter is also in the lobby. The various shopping arcade may also be in one part of the lobby or near the lobby. The various food outlets shall also be near by the lobby. Location of cloakrooms should be very much defined and planned. Another important point is that the addition to the entry from the drive in, there must be an entrance of lobby at the car parking area which usually is in the basements. Also the front office staff should be able to oversee the activities, exits, elevators, shops, etc., and if possible, the dining area and restaurant. Lobby of a large Hotel is also required to accommodate travel desk, bank counter and public as well as house telephone booths.

Lobby

The lobby is a room in a building which is used for entry from the outside. Sometimes referred to as a foyer or an entrance hall.

Many hotels go to great lengths to decorate their lobbies to create the right impression and convey an image, or power of the hotel. Size of a lobby depends upon size of Hotel. The systems used such as manual, mechanical, or automatic will also be important role while deciding the size of lobby.

The reception counter which is situated in the lobby is responsible for guest's arrival, departure, mail handling, luggage handling etc. The counter should be well planned, functional and operational. The following points should be kept in mind:

1. **Size:** For a large hotel using automatic system the size may be small while for a small hotel on Whitney rack system the size may be comparatively big.

2. **Shape:** Another important factor is that the counter of reception should be matching with the lobby. For example l- shape, straight-shape, curve shape, circular – shape.
3. **Dimension:** Basically the Height normally lies between 38" to 42"; width is 30 approximately and the length depending upon various factors such as size of lobby, material used for making counter etc.

TYPES OF FRONT DESKS IN A HOTEL LOBBY

1. Circular shape

2. Straight Shape

3. Curved shape

4. L- shaped

EQUIPMENTS USED IN LOBBY

In non automated and semi automated properties, the layout of the front desk is centered on a collection of mechanical racks and specialty equipment designed to produce, store, or display front office form. In semi- automated system, these racks are positioned besides posting machines, cash registers devices, and other pieces of equipment that facilitate front office desk tasks.

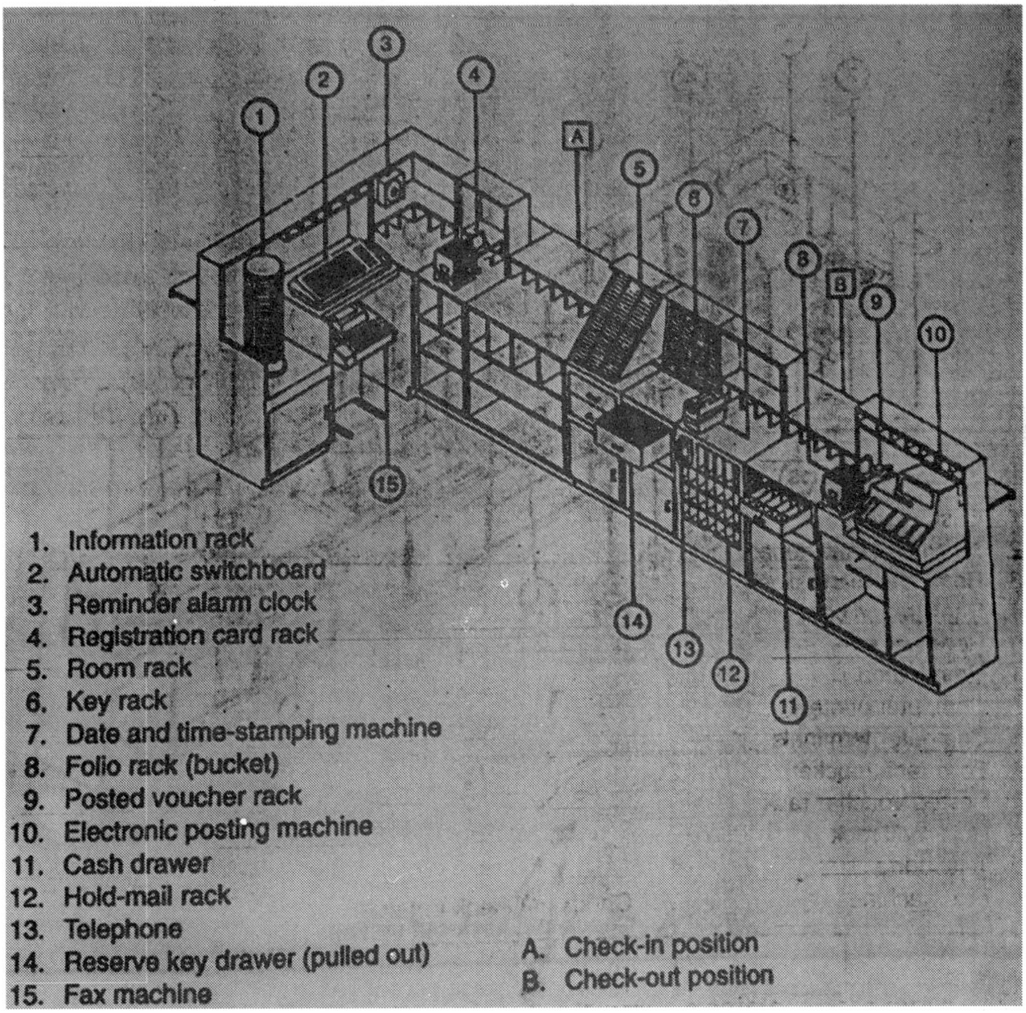

Some equipment's are as follows:

Room rack

The room rack traditionally been considered the most important piece of front equipment in non- automated hotels and semi- automated hotels. As pointed out earlier, a room rack is an array of metal file pockets designed to hold room racks slips that display guest and room status information. The room rack is normally recessed into the front desk counter, titled against the desk, or mounted below or behind the desk. When key slots are added to the room rack, it can serve as a combination room and key rack.

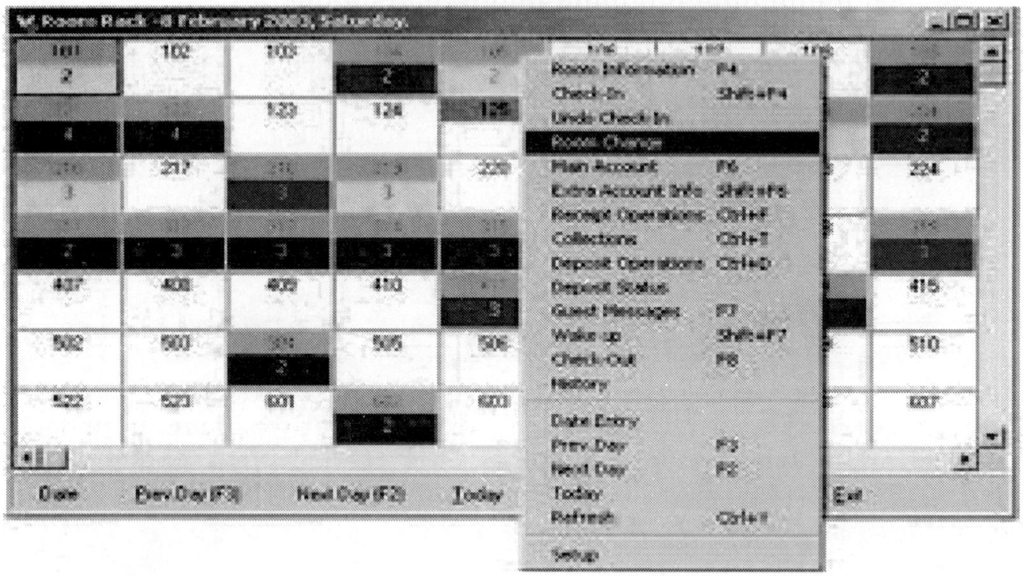

The room rack contains a summary of summary of information about the current status of all rooms in the hotel. A room rack slip or, in some hotel, the guest registration card itself can be inserted into room rack to display guest information, room number and, room rate. The intent is that one glance at the room rack should immediately inform the front desk agent of the occupancy and housekeeping status of all rooms.

Mail, message, and key rack

A key rack is an array of numbered compartments used to store guestroom keys. Historically, key racks were positioned so as to be visible to front desk agents and guest alike. The arrangements permitted guests and front office staff to know the occupancy status of a room by the number of keys present in its assigned slot. Key racks no longer are prominently featured at the front desk. Instead, they are often placed in front desk drawers to help ensure the safety and securities of guests by not disclosing occupancy information.

To minimize the number of rack in front desk area, hotels may combine the key rack with either the room rack or the mail and message rack. A combination mail, message, and key rack can be either a freestanding wall unit, an under the counter row of compartments, or a set of drawers. Some front desk uses it as room divider.

If guestroom telephones are equipped with message lights, they can be used to notify guests when they have message at the desk. In room message lights may be activated with a control switch besides each room's slot in the mail, message, and key rack.

In a fully-automated lodging property, a mail rack may be all that is necessary. The function of a key rack may be performed by the master console of an electronic locking system.

Reservation Racks

Front office of nom-automated and semi- automated hotels often use both advance and current reservation racks. In an advance reservation rack, reservation rack slips or registration cards are arranged by the guests or groups names. A current reservation rack is a portable subset of the advance reservation rack. The current reservation rack is used by front desk agents to assist in processing during registration.

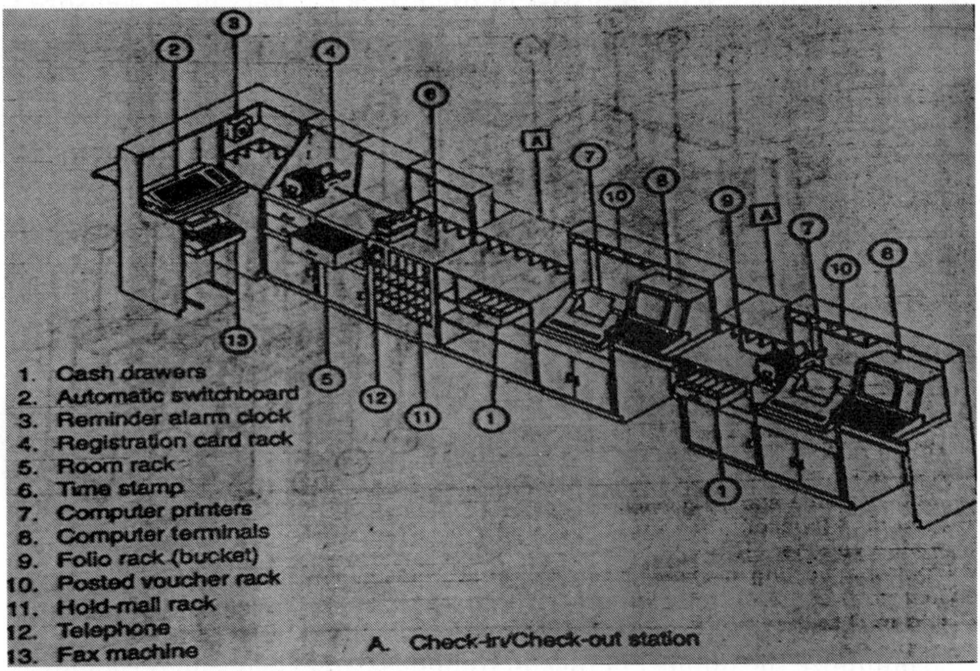

In fully automated property, both advance and current reservation racks may be eliminated. The equivalent information may be internally managed by the computer's reservation software and be accessible upon demand

Information Rack

An information rack is composed of two index listings of in- house guests, one by assigned room number. An information rack is commonly used to assist front office employees with proper routing of telephone calls, mail, messages, and visitor inquires. The information rack normally consists of aluminum slots designed to hold guest information slips. These slots can be easily arranged and re- arranged to fit the immediate needs of the hotel.

Folio Trays

In non- automated and semi automated properties, guest's folios are stored in a front office tray and arranged in ascending order by guestroom number. Guest folios remains in the tray throughout the occupancy stage of the guest cycle, except when they are used in posting transaction.

A second folio tray is normally located in the hotels accounting office. This tray contains the folios of departed guests being direct- billed or of guests who paid by credit card.

In computerized front office, the folio tray does not really hold the folios since it is held automatically electronically in the computer. The folio tray may, however, hold the completed registration card, if appropriate, and imprinted credit card voucher for each registered guest.

Account Posting Machine

Semi- automated hotels that allow guests to charge purchases to their rooms use an account posting to post, monitor, and balance the charges. A posting machine normally provides:-

- A standardized means of recording transaction
- A legible guest account statement.
- A basis for cash and deferred payment management
- An analysis of departmental sales activity
- An audit trail of charge purchase transaction

Support Devices

The front office may have numerous pieces of support equipment in addition to its racks, registers, and machines. These devices can make cumbersome functions straightforward, facilitate information handling, and provide additional storage for data, files, and ad reports used in the front office area.

Credit card imprinters presses credit card imprinters presses a credit card voucher against a guests credit card. The impact causes the raised number, expiration date, and name on the card to be recorded on the voucher for use in credit card billing and collection procedures.

A magnet strip reader reads data that is magnetically encoded and stored on the magnetic strips on the back of a credit card and transmits the data to a credit card authorization service.

Franking machine

- Franking machine can stamp hundreds of envelops quickly and efficiently by printing the correct amount of postage required and date on the envelope according to the envelops weight and size
- The franking machine records the totals of all stamps issued
- At the agreed time the amount of postage used is paid to the supplier along with a lease fee for the product.

- These are utilized mainly by large businesses and are rented from registered suppliers . they are used to process out going bulk mail.
- Franking machines are programmed by the supplier to have a certain amount of value placed for pre-programmed credit on a meter.
- When this value is reached the machine ceases to operate until more money is paid and the meter is reset.

Paper shredders

- Sometimes your organization will want to destroy letters or documents that are confidential or contain records that are useful to competitors
- Shredders cut paper into very thin strips so that they are very difficult to reassemble and read.

Key encoder

- Key card issuing machine which should be interfaced with Fidelio/ opera (PMS)
- The purpose of this machine is to issue keys assigned to the rooms which are then handed over to the guest

Photocopier

- A photocopier similar to a fax machine will produce an exact copy of a document. It enables to reproduce documents without the need to retype or reprint them.
- Rapidly copying several one or two sided pages
- Stapling collated documents
- Reducing or increasing the size of the copied documents
- Reproducing in colour or black and white.

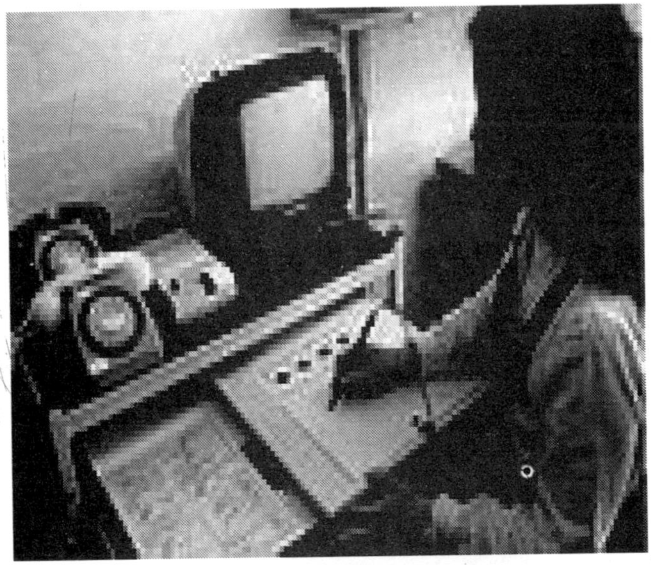

The operator telewriter writers with a pen like stylus on a specially designed surface. The handwritten message on this surface is displayed on a similar device located elsewhere. Similar to a fax machine, the telewriter is used to transmit written communication from one location to another (for example from front office to housekeeping).

Folios, mail, and other front office paperwork are inserted into a time stamp device to record the current time and date. This recording can be very important in establishing a chronology of events and transactions.

Wake up device

- Despite advances in technology some hotels may prefer that front desk agents or telephone operators make wake up calls to provide a more personal touch
- Typically the clock relied upon for wake up call purposes is the hotel clock , therefore this clock should be checked regularly to ensure that it is correct .
- In some hotels guests can dial a special telephone extension from the guestroom phone and follow instructions provided by the system to request an automated wake up call.

Securities Monitors

Such as closed circuit cameras television monitors, allow front office or securities personnel to monitor certain areas of the hotel from a central location.

A non- automated wake-up device is usually a specially designed clock with multiple alarm settings to remind front office desk agents or telephone operators to place wake up calls. A wake up call log kept beside the clock informs the agents or operators which room numbers are to be called at what times. This clock is usually known as hotel clock.

International travelers are likely to make hotel reservation by the telex network connection. The caller directs a message from a local telex machine to the hotel's telex machine. A return telex is used to confirm the reservation. Telex communication is faster than the postal service and more reliable than telephone networking since the hotel receives a written since the hotel receives a written message.

Fully automated hotels may provide self check in and check out to the guests.

Telecommunication

Hotels must be able to support a broad range of telephone calls with adequate equipment to ensure an efficient and effective telecommunications system. There are many types of calls a guest may during a hotel stay:

- **Local calls:** A local call terminates within a local calling area and typically is billed on a per call basis rather than on a per minute basis. Local telephone calls are handled by the local phone company.
- **Direct dial long distance calls:** These are most common call placed by hotels guests. A long distance call terminates outside the local calling area. Once a long distance number is dialed, it is distributed over the hotel's telephone lines the local phone company office.
- **Calling card:** These are typically billed to a code number on a calling card issued by either a local phone company or by a long distance company.
- **Credit card calls:** Many telephone companies accept credit card calls such as visa, master card, and American express as valid phone charge cards. Call placements is similar to calling card procedure.
- **Collect calls:** A guest dials '0' and then the full telephone number, and then waits several seconds for an operator. The guest informs the operator that the call is collect- the call is to be billed to the receiving party.
- **Third party calls:** These are similar to collect, except that the billed number is not the called number.
- **Person to person calls:** These are not connected unless a specific party, named by the caller, verifies that he or she is on the line. This is an expensive call, but has no cost if the requested party is not available.
- **Billed to room calls international:** Billed to room call operator assists calls. An operator places the calls for the guest and later informs the hotels of the amount of the charge.
- **International calls:** It can be direct dialed or placed with operator

assistance. To direct dial international access code, a country code, city code, and the telephone number.

- **800 or 888 toll free calls:** Toll free calls can be direct dialed from a guest room as either local calls or long distances calls. In either case, the guest receives access to the outside world line and dials '1' plus the 800 or 888 number.
- **900 premium price calls:** Calls made to businesses that charge callers a fee for the call are 900 or premium calls. Problem arises when this type of call made from guestrooms. The rates for 900 calls vary.

TELEPHONE EQUIPMENTS

Systems and equipment used by hotels for placing calls are as follows:

PBX System

Historically, an important piece of equipment controlling phone service at hotels with more than forty rooms was the switchboard or private branch exchange (PBX). This equipment takes inbound calls to the hotels PBX operator's console. The hotel's operator sends these calls on to particular extensions or stations lines.

Phobic System

Before hotel began pricing their own calls, their telephone companies priced them. The system used to process these calls was called the hotels billing information system center (HOBIC). Guests call went out over special hotel Telephone Company would intercept the call, break onto the line, and arrange for the call to be billed to a collect number, a third party number, a telephone company calling card, or the callers hotel room.

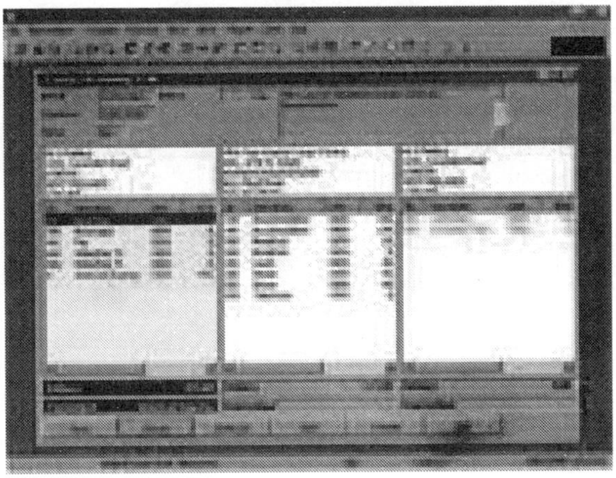

Call Accounting System

These systems enable hotels to place and price telephone calls without assistance operators or front desk staff. A call accounting system (CAS) is a set of software programs that intimate the placement, pricing and posting of calls. The CAS may interface with a hotel's computer system and electronically post charges to guest's folios.

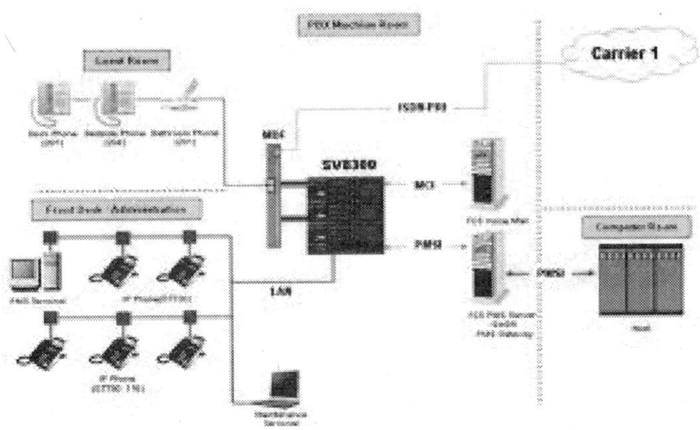

Guestroom Phones

Along with other telecommunication equipment, guestroom phones are increasing in sophistication and capabilities. For example, guests can plug personal computers or portable fax machines in to some guestroom phones. These phones have an input jack for standard computer or fax machines.

Pay Phones

Hotel rarely purchase their own pay phones due to the potentially high maintenance costs. These phones generally take a lot of abuse and are placed in public areas such as in order the hotel lobby,

Meeting rooms, conference areas, banquet rooms, and restaurants. Many hotels have their own pay phones supplied and maintained

By accompany other than their local phone company.

Pagers and Cellular Phones

Some hotels offer a pager or cellular phones and now a day's tablet rental to guests at check-in. In the case of cellular phones, the hotel bills the guest for the number of minutes of recorded use, as indicated by the phone's usage meter.

Other Technology

Often hotels install telephone systems and sophisticated features for reasons other than just cost effectiveness. Example, of these features include automatic call dispensing systems, telephone or room status systems, fax machines, computers/ laptops, call detection systems/ equipment.

QUESTIONNAIRE

1. What is lobby?
2. What are different types of lobby?
3. What are different equipments used at front desk? Explain?
4. What are different types of telephone equipments?
5. Write a note on lobby and its equipments?
6. What is telecommunication?
7. What is CAS?
8. What are different types of racks? Explain.
9. What are PBX and HOBIC system? Explain.
10. Write a short note on Folio trays?

7
BELL DESK

- INTRODUCTION
- FUNCTION OF BELL DESK
- DUTIES AND RESPONSIBILITIES OF BELL DESK STAFF
- QUESTIONNAIRE

INTRODUCTION

Bell desk section is next to the reception counter in the front office or near by the entrance. Bell desk is an extended arm of front desk. As the name suggest it is a small desk near the main entrance of the lobby. The Bell desk is headed by Senior Bell Captain. The primary duty is bellboy is to carry the luggage of the guest at the time of check-in and check-out. The department operates 24 hours.

The Bell desk should be situated in clear view of the front desk, cashier and particularly the doorman standing outside the lobby so that the doorman may signal for a bellboy at the arrival of a guest to carry the luggage. Further it is also important that the bell desk is situated near the luggage centre and luggage entrance.

FUNCTION OF BELL DESK

The senior bell captain is the in-charge of bell desk along with his staff performs various duties from here. The various function performed from here as follows:

1.Luggage Handling

Luggage handling of guest is done at various occasions such as arrival, during stay and at the time of departure. At the time of arrival when the luggage of the guest is moved from car/taxi to the lobby and further to the allotted room, the activity is called as "up bell desk activity". When the luggage of the guest is moved from room to lobby and further to the car/ taxi at the time of departure the activities called down bell activity.

LUGGAGE TAG

Room No. ____________________

Guest Name ____________________

Remarks ____________________

Handled by ____________________

Temporary of Luggage Storage

The baggage is collected from room upon request. A left luggage register is maintained in this case and an entry is made in this book. A baggage ticket (which has two parts) is used. One part is attached to the luggage and the counterfoil is given to the guest. The portion details the hotel's liability exemption clause. When the guest comes to collect his luggage he has to produce his portion of baggage ticket. The luggage store room must be secure at all times.

LEFT BAGGAGE REGISTER

Date	Room No.	Name of Guest	Bell Boy No.	Luggage Tag No.	Description of Luggage	Date of Delivery	Remarks

HOTEL XYZ LTD.

Date .... Room No................

BAGGAGE CHECK

NO. 1234

NOT RESPONSIBLE FOR GOODS LEFT OVER 30 DAYS

SUIT CASE	BRIEF CASE	SUIT BOX	GOLF BAGS
UMBRELLA	OVER COAT	PACKAGE	OTHERS

NO. 1234

NOT RESPONSIBLE FOR GOODS LEFT OVER 30 DAYS

Date............ Room No.............

SCANTY BAGGAGE PROCEDURE

Scanty baggage means no baggage or a light baggage consisting of brief case or air bag. Guests with scanty baggage are normal skippers from the hotel. Skippers are those who check out of the hotel without settling the bills. The scanty baggage guests also normally go out with their light baggage and hotel never knows that if this guest is going out with an intention to come back or not. To save guard the hotel interest, normally guests with scanty baggage are requested to pay in advance.

SCANTY BAGGAGE REGISTER
HOTEL ABC
THE MALL, DELHI

Date.............

S. No	R. No.	Name of Guest	Designation and Address	Date of Arrival	Exp Date of Departure	Checked Bell Captain	Remarks	Signature

2. Paging

Apart from luggage handling the bell desk is also responsible for paging a guest. The paging is a system of locating the guest in the hotel. Many times the in house guest expects a phone call or a visitor but decides not to wait in the room, and might decide to go the public area such as bar, restaurants; swimming pool, lobby or lounge etc. of the hotel or you may go out of the hotel. In such a case the hotel request the guest tell about his whereabouts through a location form. Usually it is filled in by the guest but many times it may be filled by hotel staff.

In hotels different systems of paging are used:-

Page Board System

The most commonly used system is called 'page board system'. This is simple system in which the bellboy is required to carry a small board which has a small handle and small bells attached to it? The receptionists write the name of the guest and his room number on the board, and the bellboy carries this board to the public area which has been mention on the location form by the guest and keeps ringing reattached bells. This attracts the attention of the guest immediately.

PAGER

With the development of electronic communication equipments some hill resorts or sea beach resorts which are spread in vast area used pager for paging

VIP guests who are given pagers where they can be immediately reached if there is a phone call or visitor for them.

3. Mail and Message Handling

The bell desk's function is also to handle and distribute mail and message received by the front desk in the absence of the guest to their respective room. Also distribution of newspaper and magazines etc. to various dooms and areas of the hotel and keeping a record of the same is done by the bell desk.

MESSAGE FORM
A B C HOTEL
CONNAUGHT CIRCUS, NEW DELHI

DATE..................

Time ....

Name of the Guest..

Room No. ....

A MESSAGE WAS RECEIVED WHILE YOU WERE AWAY

FROM:

Mr./Ms. ....

Address ....

T. No. ....

Message ....

4. Delivery of Newspapers

As per the hotel policy all hotel guests receive a copy of local newspaper each morning. The bell boy in night shift is responsible for delivering the newspaper to all occupied rooms. The bell captain obtained the room verification report. The bellboy then marks the room numbers on each newspaper. The bellboy also inserts the daily newsletters in each paper provided by the public relations the previous evening.

5. Collection of Room Keys at Departure

Another very important function of the bell desk is the collection of room key from check out guest and depositing the same at information desk.

6. Wake Call

In some hotels the wake up call to group or crew is coordinated by bell desk. In such a cases it is responsibility of the bell captain on duty in the morning shift to prepare the wake call sheets of all the groups and crews in-house.

GUEST ARRIVAL ERRANT CARD

Bell Boy................ Room No..........

Name of Guest............ Date & Day.........

LUGGAGE DESCRIPTION

Suit case	Brief case	Hand bag	Packets	Others	Remarks

Sign. of Bell Boy..................... Sign. Of Bell Captain..................

DUTIES & RESPONSIBILITIES' OF BELL DESK STAFF

SENIOR BELL CAPTAIN

1. Control and supervise the lobby staff,
2. Train the lobby staff to maximize the departmental efficiency,
3. Ensure smooth coordination between lobby and front office to facilitate smooth check in and checkout,
4. Supervise the procurement and sale of postage stamp,
5. Responsible for "left luggage" room,
6. Responsible for the safety and security in the lobby,
7. Ensure that all procedures regarding arrivals & departures are strictly followed by his staff,
8. Co-ordinates closely with tour leader regarding group baggage handling,
9. Attend to guest complaint in the absence of lobby manager to ensure prompt action,

10. Ensure delivery of morning newspaper to the guest room as well as to the executive offices,
11. Supervise daily briefing conducted by the bell captain,

BELL CAPTAIN

1. Supervise the movement of bell boys with the help of bell captain control sheet,
2. Advise the lobby manager periodically on the performance of bell boys,
3. Handle left luggage formalities and maintain the baggage check room,
4. Train the bell boys to maximize departmental efficiency,
5. Organize and supervise check in and checkout baggage formalities of guest, groups and crew,
6. Control the sale of postage stamp and postage stationery to guest,
7. Maintain record of all guest with scanty baggage and inform lobby manager about them,
8. Assist security in lobby surveillance,
9. Conduct daily briefing for bell boys,
10. Co- ordinate and control the distribution of morning newspaper,
11. Supervise the storage of essential medicine by the house doctor and be accountable of the issues made,
12. Keep the lobby area clean all the time,
13. Keep the baggage of check in and checkout guest in the lobby in an orderly fashion at the specified places.
14. Co-ordinates with:
    a) FRONT OFFICE: to execute efficiently the arrivals and departure formalities,
    b) TELEPHONE: to arrange for wake calls especially for airline crew members and groups,
    c) SECURITY: to help protect hotel property and image from undesirable persons,
    d) FRONT OFFICE CASHIER: for receiving clearance to remove baggage out of the hotel as a consequence of guest paying their bills,
    e) HOUSEKEEPING: for cleanliness and uniforms,

BELL BOY

1. Take the baggage from the car or the taxi in the porch into the lobby and then to the guest assigned room,
2. Escort the guest to the room on his arrival,
3. Place the baggage in the guest room on the luggage rack,
4. Explain the operation of light/ air conditioning control to the guest and switch them on,
5. Under instruction from the bell captain bring down the guest baggage from his room at the time of guest departure,
6. Check the departure room to ensure that the guest has not left any articles in the room by mistake,
7. Switch off the lights and air condition once the departure has taken place,
8. Obtain clearance from the front office cashier on his errand card regarding the guest bill,
9. Ensure collection of room key from the guest at the time of check out and after depositing the same at the information obtain clearance on his errand card from the information assistant,
10. Check mail message for departing guest at the time of his departure and hand over the same to the guest,
11. Take out the guest baggage from the lobby and place it in the car or taxi,
12. Handle errands requested by guest or the executives,
13. Handle guest baggage in case of room change,
14. Distribute newspaper to guest rooms and to executive offices,
15. Keep an eye on unwanted guests in the hotel,
16. Keep the lobby area clean at all times,
17. Attend to instructions of his supervisor,
18. Deliver guest message to guest room,
19. Handle and store equipment carefully and appropriately i.e. luggage trolleys& wheel chair,
20. Report guest with scanty baggage to the lobby manager
21. Run errand inside and outside the hotel as may be instructed,

QUESTIONNAIRE

1. What is bell desk and give its functions.
2. Give the layout of bell desk.
3. Give the duties and responsibilities of senior bell captain & bell captain.
4. Write in detail the duties of bell boy.
5. Write the role of bell desk in case of group check-in and check-out.
6. Draw the formats
   (i) Left baggage register
   (ii) Scanty baggage registers
   (iii) Message form
   (iv) Errant card.
7. What is scanty baggage procedure?

8

FRENCH USED IN FRONT OFFICE OPERATION BASIC FRENCH

- NOMBRES CARDINAUX
- NOMBRES ORDINAUX
- HEURE (TIME)

NOMBRES CARDINAUX

- une/une -1
- deux - 2
- trois -3
- quatre -4
- cinq -5
- six -6
- sept -7
- huit -8
- neuf -9
- dix -10
- onze -11
- douze -12
- treize -13
- quatorze -14
- quinze -15
- seize -16
- dix-sept -17
- dix-huit -18
- dix-neuf -19
- vingt -20
- vingt et un -21
- trente- 30
- trente et un -31
- quarante -40
- quarante et un -41
- cinquante -50
- cinquante et un -51
- soixante -60
- soixante et un -61

- soixante-dix -70
- soixante et onze -71
- soixante douze -72
- soixante treize -73
- soixante quatorze -74
- soixante quinze -75
- soixante seize -76
- soixante dix-sept -77
- soixante dix-huit -78
- soixante dix-neuf -79
- quatre-vingt -80
- quatre-vingt-un -81
- quatre-vingt-deux -82
- quatre-vingt-trois -83
- quatre-vingt-quatre -84
- quatre-vingt-cinq -85
- quatre-vingt-six -86
- quatre-vingt-sept -87
- quatre-vingt-huit -88
- quatre-vingt-neuf -89
- quatre-vingt-dix -90
- quatre-vingt-onze -91
- quatre-vingt-douze -92
- quatre-vingt-treize -93
- quatre-vingt-quatorze -94
- quatre-vingt-quinze -95
- quatre-vingt-seize -96
- quatre-vingt-dix-sept -97
- quatre-vingt-dix-huit -98
- quatre-vingt-dix-neuf -99

- cent -100
- cent un -101
- deux cents -200

NOMBRES ORDINAUX

1er	premier (m), 1re première (f)
2e	deuxième
3e	troisième
4e	quatrième
5e	cinquième
6e	sixième
7e	septième
8e	huitième
9e	neuvième
10e	dixième
11e	onzième
12e	douzième
13e	treizième
14e	quatorzième
15e	quinzième
16e	seizième
17e	dix-septième
18e	dix-huitième
19e	dix-neuvième
20e	vingtième
21e	vingt et unième
22e	vingt-deuxième
23e	vingt-troisième
24e	vingt-quatrième
25e	vingt-cinquième
26e	vingt-sixième
27e	vingt-septième
28e	vingt-huitième

30e	trentième
31e	trente et unième
32e	trente-deuxième
33e	trente-troisième
34e	trente-quatrième
35e	trente-cinquième
36e	trente-sixième
37e	trente-septième
38e	trente-huitième
39e	trente-neuvième
40e	quarantième
41e	quarante et unième
42e	quarante-deuxième
43e	quarante-troisième
44e	quarante-quatrième
45e	quarante-cinquième
46e	quarante-sixième
47e	quarante-septième
48e	quarante-huitième
49e	quarante-neuvième
50e	cinquantième
51e	cinquante et unième
52e	cinquante-deuxième
53e	cinquante-troisième
54e	cinquante-quatrième
55e	cinquante-cinquième
56e	cinquante-sixième
57e	cinquante-septième
58e	cinquante-huitième
59e	cinquante-neuvième
60e	soixantième
61e	soixante et unième

62e	soixante-deuxième
63e	soixante-troisième
64e	soixante-quatrième
65e	soixante-cinquième
66e	soixante-sixième
67e	soixante-septième
68e	soixante-huitième
69e	soixante-neuvième
70e	soixante-dixième
71e	soixante et onzième
72e	soixante-douzième
73e	soixante-treizième
74e	soixante-quatorzième
75e	soixante-quinzième
76e	soixante-seizième
77e	soixante-dix-septième
78e	soixante-dix-huitième
79e	soixante-dix-neuvième
80e	quatre-vingtième
81e	quatre-vingt-unième
82e	quatre-vingt-deuxième
83e	quatre-vingt-troisième
84e	quatre-vingt-quatrième
85e	quatre-vingt-cinquième
86e	quatre-vingt-sixième
87e	quatre-vingt-septième
88e	quatre-vingt-huitième
89e	quatre-vingt-neuvième
90e	quatre-vingt-dixième
91e	quatre-vingt-onzième
92e	quatre-vingt-deuxième
93e	quatre-vingt-treizième
94e	quatre-vingt-quatorzième

95e	quatre-vingt-quinzième
96e	quatre-vingt-seizième
97e	quatre-vingt-dix-septième
98e	quatre-vingt-dix-huitième
99e	quatre-vingt-dix-neuvième
100e	centième

HEURE (TIME)

What time is it?	Quelle heure est-il ?	
It's one o'clock	Il est une heure	1h00
It's two o'clock	Il est deux heures	2h00
It's 3:30	Il est trois heures et demie Il est trois heures trente	3h30
It's 4:15	Il est quatre heures et quart Il est quatre heures quinze	4h15
It's 4:45	Il est cinq heures moins le quart Il est cinq heures moins quinze Il est quatre heures quarante-cinq	4h45
It's 5:10	Il est cinq heures dix	5h10
It's 6:50	Il est sept heures moins dix Il est six heures cinquante	6h50
It's 7 a.m.	Il est sept heures du matin	7h00
It's 3 p.m.	Il est trois heures de l'après-midi Il est quinze heures	15h00
It's 6 p.m.	Il est six heures du soir Il est dix-huit heures	18h00
It's noon	Il est midi	12h00
It's midnight	Il est minuit	0h00

(Les jours de la semaine)-Days of the Week

lundi	–	Monday
mardi	–	Tuesday
mercredi	–	Wednesday
jeudi	–	Thursday

vendredi	–	Friday
samedi	–	Saturday
dimanche	–	Sunday

(Les mois de l'année)-Months of the Year

janvier	–	January
février	–	February
mars	–	March
avril	–	April
mai	–	May
juin	–	June
juillet	–	July
août	–	August
septembre	–	September
octobre	–	October
novembre	–	November
décembre	–	December

9

TARIFF STRUCTURE

- BASIS OF CHARGING
- PLANS, COMPETITION, CUSTOMER'S PROFILE, STANDARDS OF SERVICE & AMENITIES
- HUBBART FORMULA
- DIFFERENT TYPES OF TARIFFS
- RACK RATE
- DISCOUNTED RATES FOR CORPORATE, AIRLINES, GROUPS & TRAVEL

BASIS OF CHARGING

Check-in /Check-out Basis

- It is the most common way of fixation of tariff
- The hotel fixes a specific time usually 12.00 noon as check-out time which means the guest charging cycle begins from 12.00 noon and finishes at 12.00 noon on the next day.
- For a guest staying in a hotel after 12.00 noon, next day's charge may be levied.
- Accounting keeping is simple in this system.

Twenty-four Hour Basis

- In this system the charges of room starts from the time when the guest checks in and he has to pay for one day upto 24 hours from the time of arrival.
- This system is good for small and budget hotels only.

Night Basis

- In this system the guest is charged on the basis of number of nights that he spends in the hotel irrespective of time of arrival.
- If he spends two nights he will be charged for two nights with a minimum of one day charges

Day Basis

- Sometimes a guest may stay in the hotel for a few hours only and may not spend the night in the hotel at all.
- In such cases where he stays only for six hours maximum hotels may charge special discounted rate and the rate is called "day rate or day use rate".

Inclusive & Non Inclusive Rates

- Hotels also charge room rates on the basis of meals provided or not provided along with room to the guest.
- European plan: where the tariff of room includes only in the room rate for meals charged extra rate.
- Continental plan: where the room tariff includes along with room rate the continental breakfast also.
- American plan: where the room tariff includes along with room rates the English breakfast, table d'hôte lunch and dinner may also include.
- Modified American plan: where the room tariff along with room rates include English breakfast and one of the two major meals either lunch or dinner.

Rule of Thumb

- Another very traditional way of charging room rate is rule of thumb.
- In this system "one Rupee" rate is fixed for every Rs 1000/- spent on room construction cost.
- This is also called as 'cost rate formula'.

Room Tariff Card

- Room tariff is a document published by the hotel for use by the travel trade, organization and individual prospective guest.
- The list includes prices of rooms classified into different categories, such as single room, double room, twin room, suites, etc. and meal plans such as American, European and Continental etc.
- Meals such as American, European and Continental also.

HOTEL

K L G

TARIFF CARD

EXPERIENCE A ROYAL STAY WITH US.

DELUX	Single	2699.00
	Double	3299.00
SUPER-DELUX	Single	3199.00
	Double	3799.00
EXECUTIVE	Single	3699.00
	Double	4299.00
ITALIAN SUITE	Single	6500.00
	Extra Person / Bed	700.00

Taxes applicable as per law from Time to Time
Check-Out time 12.00 noon.
Equivalent dollar rate is applicable to all Foreign Nationals
All Major Credit cards accepted.
Tariff is subject to change with out prior notice.

Rack Rate

- Rack rate is a term which refers to the normal room rate of the hotel.
- This is the room rate which is published on the room tariff card.
- This is also the rate which is written on the shannon slip which is slipped in room rate of those hotels which operate on whitney system.

Corporate Rate

- This programme covers corporate offices and usually 15-25% discount can be given to the officers coming from corporate.
- The corporate rate is widely accepted as the transient target rate for most hotels.
- This is simply an average rate goal a hotel fixes achieve for a certain day or market segment.

Group Rate

- A Room tariff published in a document to group operators which is commissionable only to retail travel agents, tour operators and wholesalers.
- Generally commissionable at 10% of the published rack rate.

Government Rate and Discounted Rate

- Government employees are given per day allowance for their travelling.
- Accommodation and food by their office and some hotels offer them a rate which give them room and accommodation with in that price.
- DISCOUNTED RATE: Airlines, travel agent discounts rates should be fixed in competition to other hotels of the area.

Seasonal Rate, Crib Rate and Extra Bed Rate

- Seasonal Rate: Season and Resort hotel which usually have fluctuating demand change their rate usually as per the seasonally and offer different rates for in season and off season.
- Crib Rate: A special rate applicable to children below 12 years of age and accompanying their parents.
- Extra bed Rate: Generally one fourth of the published room rate.

Family Rate

- Special rates for families – for example, one couple and a child below 5 years, then the rate may be for one double room.
- One couple with two children below 12 years, the rate may be one double room plus one extra bed rate etc.

Food Plans

1. European Plan (EP)

This plan includes only the room charges and morning tea in some cases. All other charges are charged extra. Most commercial hotels run on this plan.

2. Continental Plan (CP.)

This plan includes room charges and a continental breakfast. All additional charges are considered extra. [A continental b/f consists of juices, toast or rolls, butter, cheese, jam, tea or coffee but no eggs.]

3. Bermuda Plan (BP)

This plan includes room charges optional early morning tea and an American breakfast.

[American b/f is a buffet breakfast not served in the room]

4. American Plan (AP)

This plan includes all principal meals. It includes room charges with morning tea, English B/F, lunch, afternoon tea and dinner. It is mostly found in resort hotels and in commercial hotels catering to groups sent by airlines and companies or travel agents. This plan is also known as 'all inclusive plan' or 'full board' or 'en pension' [English breakfast has all courses like American B/F and ham, beacon, meat is also included].

5. Modified American Plan (MAP)

This plan has evolved out of the American plan. It includes room charges with morning tea, English B/F and an option of lunch or dinner. It is also called as 'demi pension' or 'half board'. This facilitates the guests to eat out for one meal. It is usually used for groups where meal coupons are provided to the guests (coupon is valid only for a day) and the coupon cost is included in the room rent.

The use of these plans:

Commercial hotels prefer EP because:

1. Commercial hotels are situated in the urban areas, there are bound to be numerous restaurants in the vicinity. Hence the guest will prefer to keep his option open as far as meals are concerned. Moreover the hotel may not have a particular cuisine which the guest likes.
2. On the other hand hotel being situated in an urban area would get plenty of chance guests in their restaurants. Thus their F&B income is not restricted to only hotel residents. They do offer meal inclusive plans but only to groups sent by travel agents and company bookings for conventions, seminars, etc.

Resort hotels prefer AP/ MAP because

1. They may be situated in an isolated area with hardly any restaurant in the vicinity. Guests therefore prefer to have meals in the hotel. For the tourists wishing to go sightseeing during the day, an MAP will be more appropriate.
2. The hotel itself benefits from this plan since the hotel relies only on the resident guests for their food and beverage income.

The CP. & BP lie between EP & AP so they can be offered by any hotel.

Above five are food plans.

There is another plan called 'GO PLAN'

It is not a food plan. It is an adjustment made in the settlement of accounts.

If a guest stays in different hotels of the same chain in the course of his tour, his bills will be forwarded to his next destination every time he changes the place of stay. The guest can make the payment at the last hotel he visits belonging to the same chain.

HUBBART FORMULA

The Hubbart Formula is a formula that can be used in Hotel management. It is used to determine the proper average rate to set for rooms in a given hotel.

Hotel managers have to be very careful when setting prices. Unlike managers in many other businesses, they cannot manipulate supply. All they can do to make the optimal profit is to set prices in such a way that they fill as many rooms as possible every night while making the

Greatest amount of money. They do not want to set prices so high that people will not buy, but they do not want to set them too low because that would result in a loss of potential revenue.

The Hubbart Formula is used to help with setting prices. It can be expressed as a formula:

[(Operating expenses + Desired return on investment) – other income]/ projected room nights = room rate.

The Hubbart Formula, then, takes into account how much income is needed from each room to get the level of return that is desired. It can therefore be used to help determine the average rate to charge for a night's stay in a room in a given hotel.

SPECIAL RATES

Very often a room may not be sold at the tariff quoted on the tariff sheet. The rooms may be discounted or special rates may be applied under certain conditions, or as a special case.

COMPANY VOLUME GUARANTEED RATE

Based on the room night potential of different companies, certain hotels give a special rate to those companies which contribute a large volume of room nights. This special rate offered came to be called as the 'Company Volume Guaranteed Rate' (C.V.G.R) or 'Company Guaranteed Rate' (C.G.R.). The higher the volume of business, the higher was the percentage of discount given. For this purpose, all those companies which offer a large quantum of business could be 'A' rated. As the contribution figure dipped, the company rating would also drop to 'B' or even 'C' for those with a relatively poor volume of business.

Many hotels today, in order to accommodate all categories of employees from one particular organization, have gone ahead and offered very low rates to the lower down officers, and higher rates to the top brass of the company, based on their entitlements and expenditure capabilities. A record of the room night contribution (R.N.C.) of individual companies are maintained either on a computerized system or manually by an alphabetically indented register. Periodically, the companies are informed of their volume contribution. If the expected room night contribution was not maintained by any one company, they would fall to a lower rating or even be left out of the C.G.R. list after the total period of assessment.

PACKAGE RATES

Many resort hotels (especially during lean/Off season periods) and some commercial hotels from time to time coin seasonal packages for different durations (e.g.: two nights three days/three nights four days), which may include besides the room and meal, a complimentary airport transfer, sightseeing, entertainment etc.

OFF-SEASON RATES

Most resorts and other seasonal hotels have separate tariffs for peak and off-seasons. The off-season rates are much lower than regular or peak-season rates.

EMPLOYEE RATE

Employees of major hotel chains have a special employee rate for all employees at their member hotels within the chain. This is however based on the availability of space and policy of the individual hotel.

F.H.R.A.I DISCOUNT

The Federation of Hotel and Restaurants Association of India (F.H.R.A.I) is a major association of hotels and restaurants in India. As a gesture of goodwill for members of the same fraternity, the association issues membership cards to the Proprietor / Partners / Chairman / M.Ds of these establishments, which entitles them to a special discount (presently 30% on room rent, food and beverage

(Excluding liquor), if paid by cash and 25% if settled through a credit card. The percentage of discount and other conditions are subject to change).

AIRLINE CREW

Most airlines enter into a contract with hotels in different cities where its flights commute, wherein staff of the airline (crew) are given a very special rate for a fixed period. Their duration of stay may be a few hours up to a maximum of 24 hours. There is also another special rate negotiated for the lay-over passengers. The food-plan applied would be based on the requirement, but the food element computed is also on a discounted basis

GROUPS

Groups (G.I.T - Guest in Transit) are given special rates due to the number of rooms taken by them at a time. A group under standard stipulation, comprises of 15 guests or more. Based on the discretion of the Management, the group leader may be given a complimentary room for a minimum of 15 paying customers.

Guests who do not come into any of the above groups are called as 'F.I.Ts' or Free Individual Travelers. i.e., they are not part of any group or company enjoying special rates. When these are Indians or Domestic clientele, they are referred to as 'D.F.I.T'. Or 'Domestic Free Individual Traveler'. Similarly, if the guest is not a domestic traveler i.e., if he is a foreigner, then he is called as 'F.F.I.T'. Or 'Foreign Free Individual Traveler'.

CRIB RATE

This is a special rate applicable in some hotels to children. Most Indian hotels prefer to compliment up to a maximum of two children below the age of twelve.

EXTRA BED / EXTRA PERSON CHARGES

As most five star hotels today do not have single rooms, but have only double rooms which could accommodate a minimum of two guests, a third person if present, is given an extra bed and charged. This charge is in most hotels.

Levied even if an extra bed is not given. The rate charged could be approximately 20 to 25% of the room rate.

Besides the above, special rates may also be given to a hoard of other category of people based on the discounting policies of the management. Some of these might be commercially important persons (C.I.Ps) for publicity and promotion purposes, influential persons like company directors, decision makers, top executives, travel writers, etc. Such discounts have to be authorized by a senior member of the Management.

MARKET BASED PRICING

It is setting a price based on value of the product in the perception of the customer.

A) Competition: Rate must be competitive (at the same time it should be able to produce adequate revenue to meet fixed obligation) with other hotels of the same standards and providing almost similar services and facilities as provided by other hotels situated in the same vicinity of the city.

B) Rate Cutting: lowering of rates to increase occupancy level, especially during off season also at a time of the year or day of the week when you need business.

C) Guest Requirements: Various room tariffs as per guest requirements e.g.: early check-in on CP basis or late check out on MAP basis. Various amenities the hotels is going to provide to the guest such as air conditioning in all rooms, carpeting ,provision of swimming pool, tennis court equipment, arrangement for conferences halls , lobbies, lawns ,parking spaces ,special aspect of Continental & Indian cuisine, cutlery and crockery, modern equipments and machinery.

D) Market Tolerance: Checking competing hotels best available rates for a room. These rates can be found out by hotels by calling up the competing hotels without disclosing their identity.

E) Inclusive and Non Inclusive Rates: Charging room rates on the basis of meals provided on a CP/MAP/AP basis.

OTHERS ARE:

- Customer Profile: Category of customer coming to your hotel .The social status and financial status i.e. Paying Capacity, should be kept in mind.
- Locality: Locality where hotel is situated whether posh area-Shopping & other facilities.
- Room Location: Front room and rooms opening to better view would cost more than dark rooms, corner rooms.
- Publicity: The amount of publicity done by hotel. The type of expense has to be adjusted somehow as it has no source of return but is a must in popularizing the various service of a hotel.
- • Standard Of service: More amenities, higher the standard and so also higher the room rate

QUESTIONAIRE

1. What is tariff structure?
2. What is the basis of charging in tariff structure?
3. What are the two common methods of fixing the room tariff?
4. What are the points which are to be considered which are kept in mind for fixing hotel tariff?
5. What are the methods for establishing room rates?
6. What do you mean by rule of thumb?
7. What is Hubbart Formula?

10

FRONT OFFICE AND GUEST HANDLING

- PRE ARRIVAL
- ARRIVAL
- DURING GUEST STAY
- DEPARTURE
- QUESTIONNAIRE

INTRODUCTION

Guest Cycle

A division of the flow of business through a hotel that identifies the physical contacts and financial exchanges between guests and hotel employees.

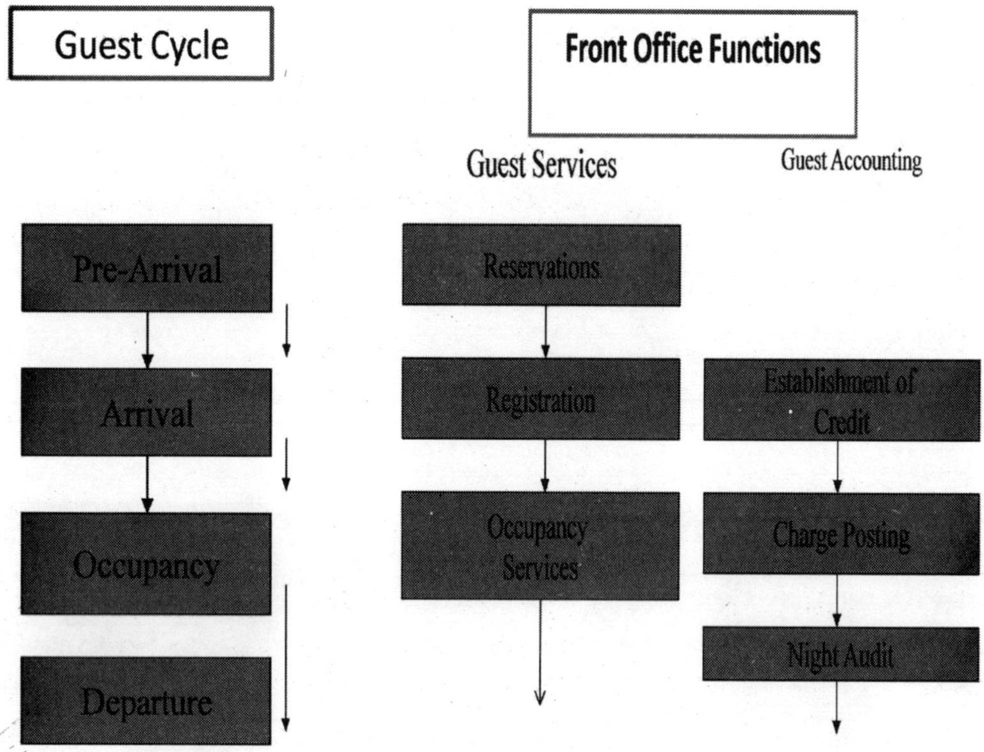

Pre-Arrival

The guest chooses a hotel during the pre-arrival stage of the guest cycle.

The guest's choice can be affected by many factors:

- Previous experiences with the hotel;
- Advertisements;
- Recommendations from travel agents, friends, or business associates;
- The hotel's location or reputation and preconceptions based upon the hotel's name or chain affiliation;

- Ease of making reservations;
- How the reservations agent describes the hotel and its facilities, room rates, amenities;
- The attitude, efficiency, and knowledge of the front office staff may influence a caller's decision to stay a particular hotel.

Reservations

An agreement between the hotel and a guest that the hotel will hold a specific type of room for a particular date and length of stay.

The most important outcome of the reservations process is having a guestroom ready and waiting when the guest arrives

If a reservation can be accepted as requested, the reservation agents create a reservation record.

The creation of a reservation record initiates the hotel guest cycle.

This enables the hotel to personalize guest service and appropriately schedule needed staff and facilities.

By confirming reservation, the hotel verifies a guest's room request and personal information, and assures the guests that his or her needs will be addressed.

Based on information collected during the reservations process, a hotel may also be able to perform pre-registration.

Such activities include assigning a specific room and rate for guests who have not yet arrived, and creating guest folios.

A ***guest folio*** is a record of the charges incurred and credits acquired by the guest during occupancy.

A reservation agent must be able to respond quickly and accurately to requests for future accommodation.

The proper handling of reservation information can be critical to the success of a lodging property.

Efficient procedures will also open up more time for the reservation agent to attend to detail and to market hotel services.

Arrival

This stage includes the following activities:

a. Registration Function;

b. Rooming Function.

The front desk agent should determine the guest's reservation status before beginning the registration process.

Guests with reservations may have already undergone pre-registration activities.

Guests with without reservations – or walk-in guests – present an opportunity for front desk agents to sell guestrooms.

To sell successfully, the front desk agents must be very familiar with the hotel's room types and guest services, and be able to describe them in a positive way.

A guest will not register if he or she is not convinced of the value of renting a particular hotel room.

Registration

Begins when the front desk agent extends a sincere welcome to the guest.

The procedure by which an incoming guest signifies his or her intent to stay at a property by completing and signing a registration card.

- To a great degree, registration relies on the information contained in a reservation record.
- A registration record completed either as a part of registration activity or at the time of check in, is essential to efficient front office operation.
- A registration record should include information about the guests intended method of payment, the planned length of stay, and any special guest
- Needs such as a rollaway bed, crib or a preferred guest
- Location. It should also include the guest's billing address,
- Telephone number and signature.
- Gathering all requisite information at the time of registration enhances the front office's ability to satisfy special guest needs, forecast room occupancies, and settle guest accounts properly.
- At check out the guest registration card is the primary source for guest history records.

- The front desk agent uses the registration information to assign a room type and a room rate for each guest. It also depends on reservation information.

Occupancy

The center of front office activity, where the front desk is responsible for coordinating guest services.

A major front office objective throughout the guest cycle is to encourage repeat visits.

Sound guest relations are essential to this objective.

Guest relations depend on clear, constructive communications between the front office, other hotel departments and divisions, and the guest.

Security is another primary front office concern during occupancy.

The guestroom is usually the largest single charge on the guest account. Additional expenses can be charged to a guest's account if he or she established acceptable credit at the front desk during the arrival stage.

Goods or services purchased from the hotel may also be charged to guest accounts. Front desk accounting records must be periodically reviewed for accuracy and completeness. This need is met through the ***night audit***.

Although the name implies that this process takes place in the evening, this is not necessarily the case. In hotels with computerized front office accounting system, the audit can be conducted at any time during the day. Some computerized properties choose to call the audit the ***front office audit or update.***

Departure

This is the final element of guest service. Checking the guest out of the hotel and creating a guest history record.

At check-out, the guest vacates the room, receives an accurate statement of account for settlement, returns the room keys, and departs from the hotel.

Once the guest has checked out, the front office updates the room's availability status and notifies the housekeeping department.

During the check-out, the front office determines whether the guest was satisfied with the stay and encourages the guest to return to the hotel – or another property in the chain.

The final element of guest accounting is settlement of the guest's account.

The purpose of account settlement is to collect money due the hotel. Depending on the guest's credit arrangements, the guest will pay cash, sign a credit card voucher, or verify direct billing instructions.

Account balances should be verified and errors corrected before the guest leaves the hotel. Problems may occur in guest account settlement when charges are not posted to the guest's account until after the guest checks out. These charges are called ***late charges***.

Settling accounts for departed guests is generally handled by the accounting department – not the front office. However, the front office is responsible for providing complete and accurate billing information, to assist the back office accounting division in these efforts.

Once the guest has checked out, the front office can analyze data related to the guest's stay. Front office reports can be used to review operations, isolate problem areas, where corrective action may be needed, and pinpoint out business trends.

Operation analysis can help managers establish a standard of performance which can be used to evaluate the effectiveness of front office operations.

Front Office Accounting

A front office accounting system monitors and charts the transactions of guests and businesses, agencies, and other non-guests using the hotel's services and facilities.

An effective guest accounting system consists of tasks performed during each stage of the guest cycle.

In brief, a front office accounting system:

- Creates and maintains accurate accounting file for each guest or non-guest account;
- Tracks financial transactions throughout the guest cycle;
- Ensures internal control over cash and non-cash transactions;
- Records settlement for all goods and services provided.

QUESTIONNAIRE

1. What do you understand by guest cycle
2. Discuss briefly the activities involved in pre arrival
3. What are the major functions performed at the time of reservation
4. Discuss various during the stay activities involved in a guest cycle
5. What do understand by occupancy
6. Mention the importance of front office accounting

11
RESERVATIONS

- IMPORTANCE OF RESERVATION
- MODES OF RESERVATION
- CHANNELS AND SOURCES (FITS, TRAVEL AGENTS, AIRLINES, GITS)
- TYPES OF RESERVATIONS (TENTATIVE, CONFIRMED, GUARANTEED ETC.)
- SYSTEMS (NON AUTOMATIC, SEMI AUTOMATIC FULLY AUTOMATIC)
- CANCELLATION
- AMENDMENTS
- OVERBOOKING

INTRODUCTION

A **hotel reservation system**, also known as a **central reservation system** (CRS) is a computerized system that stores and distributes information of a hotel, resort, or other lodging facilities.

A central reservation system is a tool to reach the global distribution system as well as internet distribution systems from one single system. A CRS assists hotel managers in managing their online marketing and sales, allowing them to upload their rates and availabilities to be seen by sales channels that are using the CRS. Sales channels may include conventional travel agencies as well as online travel agencies.

Online hotel reservations are a popular method for booking hotel rooms. Travelers can book rooms on a computer by using online security to protect their privacy and financial information and by using several online travel agents to compare prices and facilities at different hotels.

Prior to the Internet, travelers could write, telephone the hotel directly, or use a travel agent to make a reservation. Nowadays, online travel agents have pictures of hotels and rooms, information on prices and deals, and even information on local resorts. Many also allow reviews of the traveler to be recorded with the online travel agent.

Online hotel reservations are also helpful for making last minute travel arrangements. Hotels may drop the price of a room if some rooms are still available. There are several websites that specialize in searches for deals on rooms.

Modules in a CRS include:

- Reservations
- Profiles
- Groups and blocks
- Rate and inventory control
- Administration
- Reporting
- Global distribution interface
- PMS interface

Information commonly stored in a CRS includes

- Room types

- Rate plans architecture
- Room rates and conditions (guarantee, deposit, customized cancellation rules, minimum length of stay, maximum length of stay, closed to arrival, arrival not allowed, departure not allowed...)
- Room inventories
- Generic hotel information (address, phone number, fax number)
- Distribution content (descriptions, amenities, pictures, videos, local attractions...) are stored in the CRS or in a content management system
- Reservation information
- Nearby IATA cities and airports

Reservations

- Individual, group, shared, and multi-rate reservations
- Add, change, and cancel bookings including multiple legs
- Standard, package, negotiated, and group rates (via on screen button)
- Multi-Currency rate displays
- Sell messages dynamically linked to CRO office, property, rate or allotment code
- Geographical and regional single or multi-property search
- Property details including pictures, raster maps, rate and room type lists, nearby attractions, and point of interest information
- Links to external context databases to provide in-depth property, rate, and room details
- List of room types and rate codes
- List of rate availability strategies and restrictions
- User definable products by rate code
- Waitlist capabilities
- Quote rates system set up initial and secondary rates per property, per day
- Query system for reservation action items
- Intuitive, logical sales process flow

The main function of the reservation process is to **match room requests** with **room availability**. Below is the detailed process of reservation:

a) Conduct the reservation inquiry
b) Determine room and rate availability
c) Create the reservation record
d) Confirm the reservation record
e) Maintain the reservation record
f) Produce reservation reports

Reservation and Sales

- Prior to Computerization era, the main function of the Reservation Process is only to determine Basic Room Availability. That is to say, the reservation clerk can only tell the potential guest that a room is reserved for him/her. However, the reservation clerk cannot tell you the type of the room, rate honored. Therefore, the selling function shifted from the front office to the reservation department. Hence, projections of Room Revenues and Profitability Analysis became one of the basic functions of the Reservation Department.
- In parallel, reservation department and reservation agents should have sales goals to achieve which might focus on number of room nights, average room rate, and/or booked room revenue.

Modes of Reservation

The process of booking begins with an enquiry. There are number of means by which guest can contact hotels.

They are:

a. In person
b. Letter
c. Telephone
d. Fax
e. E-mail
f. Telex
g. Travel agents

Sources of Reservation

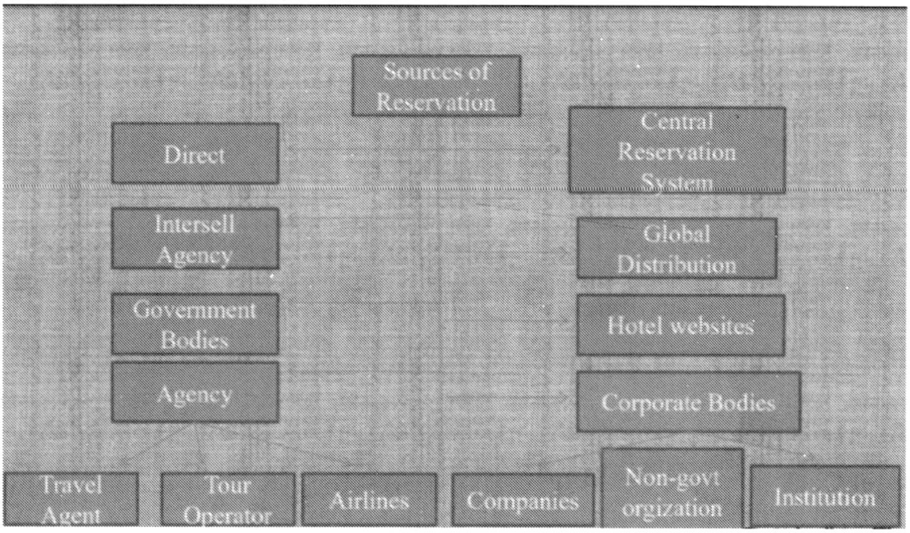

A hotel receives reservation requests from different sources like:

- Direct reservation
- Central reservation system
- Inter-sell agencies
- Global distribution system
- Corporate bodies
- Government sector

Direct Reservation :

A reservation request that a hotel receives directly from an individual or a group without a mediator is known as a direct reservation.

• The direct reservation request is processed by the reservation manger and his team of reservation assistant in large hotel. In case of a small hotel the same may be processed even by receptionist

Central Reservation System :

Central reservation system (CRS) is a computer-based reservation system, which enables guests to make reservations in any of the participating lodging properties at any destination in a single call. The central reservation office typically deals with direct guests, travel agents, corporate bookers, etc. by means of toll-free telephone numbers. • The CRS is of two types: – Affiliated system: In affiliated reservation systems, all the participating hotel units belong to the same chain or group, like Welcome net by Welcome group of Hotels, Holidex by Holiday Inn Hotels, Image by Hyatt Hotels, and ITT by Sheraton Hotels. – Non-affiliated system: Non-affiliated system is a subscription-based system, designed to connect independent or non chain properties, like the Leading Hotels of the World (LHW), Small Luxury Hotels of the World (SLH). This enables non-chain properties to enjoy the benefits of CRS.

Intersell agencies

An intersell agency is an agency that deals with many products such as hotel reservations, car rentals, travel arrangements, tour operations, airline reservations, railway bookings, etc.

- **EG :** make my trip, travel guru

Corporate bodies

Hotels also receive bookings from companies (FMCGs, pharmaceutical, etc.), non-governmental organizations (such as Care, Oxfam, Red Cross, WHO, etc.), and institutions (which may be educational, financial, banking, etc.). • Government sector: Hotels receive bookings from government sectors such as public sector undertakings, embassies, and consulates.

Hotel websites

A hotel's website is another potential source for receiving reservations. The website contains a link for reservation requests. By clicking the link, guests can make a hotel reservation as per their requirements from the comforts of their house/office/cyber cafe.

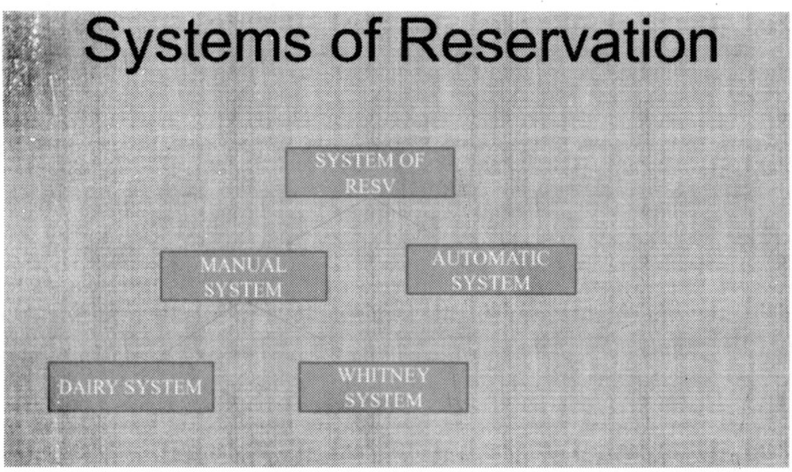

Systems of Reservation Depending on the needs of the hotel **and the** volume of business, a hotel may adopt either:

- **Manual System :**

In a manual system, all the reservation records are maintained manually. This old system of reservation is suitable for a small property, where the number of rooms is less and the volume of reservation requests is also low.

- **Automatic System:**

Automated reservation systems are computerized reservation systems that are used to store and retrieve room status information and conduct transactions. – The information stored in the automatic system is the same as in a manual system. However, the processing of reservation request does not require manual study of bed room journals, density charts, or conventional charts. – The reservation assistant can check the availability of rooms by clicking on a link on the computer. – In this system, the reservation information is keyed into the electronic format of the reservation form, and this information is transferred to the central server where the room status is updated automatically.

Manual System of Reservation

- The hotel may use one of the following systems of manual reservation: Diary System of Reservation ¬ Whitney system of reservation
- Diary system of reservation: As the name suggests, in this system a daily diary is kept, in which the reservation agent lists all arrivals due on a particular day. – It is usually kept on a loose-leaf basis. – The top page represents arrivals on the current date; this is removed – and sent to the front desk for receiving the guests. – The hotel booking diary may be hard bound also. The diary system of – reservation is only suitable for very small properties. – The tools used in diary system of reservation are as under:
- Booking diary
- Room status board/ reservation journal
- Expected arrival list/ Movement list
- Cancellation register
- Black list

DIARY SYSTEM

s.no	Date of booking	Name of the Guest	No.of Pax	Address and Tel	ETA	Type and no.of rooms	Room rate	Date of Departure	Booked by and tel	Billing inst	Remarks	Signature of clerk
1	10.02.02	Mr.James	1		8.00 AM	Single	EP / 800/-	13.04.02	TCI	Bill to TCI	Late arrival	
2	15.02.02	Mr&Mrs Kamal	2		10.00AM	Double	AP/1500/-	16.04.02	Direct	Direct	Facing pool side	
3	18.02.02	Mr&Mrs.Sunil	2		1.00 AM	Double	MAP/ 1400/-	21.4.02	SITA	Direct	Quiet Room	
4	1903.02	Mr Balu	1		2:00 PM	Single	CP/700/-	21.4.02	Caltex India	Direct	Car at Airport	

Whitney system of reservation:

- This system of room reservation, developed by the American Whitney Duplicating Check Company, is suitable for small and medium properties–with up to 150 rooms. It is based on the use of standard size slips, known as Whitney slips or Shannon slips, which can be held on a metallic carrier on Whitney racks.
- The advantages of using Whitney system are as under: – Bookings can be kept in order of the date of arrival. – Booking records may be arranged in alphabetical order. – The racks and carriers can be used over and over again. The running expense is only of the slips. – The Whitney racks are placed vertically, saving storage space.

WHITNEY SLIP

DATE OF ARRIVAL	NAME OF THE GUEST	ROOM TYPE	RATE	DATE OF DEPARTURE
MODE OF RESERVATIO N	RESERVED BY	DATE RECEIVED		
AGENCY IF ANY				
BILLING INSTRUCTIO NS			CONFIRMATI ON DATE	

Density Chart

- It is developed to over come the problems of conventional chart
- It has rooms catergory for the duration one month
- Vertical coloum indicates date and horizontal coloum indicates individual rooms
- It is indicated by (/) for indicating reservations
- It can take over bookings

ADVANTAGES:

- 1. short stay problems are solved
- 2. large hotels will use this system
- 3. counting or rooms will be easy

DENSITY CHART

MONTH : JAN. 2010									
TYPE OF ROOM	SINGLE								
DATE	NO.OF ROOMS								
1	1	2	3	4	5	6	29	30	31
2	/	/	/	/	/	/			
3						/	/	/	/
4			/	/	/	/			
31				/	/				

ADVANCE LETTING CHART

Dates	1	2	3	4	5	6	7	8	9
101	Mr. Patriks					Mr. Percival+1			
102		Ms. Gorge							
103									
104									
105	Ms. Alicia								
106			Mr. Methew+1						
106									

TYPES OF RESERVATIONS

Guaranteed Reservation

Insures that the hotel will hold a room for the guest until a specific time following the guest's scheduled arrival date [i.e. Check-out time or start of the hotel's day Shift or any time the lodging property chooses]. On return, the guest shall guarantee his/her reservation of room unless reservation is properly canceled. In order to guarantee a reservation, guests might opt for one of the following methods:

a) Prepayment guaranteed reservation

b) Credit card guaranteed reservation

c) Advance deposit or partial payment

d) Travel agent guaranteed reservation

e) Voucher or **M**iscellaneous **C**harge **O**rder [**MCO**]

f) Corporate guaranteed reservation

Non-guaranteed Reservation

Insures that the hotel agrees to hold a room for the guest until a stated reservation cancellation hour (Usually 6 p.m.) on the day of arrival.

- Reservation agents shall make sure to encourage their guests to guarantee their reservations especially in the high season

Reservation Inquiry

- Guests can communicate their reservation inquiries in person, over the telephone, via mail, through facsimile, telex, e-mail... Moreover, reservation inquiries can be made through a **Central Reservation System** or an **Intersell Agency.**
- While getting a reservation inquiry, the reservation agent shall obtain the following guest-related information:

  a) Guest's name, address and telephone number

  b) Company or travel agency name

  c) Date of arrival and departure

  d) Type and number of rooms requested

  e) Desired room rate

f) Number of people in the group, if applicable

g) Method of payment and/or guarantee

h) Any other special requests

- Most of the above mentioned information is used to create a **reservation record.**

SOURCES OF RESERVATIONS

1. Central Reservation Systems
2. Intersell Agencies
3. Property Direct Reservation System

Central Reservation Systems

- The majority of Lodging Properties belongs to one or more Central Reservation Systems
- A central reservation system is composed of a central reservation office, member hotels connected together via communication devices, and potential guests.
- Central **R**eservation **O**ffice [**CRO**] offers its services via a 24-hours toll free telephone number(s).
- On return, central reservation offices charges a fee for the utilization of its services which might take the form of a flat fee and a variable fee, or a flat percentage of potential room revenue, actual room revenue, and/or Rooms Division gross profit.

Central Reservation Offices are divided into two:

A) Affiliate reservation network:

- This very network is referred to as the hotel chain's reservation system. In fact, it is composed of a CRO, and hotels, which are members of the same chain. The main advantages of affiliate reservation network are:

  a) Streamline the process of reservation

  b) Reduce overall system costs

  c) Attract business for or refer business to another chain property

d) Affiliate reservation networks might serve, in addition to its main function, other duties like:

- Serve as an inter property communication network
- Serve as an accounting transfer tool
- Serve as a destination information center
- Serve as a connection with Global Distribution Systems

[GDS]⇒ System including several Central Reservation Offices connected to each other.

B) Non-affiliate reservation network:

- A non-affiliate reservation network is composed of a central reservation office, potential guests, and member independent hotels.

Intersell Agencies

- Intersell Agencies are special types of central reservation offices contracting to handle reservation for more than one Product Line [ex: Handle at the same time Airline Tickets, Car Rental, Hotel Reservation.]

Property Direct Reservation System:

- Even though many of the five-star hotels rely heavily on central reservation offices and intersell agencies, some potential guests might still find it convenient, and personal to call directly the hotel to communicate a reservation inquiry.

Group Reservations

Conducting a reservation request for a group shall be treated differently than accommodating a reservation of individual guests (i.e. Frèquent Independent Traveler).

The main reason is that individual reservation requests are treated by the reservation department, while group reservations are initiated by the Sales & Marketing division, and finalized through a careful coordination of the reservation from one hand and the marketing from the other.

Here are some other differences between handling individual and group reservations:

Individual Reservation	**Group Reservation**
Reservation Department	Sales Department
• Usually one person calls to reserve for himself / herself	• Usually one person reserves for the whole members of the group (Group representative, Group leader, Member of the travel agency / Tour operator...)
• One Reservation record for each potential guest	• One Reservation rerecord for the whole group
• One Guest Folio for each potential guest opened as part of the pre-registration process	• One Master Folio for the whole group opened as part of the pre-registration process
• Higher price assigned for room	• Low price assigned for room
• Upon matching room inquiry with room availability, reservation agent reserves a room	• Upon signature of allotment contract, **first block** rooms needed. Later, upon **receipt** of Final List by Cut-off date, **deblock the block**, reserve for those **rooms conveyed in the List and release the remaining for sale.**
• Reservations can be either Guaranteed or Non-guaranteed.	• Reservations are usually on a Guaranteed basis.

- **Below is a detailed procedure of how group reservation, in a typical hotel, is conducted:**

    1. A group **representative**, a member of the travel agency or the **tour** operator, not **individuals**, shall **communicate** group **reservations**' request to the hotel's **marketing** department
    2. Upon availability, the hotel's **reservation** department shall **block the** requested number of rooms **for this** very group
    3. The Hotel shall give a deadline for the group, in order to receive their final list. That deadline is called **Cut-off Date**
    4. After receiving the final list, the reservation department shall change the desired number of rooms' status from **blocked** to **booked** (or reserved) rooms, and release the remaining rooms (if any left) as **vacant**
    5. If the hotel did not receive the final list by the cut-off date, then the reservation department has all the right to cancel the group reservation and release all the initially booked rooms into vacant rooms.
    6. However, management shall use this right with precautions especially

when it comes to groups reserving from travel agencies and tour operators of which the hotel is frequently operating.

Reservation Availability

- After receiving a reservation request, the hotel might accept it, as it is, if there is room availability. If not, the reservation department should suggest *alternative* room types, dates, and/or rates, to the potential guest. If, however, the potential guest insists on his/her previous request, the hotel should suggest an *alternative* hotel.
- The reservation department should always compare *historical reservation volumes* against *actual arrivals*. The main reason is to cope with ***overbooking***, which a situation occurring when the total number of rooms reserved for a certain period of time exceeds the total number of rooms available for sale, for the same period of time.
- In order to cope with the overbooking problem, some statistical and historical data should be stored and processed by the hotel and should be continuously updated. Such data should include:

  a) Number of rooms reserved for a speci[illegible]e

  b) Number of rooms occupied by stayovers (for a certain specific date)

  c) Forecasted no-shows percentage

  d) Forecasted understays percentage

  e) Forecasted overstays percentage

  f) Forecasted cancellation percentage

  g) Number of out of order rooms for a specific date

Let's consider the Following Problem

Fatma Hotel consists of 100 Rooms. Mr. John Green has been newly hired for the position of a Reservation Assistant manager. One of the responsibilities of John is to calculate how many rooms above 98 (i.e. the Maximum Number of Rooms in the Hotel) does management need to overbook for the night of October 29th, 2002. Mr. Green was given the following data, at hand, both updated and concerning the night of October 29th, 2002:

- Number of rooms reserved: 50 Rooms
- Number of rooms occupied by stayovers: 45 Rooms
- Forecasted no-shows percentage: 10%

- Forecasted understays percentage: 05%
- Forecasted overstays percentage: 10%
- Forecasted cancellation percentage: 07%
- Number of out of order rooms: 02 Rooms

1. Potential Solution:
   - Total number of rooms expected to be occupied for the night of October 29th, 2002 = 50 reserved rooms + 45 stayover rooms = **95 Rooms**
   - Adjustment due to no-shows % = -10%*50 = **-5 Rooms**
   - Adjustment due to understays % = -5%*45 = **-2.25 Rooms**
   - Adjustment due to overstays % = 10%*45 = **+4.5 Rooms**
   - Adjustment due to cancellation % = -7%*50 = **-3.5 Rooms**
   - Total adjustment = -5-2.25+4.5-3.5 = **-6.25 Rooms**
   - Total number of rooms expected to be occupied for the night of October 29th, 2002 (i.e. after adjustment) = 95 - 6.25 = **88.75 Rooms**
   - Total number of rooms available for sale for the night of October 29th,2002 = 100-2 = **98 Rooms**
   - Additional number of rooms to be reserved for the night of October, 29th, 2002 = 98-88.75 = **9.25 Rooms**
   - Total number of rooms expected to be reserved and occupied for the night of October 29th, 2002 = 95+9.25 = **104.25 Rooms**
   - Expected occupancy rate with adjustments = 104.25/98 * 100 = **106.38%**
   - Overbooking factor = 106.38% - 100% = **6.38%**

SYSTEMS OF RESERVATION

All reservations received in a hotel are entered somewhere so that as and when required it can be retrieved in a shortest possible time.

There are numerous systems of reservations which may be suitable to different types and sizes of hotels. These methods can be broadly classified into the following:

1. Non - Automatic (manual)
2. Fully – Automatic (computerized)
3. Semi – Automatic

Equipment Tracking Room Availability

- In order to function properly, the reservation department shall maintain control books, wall charts, and/or a computerized system. Whatsoever system chosen, the reservation department shall maintain and update that system to include any reservation transaction (i.e. whether a reservation, cancellation, modification...). Below is a description of the three commonly used sets of equipment to track room availability under the manual, semi-automated and fully-automated systems:

1. **Control books:**

   - Control books are standard three-ring, loose-leaf binders with a tally Page assigned to each day of the year. Under this very system, when a potential guest calls to have a reservation, the reservation clerk shall check the cells corresponding to rooms.
   - If there is an empty cell for all the length of stay of the guest then the reservation clerk mark it as X (i.e. reserved). If the guest is expected to continue staying the next day, then the reservation clerk shall mark the next day's respective room cell as O (i.e. Stayover).
   - Lastly, the reservation clerk is encouraged to use colors while updating information or the cells on the control book.

2. **Wall charts**:

   These are charts stapled on the wall depicting days of the month versus hotel rooms.

   - Moreover, upon need and convenience, these charts might be customized to track appropriate room Numbers, rates, and codes, hence, is advantageous to control books.
   - Moreover, in this very system, different colors are used to differentiate between different reservation transactions, types of guest reserving.
   - Lastly, wall charts eliminates the erasures and rewriting associated with control book, hence lees errors might occur.

3. **Computerized systems:**

   Computerized systems are by far the best systems that track room availability.

   - In fact, these very systems control room availability data and automatically generate many reservation-related reports in an accurate manner.

- Moreover, computerized systems can itemize room availability for future periods by *open dates*, *closed dates*, versus *special event dates.*
- Lastly, this very system can forecast room availability for any reservation horizon needed in the future.

In the case of non-availability of room type, the system can further suggest alternative room types, rates, or even other nearby hotels.

Reservation Record

Each reservation department shall prepare a reservation record, which depicts the various personal and financial data of guests, for each reservation transaction.

- The aim is to identify guests and their occupancy needs before guest's arrival. Moreover, the hotel can personalize or customize guest services and better schedule staff accordingly

In order to create a reservation record, the following items are needed:

a) Guest name (and group name, if applicable)

b) Guest's home or billing address

c) Guest's telephone number, including area code

d) Name, address, and telephone number of guest's company, if appropriate

e) Name of and pertinent information about the person making the reservation, if not the guest

f) Number of people in the group, and perhaps ages of any children

g) Arrival date and time

h) Number of nights required or expected departure date, depending on how the system is programmed

i) Reservation type [Guaranteed versus Non-guaranteed]

j) Special requirements [i.e. infant, disabled guest, or no-smoking accommodation

k) Additional information, if needed [i.e. late arrival, method of transportation, flight number, room preferences...]

- At the reservation process, reservation agents shall keep in mind that a rate quoted and confirmed must be honored.

Moreover, reservation clerks should be aware of the following:

a) Supplementary charges for extra services or amenities

b) Minimum stay requirements in effect for dates requested

c) Special promotions in effect for dates requested

d) Applicable currency exchange rates, if quoting rates to an international tourist

e) Applicable room tax percentages

f) Applicable service charges or gratuities

Reservation Confirmation:

The hotel should communicate guests by telephone, telex, mail, or e-mail a *Letter of Confirmation*, which confirms the important points of the reservation agreement.

- This very letter might be shown at the registration process in order to accelerate the pace of registration and prove that the guest has the right to have a room at the hotel.

The Hotel shall send a confirmation letter to all reserved potential guests, whether their reservations are guaranteed or non-guaranteed. Below are the main points that should be communicated in a confirmation letter:

a) Name and address of the guest

b) Date and time of arrival

c) Room type and rate

d) Length of stay

e) Number of persons in a group, if any

f) Reservation type [guaranteed or not]

g) Reservation confirmation number

h) Special requests, if any

Confirmation Numbers

- Hotels shall communicate meaningful confirmation numbers to their potential guests.

These numbers shall have statistical meanings, which might help the hotel in maintaining an efficient historical database.

Here is an example:

32 02 G JC 63

a) 32: Guest's scheduled arrival date on Julian dates calendar.

b) 02: Group reservation. In this very system, 01 might mean Frequent Independent Traveler.

c) G: means that the reservation is guaranteed. If N is written, it means non-guaranteed.

d) JC: are the initials of the reservation agent who processed the reservation (ex: Jamel Chafra)

e) 63: Consecutive numbering of all reservation confirmation numbers issued in the current year.

Reservation Reports:

In the reservation department, the widely used management reservation reports include:

a) Reservation transaction report

b) Commission agent report

c) Turnaway report (sometimes called the refusal report)

d) Revenue forecast report

Expected Arrival, Stayover, and Departure Lists

- On a daily basis, the reservation department shall prepare the expected arrival, stayover, and departures lists and communicate them to the front office department.

    1. **Arrival list**: List of the names, and surnames along with respective room number of the guests who are expected to arrive the next day.
    2. **Stayover list**: List of the names, and surnames along with respective room number of the guests who are expected to continue occupy their rooms the next day.
    3. **Departure list**: List of the names, and surnames along with respective room number of the guests who are expected to depart the next day.

SAMPLE RESERVATION FORM

PERSONAL DETAILS: □ *Mr.* □ *Mrs.*

Surname: ____________________ ***First name:*** ____________________

Company: ____

Address: ____

Postal Code/City: ____________________ ***Country:*** ____________________

Email (needed for confirmation): __________________________

Arrival Date: ____________ ***Departure Date:*** ___________ ***No. of nights:*** ____

Guest room check- in time: 15:00 Check-out: 12:00 (noon)

Room Rate: □ ***110 EUR single Deluxe room*** □ ***120 EUR double Deluxe room***

Room rate is per night, inclusive of Full American breakfast, 9% VAT, Wi-Fi Internet, use of sauna, Jacuzzi and fitness.

Supplements for room upgrade - please tick the category your are interested in booking:

□ ***Superior room*** *with Prague Castle view: 20 € per night*

□ ***Executive Floor:*** *50 € per night (incl. luxurious cosmetics, newspaper delivery, access to the Executive Lounge and El Greco meeting room, free use of swimming pool next door, Light-Hot Snack Menu)*

□ ***Junior Suite:*** *30 € per night*

□ ***Junior Suite Executive Floor****: 80 € per night*

Other Requirements: □ *smoking* □ *non smoking* □ *diet/vegetarian*__________

CREDIT CARD GUARANTEE □ **EC/MC** □ **Visa** □ **Amex** □ **Diners**

CC Number: ________________________***Expiry Date:***____________________

CC Holder:____

The cardholder´s signature is required: ________________________

AIRPORT TRANSFER (airport–hotel–airport): □ *1550 CZK/Hotel Limousine - Mercedes E class*

□ *2500 CZK/Hotel Shuttle up to 8 pax*

Arrival: flight number______ ***/ time***_____ ***Departure: flight number***______ ***/ time***______

DEADLINE: **8.1.2010** ***(After this date room rate will be confirmed upon availability)***

CANCELLATION CONDITIONS:

Any cancellation later than 48 hours prior arrival or no show will result in cancellation charge at the contracted room rate for one night stay to given credit card.

Please forward the filled-out registration form to the attention of: *Zuzana Neumannová, Event coordinator; e-mail: events@hotelpresident.cz* *phone: +420 234 614 143, fax: +420 234 614 117*

EXAMPLE OF A RESERVATION:

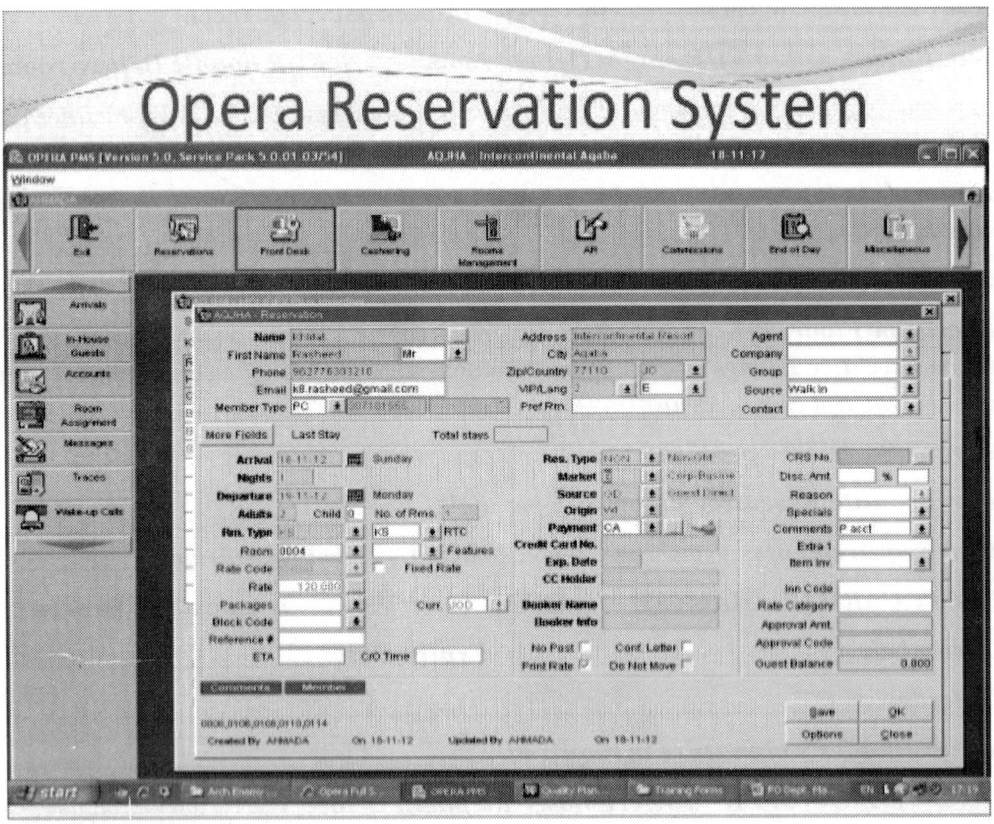

STEP-BY-STEP PROCEDURE OF RESERVATION

1. Check rates and book a hotel reservation as far in advance of the departure date as possible. Hotels tend to raise rates as availability declines; however, it is possible to get a last minute deal.

2. Use an online travel site to identify hotels in the city you are visiting or near a specific attraction, address or airport.
    - Sites that book hotels, flights, rental cars, vacation packages and more include Orbitz.com, Expedia.com and Travelocity.com. These sites have features that make it easy to adjust dates and see how it affects hotel rates.
    - Hotels.com (an Expedia company) and HotelDiscounts.com specialize in lodgings but also book vacation packages.
    - Sidestep.com is a search engine for other travel sites and makes it easy to compare hotel reservations and other rates.
    - If you aren't picky about arrival and departure dates or location, you might consider Priceline.com. However, you won't know which hotel you are staying in until you book it.
    - Determine whether you need a standard room, one-bedroom, two-bedroom or something larger.

1. Identify what amenities you need.
    - In-room conveniences to consider include high-speed Internet, a refrigerator, a kitchen or kitchenette, and a pull-out sleeper sofa. Some hotels will bring a crib or cot into the room if you need it.
    - Hotel amenities might include an indoor or outdoor pool, fitness center, business center, restaurants and room service.'
2. Enter your arrival and departure dates as well as how many adults and children will be staying in the room.
3. Narrow down the list to one or two hotels with the amenities you need and the best rates, and then go to those hotel websites to check rates there.
    - Compare rates with discounts (e.g., for seniors, AAA members, frequent flyer members) and taxes applied.
    - If you are bringing pets, verify that pets are allowed and whether an additional fee is charged.
    - Take into account whether a free breakfast is included, or a happy hour offers free drinks and/or food.
4. Look at the photos and virtual tours available online to get a feel for what the hotel and its rooms look like. You may need to call the hotel to get specific information, such as the year built/remodeled, check-in/check-out times and cancellation policy.

5. Book the hotel room online or by phone. You will need to give a credit card number, but the card will not be charged unless you don't cancel according to the cancellation policy.
6. Print or write down your confirmation number and bring it with you on the trip.

TIPS

- When calling the hotel directly to make a hotel reservation, don't be afraid to ask for a better deal or free room upgrade.
- Contact the hotel's sales department if you need to book a hotel reservation for a group.

Overbooking

- the term overbooking is a common practice in hotel or resort. Overbooking occurs when more rooms are booked than availability. Overbooking is done based on estimating the number of no show reservations, under stays, walk-ins and stayovers in order to meet 100% occupancy.
- Overbooking is considered as a complex policy for any hotel which is generally administered by the front office manager. According to the American courts overbooking is praised as "in many cases to overcome the problem of no shows and late cancellations may produce advantages by way of operating efficiencies that far compensate the occasional inconveniences to guests and travellers". The American courts have apprehended hotel overbooking as an expected and justifiable practice which can compensate the losses that are occurred from no shows. No show factors are determined based on past experiences with guests with confirmed or guaranteed reservations generally who did not come.
- Though the policy of overbooking could bring inconvenient to the guests or travelers but hotel authority or front office managers do not practice overbooking intentionally , they overbook the room to fulfill the financial objectives and to make up the losses arises from no shows.

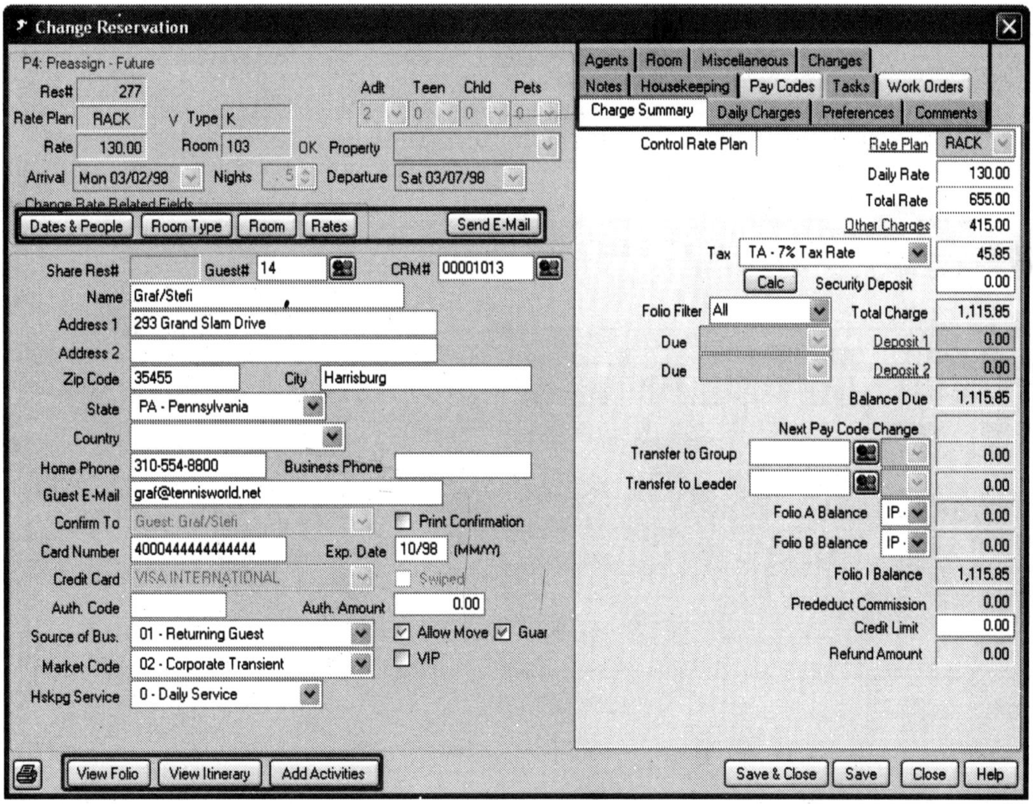

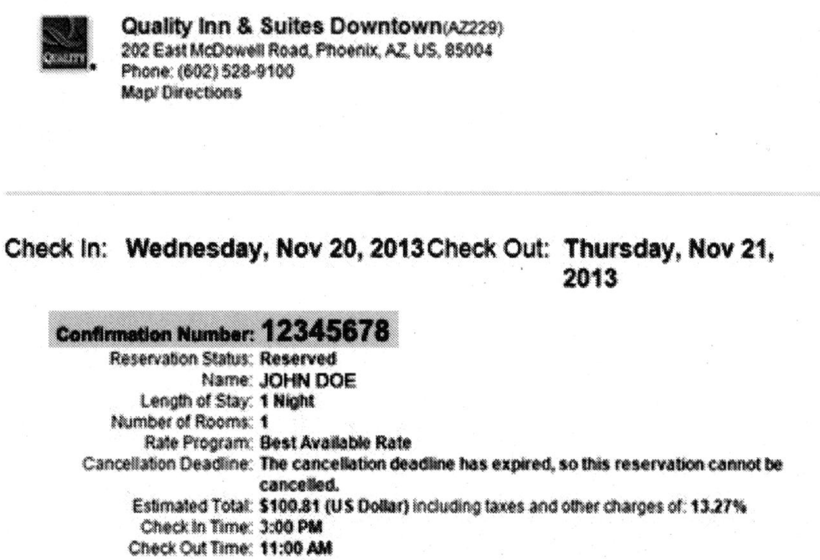

Quality Inn & Suites Downtown(AZ229)
202 East McDowell Road, Phoenix, AZ, US, 85004
Phone: (602) 528-9100
Map/ Directions

Check In: Wednesday, Nov 20, 2013 Check Out: Thursday, Nov 21, 2013

Confirmation Number: 12345678

Reservation Status: **Reserved**
Name: **JOHN DOE**
Length of Stay: **1 Night**
Number of Rooms: **1**
Rate Program: **Best Available Rate**
Cancellation Deadline: **The cancellation deadline has expired, so this reservation cannot be cancelled.**
Estimated Total: **$100.81 (US Dollar)** including taxes and other charges of: **13.27%**
Check In Time: **3:00 PM**
Check Out Time: **11:00 AM**

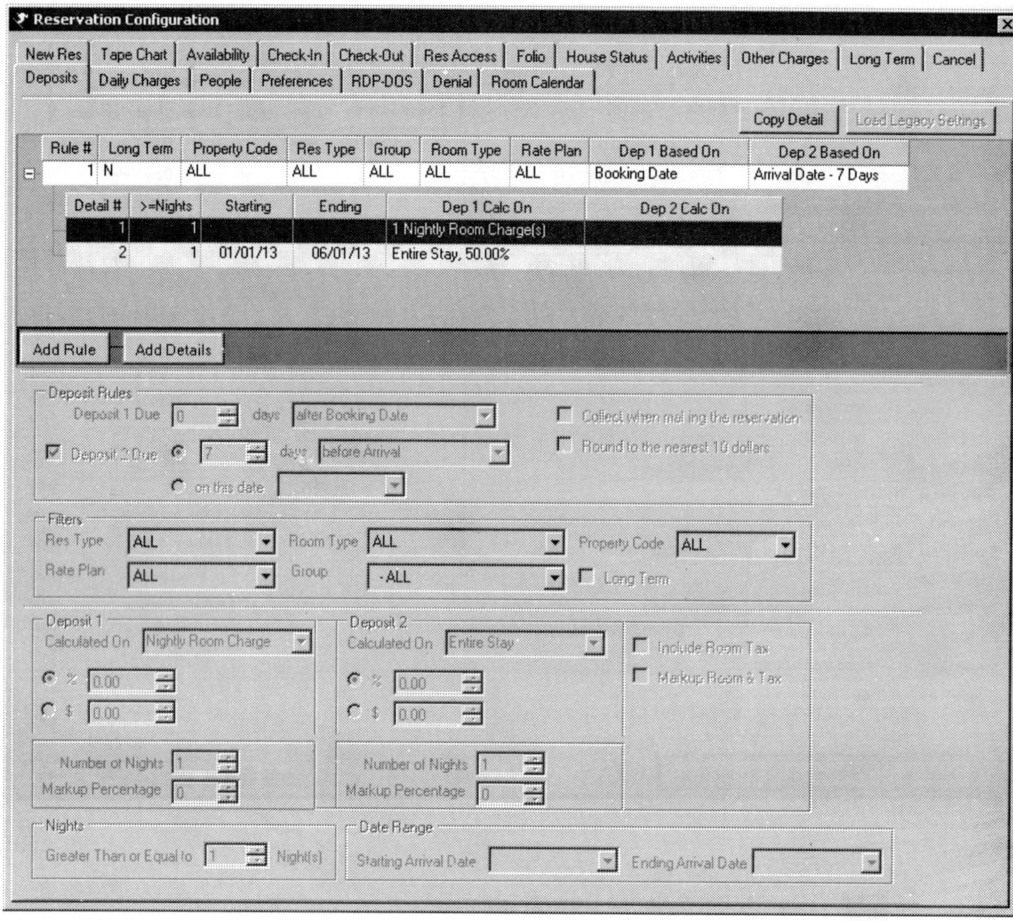
Reservation Configuration
New Res
Tape Chart
Availability
Check-In
Check-Out
Res Access
Folio
House Status
Activities
Other Charges
Long Term
Cancel
Deposits
Daily Charges
People
Preferences
RDP-DOS
Denial
Room Calendar
Copy Detail
Load Legacy Settings
Rule # | Long Term | Property Code | Res Type | Group | Room Type | Rate Plan | Dep 1 Based On | Dep 2 Based On
1 N ALL ALL ALL ALL ALL Booking Date Arrival Date - 7 Days
Detail # | >=Nights | Starting | Ending | Dep 1 Calc On | Dep 2 Calc On
1 1 1 Nightly Room Charge(s)
2 1 01/01/13 06/01/13 Entire Stay, 50.00%
Add Rule
Add Details
Deposit Rules
Deposit 1 Due
days
after Booking Date
Deposit 2 Due
before Arrival
on this date
Collect when making the reservation
Round to the nearest 10 dollars
Filters
Res Type
ALL
Room Type
ALL
Property Code
ALL
Rate Plan
ALL
Group
- ALL
Long Term
Deposit 1
Calculated On
Nightly Room Charge
Deposit 2
Calculated On
Entire Stay
Include Room Tax
Markup Room & Tax
Number of Nights
Markup Percentage
Nights
Greater Than or Equal to
Night(s)
Date Range
Starting Arrival Date
Ending Arrival Date

IEEE Ultrasonics Symposium
October 4, 2003 through October 10, 2003

HILTON HAWAIIAN VILLAGE ROOM RESERVATION REQUEST

Ms.
Mrs.
Mr.____ No. of Persons: ______________

Arrival Date: ________________ Time: ________AM/PM Departure Date: ________________
Check-in time: 2:00pm / Check-out time: 11:00am

CIRCLE RATE DESIRED: * (rates are for single or double occupancy)

Village Garden View	**$158.00**
Run of Ocean	**$199.00**
Additional Person(s) - (Third & Fourth Occupant)	**$30.00 per person**
* **Children under 18 Free in same room as parent**	

All rates are plus 7.25% Hotel Occupancy Tax and 4.16% Hawaii Excise Tax (Total 11.41% Tax).

If sharing, please give name of other person ________________________________.

☐ Check here for Accessible Accommodation

To make a reservation by telephone, call 1-800-HILTONS (1-800-445-8667)

As there is a limited amount of rooms available in each category, requests will be fulfilled on a "first come, first served" basis. If your requested category is not available, you will be confirmed in the next higher available category.

Confirmation to be mailed to: (Please print or type)

Name		Telephone: ( )			
Affiliation		Fax: ( )			
Address					
City		State		Zip	

This reservation request **must be accompanied by a one-night deposit** and received no later than **September 4, 2003**. After this date, reservation will be subject to availability. Cancellations received within 72 hours of arrival date will be assessed a "late cancellation" charge of a one night room rate plus 11.41% Hawaii state tax. **After check-in, any departure prior to the stated departure date will be assessed a $50.00 charge.** Please send a check or money order payable to the Hilton Hawaiian Village, or complete the following for credit card deposits:

☐ Visa ☐ Mastercard ☐ American Express ☐ Other ____________

Credit Card Number: ______________________ Expiration Date: __________

☐ HILTON HHONORS MEMBER NUMBER ______________

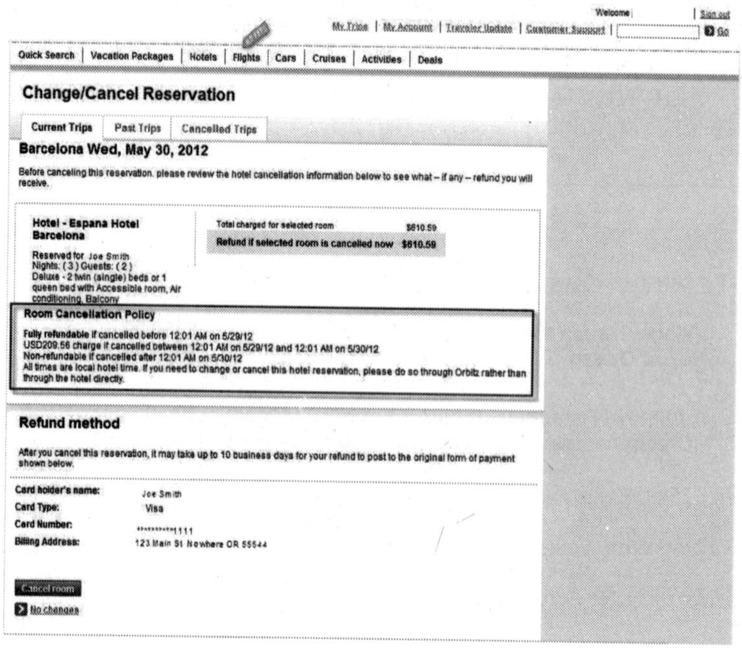
Welcome | Sign out
My Trips | My Account | Traveler Update | Customer Support | Go
Quick Search | Vacation Packages | Hotels | Flights | Cars | Cruises | Activities | Deals
Change/Cancel Reservation
Current Trips | Past Trips | Cancelled Trips
Barcelona Wed, May 30, 2012
Before canceling this reservation, please review the hotel cancellation information below to see what – if any – refund you will receive.
Hotel - Espana Hotel Barcelona
Reserved for Joe Smith
Nights: (3) Guests: (2)
Deluxe - 2 twin (single) beds or 1 queen bed with Accessible room, Air conditioning, Balcony
Total charged for selected room $610.59
Refund if selected room is cancelled now $610.59
Room Cancellation Policy
Fully refundable if cancelled before 12:01 AM on 5/29/12
USD209.56 charge if cancelled between 12:01 AM on 5/29/12 and 12:01 AM on 5/30/12
Non-refundable if cancelled after 12:01 AM on 5/30/12
All times are local hotel time. If you need to change or cancel this hotel reservation, please do so through Orbitz rather than through the hotel directly.
Refund method
After you cancel this reservation, it may take up to 10 business days for your refund to post to the original form of payment shown below.
Card holder's name: Joe Smith
Card Type: Visa
Card Number: **********1111
Billing Address: 123 Main St Nowhere OR 55544
Cancel room
No changes

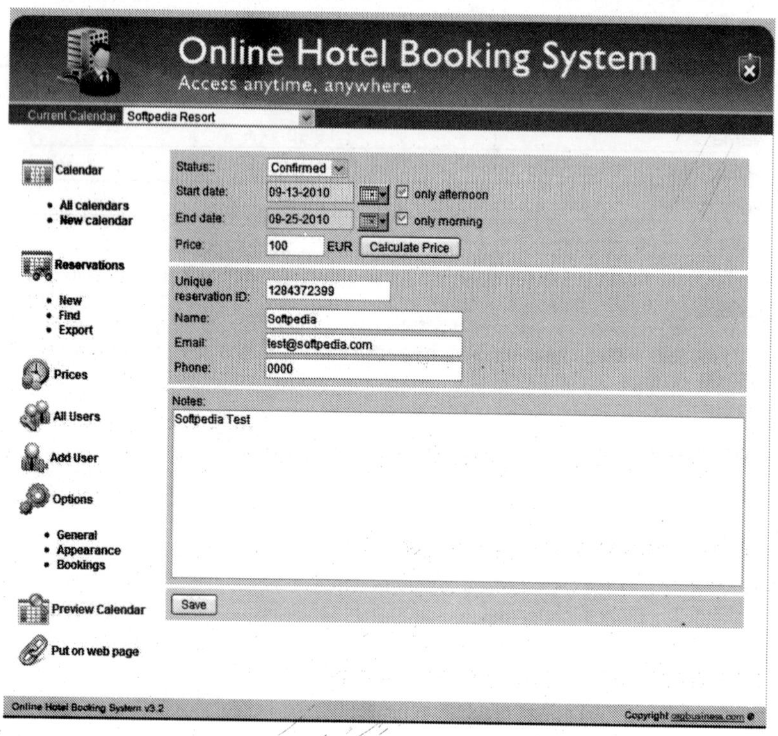
Online Hotel Booking System
Access anytime, anywhere.
Current Calendar Softpedia Resort
Calendar
All calendars
New calendar
Reservations
New
Find
Export
Prices
All Users
Add User
Options
General
Appearance
Bookings
Preview Calendar
Put on web page
Status: Confirmed
Start date: 09-13-2010 only afternoon
End date: 09-25-2010 only morning
Price: 100 EUR Calculate Price
Unique reservation ID: 1284372399
Name: Softpedia
Email: test@softpedia.com
Phone: 0000
Notes:
Softpedia Test
Save
Online Hotel Booking System v3.2
Copyright

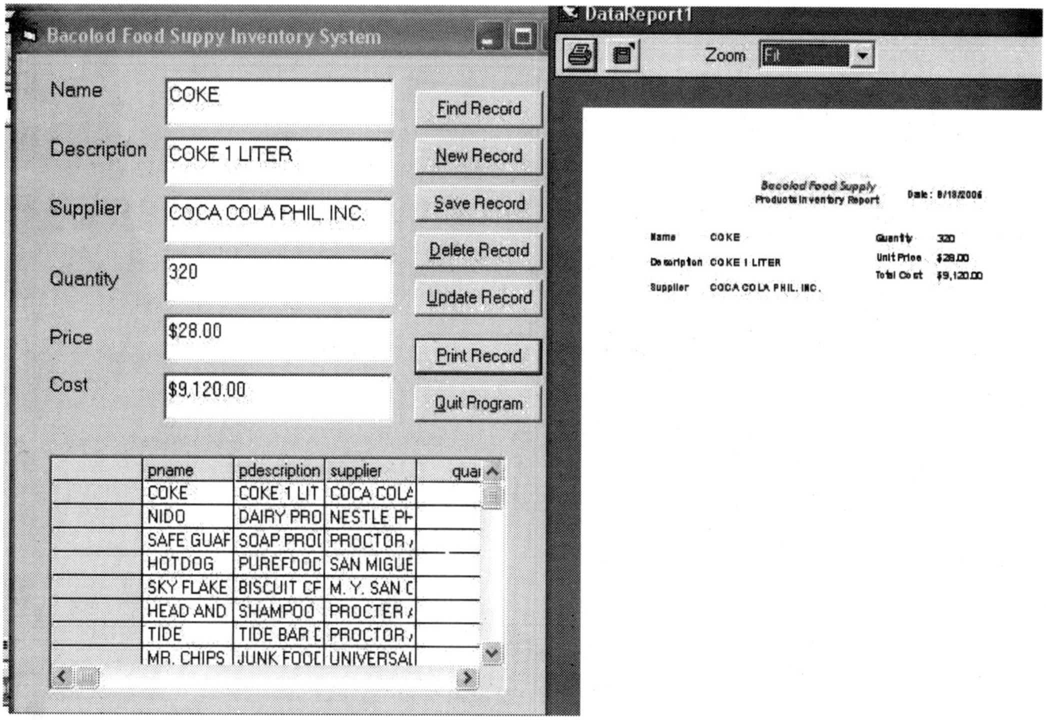
Bacolod Food Suppy Inventory System
Name
COKE
Description
COKE 1 LITER
Supplier
COCA COLA PHIL. INC.
Quantity
320
Price
$28.00
Cost
$9,120.00
Find Record
New Record
Save Record
Delete Record
Update Record
Print Record
Quit Program
pname
pdescription
supplier
COKE
NIDO
SAFE GUAF
HOTDOG
SKY FLAKE
HEAD AND
TIDE
MR. CHIPS
DataReport1
Zoom
Fit
Bacolod Food Supply
Products Inventory Report
Name
COKE
Description
COKE 1 LITER
Supplier
COCA COLA PHIL. INC.
Unit Price
$28.00
Total Cost
$9,120.00

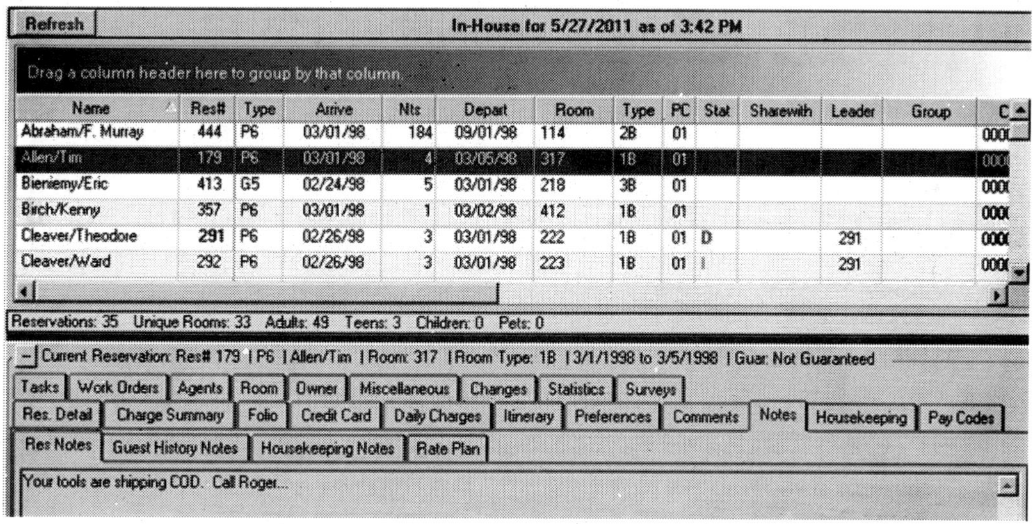
Refresh
In-House for 5/27/2011 as of 3:42 PM
Drag a column header here to group by that column
Name
Res#
Type
Arrive
Nts
Depart
Room
Type
PC
Stat
Sharewith
Leader
Group
Abraham/F. Murray
Allen/Tim
Bieniemy/Eric
Birch/Kenny
Cleaver/Theodore
Cleaver/Ward
Reservations: 35 Unique Rooms: 33 Adults: 49 Teens: 3 Children: 0 Pets: 0
Current Reservation: Res# 179 | P6 | Allen/Tim | Room: 317 | Room Type: 1B | 3/1/1998 to 3/5/1998 | Guar: Not Guaranteed
Tasks
Work Orders
Agents
Room
Owner
Miscellaneous
Changes
Statistics
Surveys
Res. Detail
Charge Summary
Folio
Credit Card
Daily Charges
Itinerary
Preferences
Comments
Notes
Housekeeping
Pay Codes
Res Notes
Guest History Notes
Housekeeping Notes
Rate Plan
Your tools are shipping COD. Call Roger...

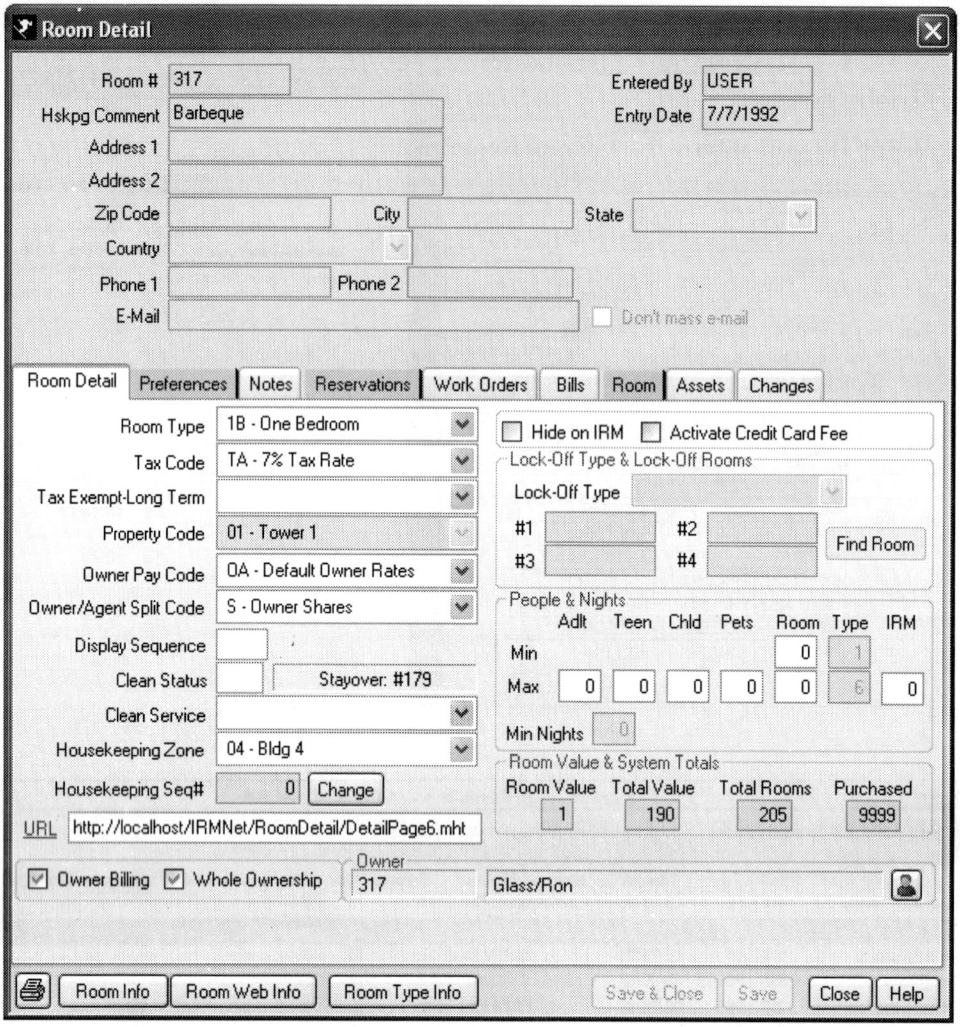
Room Detail
Room # 317
Hskpg Comment Barbeque
Address 1
Address 2
Zip Code
City
State
Country
Phone 1
Phone 2
E-Mail
Don't mass e-mail
Entered By USER
Entry Date 7/7/1992
Room Detail
Preferences
Notes
Reservations
Work Orders
Bills
Room
Assets
Changes
Room Type 1B - One Bedroom
Tax Code TA - 7% Tax Rate
Tax Exempt-Long Term
Property Code 01 - Tower 1
Owner Pay Code 0A - Default Owner Rates
Owner/Agent Split Code S - Owner Shares
Display Sequence
Clean Status Stayover: #179
Clean Service
Housekeeping Zone 04 - Bldg 4
Housekeeping Seq# 0 Change
URL http://localhost/IRMNet/RoomDetail/DetailPage6.mht
Hide on IRM
Activate Credit Card Fee
Lock-Off Type & Lock-Off Rooms
Lock-Off Type
#1 #2 #3 #4
Find Room
People & Nights
Adlt Teen Chld Pets Room Type IRM
Min
Max
Min Nights
Room Value & System Totals
Room Value 1
Total Value 190
Total Rooms 205
Purchased 9999
Owner Billing
Whole Ownership
Owner 317 Glass/Ron
Room Info
Room Web Info
Room Type Info
Save & Close
Save
Close
Help

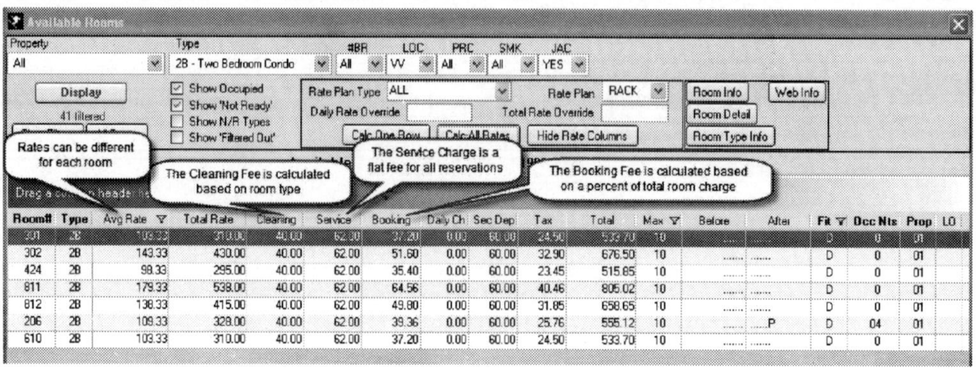
Rates can be different for each room
The Cleaning Fee is calculated based on room type
The Service Charge is a flat fee for all reservations
The Booking Fee is calculated based on a percent of total room charge

QUESTIONNAIRE

1. What is a reservation? List the sources and modes of reservation in hotels. Briefly describe them.
2. What do you mean by 'Group Reservation'? Explain its importance for a hotel and the procedure to be followed while processing group reservation.
3. Explain in brief the following:
   a) Density Chart
   b) Guaranteed Reservation
   c) Modes & Channels of Reservation
   d) Whitney system of reservation
   e) Commission Terms
   f) Hotel Tariff Terms
   g) Inter-Sell Agencies
   h) Group reservations
   i) Central Reservation System(CRS)
   j) Cancellation.
4. Give the job description of the following:
   a) Reservation Assistant
   b) Density Chart Controller
   c) Reservation Manager
5. Give step – by – step procedure of reserving a room. Draw the format of a sample room reservation form.
6. What are the advantages of reservation for a guest & for the hotel as well?
7. List the sources and modes of reservation for a hotel.
8. List the systems of reservation. Explain any of them in detail with formats.
9. What do you mean by over-booking? Explain in detail over booking with its advantages and disadvantages.
10. Give the reservation department's layout and the organization chart of a large super deluxe hotel.
11. Which system of reservation will be most suitable for a large busy hotel and why?

12. Which system of reservation will be most suitable for a small resort hotel and why?
13. What is the importance of telephone in room reservation? What points should be kept in mind while handling a telephone?
14. Give reservation department's layout and the organization chart of a large super deluxe hotel.
15. Why advance is asked while making a reservation? How will you treat advance received along with the reservation request?

12

ROOM SELLING TECHNIQUES

- INTRODUCTION
- UP SELLING
- DISCOUNTS

INTRODUCTION

The sales function has become an important and vital part of front office work, with more and more companies entering the hotel and catering field, the public now have a much wider choice, so it is essential for an establishment to present and attractive and economic product.

The consumer must be persuaded to buy the product and this factor of front office work has influenced the training and selection of the reception staff. The receptionist must be capable of making a sale, since front office efficiency is judged on selling success. Sales techniques can be learned, although without a doubt some people will; have more flair for work.

Although the marketing strategy will usually be devised by senior personnel, it is the reception staff who will implement it. So it is importance that front office staff should be aware of main objectives of marketing a hotel.

To plan for a point of sale front office, a front office staff must promote other profit centers of the hotel. This planning includes setting objectives, brainstorming areas of promotion, evaluating alternatives, drawing up budgets, and developing an evaluation tool for feedback.

UPSELLING

Upselling is a valuable technique for increasing a hotel's growth and profitability. However, it's not just a tool for increasing profits, but also a means of increasing customer satisfaction because you are suggesting additional products or services that will enhance their stay. Upselling is particularly effective when you have established trusting relationships with existing clients. Because these customers know and trust your business practices and service level, there's an expectation of quality. These techniques can be both simple and profitable.

Some of the goals for the front office as it adopts a sales department attitude include the following:

- Sell rooms to guests who have not made prior reservations
- Up sell (encourages a customer to consider buying a higher-priced product or service than originally anticipated) to guests who have made prior reservations.
- Maintain the inventory of the product i.e. the rooms.
- Convey information to guests about the other products available for sale at the property .for example food and beverages. The objective of front office

is to sell all available facilities at the hotel to the guests. Front office staff is probably the most important means of letting guests know what services are available.

- Ensure that maximum revenue is generated from the sale of rooms by striking a balance between overbooking and a full house
- Obtain guest feedback

Up selling rooms

The front office assistant should be confident nod business like when making suggestions. Rarely does a clerk quote minimum rate. The preferred approach is to provide guests with a choice of rates.

1. Know the product
2. Control the encounter. Ask specific questions such as "we have a quiet double room in our club floor. Is that suitable for you?" avoid vague, open ended questions such as "what kind of a room are you looking for?"
3. Sell high, but avoid high pressure selling techniques
4. Always quote the full rate plus tax
5. Turn negative aspect of a room or rooming situation into an advantage for the guest. For example, a room without a view becomes "quiet room". A room near the elevator may be busy but quote it as handy and easily accessible.
6. Sandwich the price between descriptive phrases. For example" one of our extra rooms at Rs 7500 plus tax, overlooking the park". Or quote the price of more than one room, giving the guest a choice," we still have double rooms for Rs 6500 but the ones with new minibar are RS 7500".
7. Ask for the sale. Once all information has been presented to the guest, the front office assistant must gently but resolutely close the sale." if that is a suitable choice may I ask you to sign the registration card?" is an effective way to move negotiations to a close.
8. Listen to guests' conversational comments, "wow what a hot day. I could do with something cool." they will help to determine their needs better and to sell other services of the hotel: "our poolside bars are open..."
9. Sell the whole hotel by making suggestions for dinner ("just dial 5 on your room phone to make a reservation") or for drinks in the lounge "the new entertainer is fantastic!"), or for recreational facilitate ("there is no charge for the use of sauna").

10. Try to anticipate guest's' needs and offer services, suggestions and assistance.

Brainstorming Areas for Promotion

When developing a program to increase front office sales activity, the front office manager in conjunction with other department should identify as specifically as possible, the hotel products and services to be promoted.

A typical outline of promotional areas would be as follows:

1. FRONT OFFICE

A. Reservations

1. Up selling when reservation is placed
2. Additional reservation during registration and checkout

B. ROOMS

1. Upgrading of reservation during registration
2. Promotional packages
3. Office rentals
4. Movie library rental
5. Computer games for children

C. SECRETARIAL SERVICES

1. Photocopies
2. Dictation
3. Typing
4. Fax transmission
5. Laptop computer rental

D. PERSONAL SERVICES

1 Baby sitting
2. Shopping malls
3. Bell staff assistance with luggage and equipment
4. Concierge

A. theatre/music/art tickets
B. general tourist information
C. tours of the area
D. airline reservations
E. emergency services
F. information on local transportation

FOOD AND BEVERAGE DEPARTMENT

A. RESTAURANTS

1. special menu items for the day
2. signature menu items
3. special pricing combination for diners
4. reservations
5. gift certificates

B. ROOM SERVICE

1. meals
2. party service
3. snacks
4. beverage/alcohol

C. BANQUET SERVICE

D. LOUNGE

1. specials of the day
2. special theme of the day
3. featured entertainer
4. promotional package

GIFT SHOPS

A. Emergency items

1. Clothing

2. Toiletries

B. Souvenirs

C. Promotional sales in progress

HEALTH SERVICES

A. Swimming pool

1. Availability to guests
2. Membership/gift certificates

B. Jogging paths and time of organized daily group runs

C. Health club

1. Availability to guests
2. Memberships/gift certificates

TYPES OF DISCOUNTS

Prompt Payment Discount

Trade Discounts are deductions in price given by the wholesaler or manufacturer to the retailer at the list price or catalogue price. *Cash Discounts* are reductions in price given by the creditor to the debitor. These discounts are intended to speed payment and thereby provide liquidity to the firm. They are sometimes used as a promotional device. we also explain that discount is relaxation in price.

Preferred Payment Method Discount

Some retailers (particularly small retailers with low margins) offer discounts to customers paying with cash, to avoid paying fees on credit card transactions.

Partial Payment Discount

Similar to the Trade discount, this is used when the seller wishes to improve cash flow or liquidity, but finds that the buyer typically is unable to meet the desired discount deadline. A partial discount for whatever payment the buyer makes helps the seller's cash flow partially.

Sliding Scale

A discount offered based on one's ability to pay. More common with non-profit organizations than with for-profit retail.

Forward Dating

This is where the purchaser doesn't pay for the goods until well after they arrive. The date on the invoice is moved forward - example: purchase goods in November for sale during the December holiday season, but the payment date on the invoice is January 27.

Seasonal Discount

These are price reductions given when an order is placed in a slack period (example: purchasing skis in April in the northern hemisphere, or in September in the southern hemisphere). On a shorter time scale, a happy hour may fall in this category. Generally, this discount is referred to as "X-Dating" or "Ex-Dating". An example of X-Dating would be:

- 3/7 net 30 extra 10 - this means the buyer must pay within 30 days of the invoice date, but will receive a 3% discount if they pay within 7 days after the end of the month indicated on the invoice date plus an extra 10 days.

Trade Discount

Trade discounts, also called functional discounts, are payments to distribution channel members for performing some function. Examples of these functions are warehousing and shelf stocking. Trade discounts are often combined to include a series of functions, for example 20/12/5 could indicate a 20% discount for warehousing the product, an additional 12% discount for shipping the product, and an additional 5% discount for keeping the shelves stocked. Trade discounts are most frequent in industries where retailers hold the majority of the power in the distribution channel (referred to as channel captains).

Trade discounts are given to try to increase the volume of sales being made by the supplier.

The discount described as trade rate discount is sometimes called "trade discount".

Trade Rate Discount

A trade rate discount, sometimes also called "trade discount", is offered by a seller to a buyer for purposes of trade or reselling, rather than to an end user. For example, a pharmacist might offer a discount for over-the-counter drugs to physicians who are purchasing them for dispensing to the physicians' own patients. A seller supplying both trade or resellers, and the general public will have a general list price for anybody, and will offer a trade discount to bona-fide trade customers.

Trade-in credit

Trade-in credit, also called trade-up credit, is a discount or credit granted for the return of something. The returned item may have little monetary value, as an old version of newer item being bought, or may be worth reselling as second-hand. The idea from a seller's viewpoint is to offer some discount but have the buyer showing some "counter action" to earn this special discount. Sellers like this as the discount granted is not just "given for free" and makes future price/value negotiations easier. Buyers have the advantage of getting some value for something no longer used. Examples can be found in many industries.

Cumulative Quantity Discount

Cumulative quantity discounts, also called accumulation discounts, are price reductions based on the quantity purchased over a set period of time. The expectation is that they will impose an implied switching cost and thereby bond the purchaser to the seller.

Non-cumulative Quantity Discount

These are price reductions based on the quantity of a single order. The expectation is that they will encourage larger orders, thus reducing billing, order filling, shipping, and sales personnel expenses.

Dependence of Price on Quantity

An extreme form of quantity discount is when, within a quantity range, the price does not depend on quantity:

- if one wants less than the minimum amount one has to be pay for the minimum amount anyway

- if one wants an amount between two of the fixed amounts on offer, one has to pay for the higher amount

These also apply in the case of a service with "quantity" referring to time. For example, an entrance ticket for a zoo is usually for a day; if one stays shorter, the price is the same. It is a kind of pass for unlimited use of a service during a day, where one can distinguish whether or not, when leaving and returning, one has to pay again. Similarly a pass can be for another period. In the case of long periods, it is obvious that one can leave and return without paying again.

If one has to buy more than one wants, we can distinguish between the surplus just not being used, or the surplus being a nuisance, e.g. because of having to carry a large container.

Disability Discount

A discount offered to customers with what is considered to be a disability.

Educational or Student Discount

These are price reductions given to members of educational institutions, usually students but possibly also to educators and to other institution staff. The provider's purpose is to build brand awareness early in a buyer's life, or build product familiarity so that after graduation the holder is likely to buy the same product, for own use or for an employer, at its normal price. Providers also offer student discounts as means of offering a product within the budget of a student, which would otherwise be too expensive, thus gaining extra sales. Educational discounts may be given by merchants directly, or via a student discount program, such as CollegeBudget in the United States or NUS and Studentdiscounts.co.uk in the United Kingdom.

Employee Discount

A discount offered by a company to employees who buy its products.

Military Discount

A discount offered to customers who are or were members of a military service. A discount is the value that deduct from a service or from goods. Types of military discounts include discounts for active duty military, veterans, retired military personnel, and military spouses or dependents. In the United States, military discounts frequently require proof of ID to show eligibility such as a

DD Form 214, DD Form 215, or DD Form 217 from any branch of the Armed Forces, TRICARE Cards, Veterans Affairs Cards Uniformed Services Privilege and Identification Cards (USPIC) or other official documentation. Eligibility for military discounts can also be verified online or via mobile by verification companies likeSheerID .

Toddler Discount, Child Discount, Kid Discount

A discount, or free service, offered to children younger than a certain age, commonly for admission to entertainments and attractions, restaurants, and hotels. There may be a requirement that the child be accompanied by an adult paying full price. Small children often travel free on public transport, and older ones may pay a substantially discounted price; proof of age may be required.

Young Person's Discount

Discounts are sometimes offered to young people below a certain age who are neither children nor in education.

Senior Discount

A discount offered to customers who are above a certain relatively advanced age, typically a round number such as 50, 55, 60, 65, 70, and 75; the exact age varies in different cases. The rationale for a senior discount offered by companies is that the customer is assumed to be retired and living on a limited income, and unlikely to be willing to pay full price; sales at reduced price are better than no sales. Non-commercial organizations may offer concessionary prices as a matter of social policy. Free or reduced-rate travel is often available to older people (see, for example, Freedom Pass).

Special Prices Offered to Friends of the Seller

A discounted price offered to friends of the salesperson.

Special Prices Offered to Local Residents

Discounts are common in tourist destinations. In Hawai'i, for example, many tourist attractions, hotels, and restaurants charge a deeply discounted price to someone who shows proof that they live in Hawai'i; this is known as a "Kama'aina discount," after the Hawaiian word for an old-timer or native.

Types of Allowances

Promotional allowances

These are price reductions given to the buyer for performing some promotional activity. These include an allowance for creating and maintaining an in-store display or a co-op advertising allowance.

Brokerage allowance

From the point of view of the manufacturer, any brokerage fee paid is similar to a promotional allowance. It is usually based on a percentage of the sales generated by the broker.

Specific Allowance

This is allowance created in respect of specific receivables which are known to be facing serious financial problems or have a trade dispute with the entity. Such balances may be identified by examining an aged receivable analysis which details the time lapsed since the creation of a receivable. Long outstanding balances identified from such analyses could be considered for inclusion in the allowance for doubtful debts.

The difference between the treatment of a bad debt and a specific allowance for doubtful debt is that in the latter case, the receivable ledger of the specific debt is not removed in case the debtor actually pays whereas in the case of bad debts, the receivable ledger is reduced to nil. Also, specific allowance may not be created for the entire amount of the doubtful receivable but only a portion of it. For instance, if there is a 50% chance of recovering a doubtful debt in respect of a certain receivable, a specific allowance of only 50% may be required. On the contrary, bad debt is normally recognized in full.

General Allowance

Past history of a business may show that a portion of receivable balances is not recovered due to unforeseen circumstances. Therefore, it may be prudent to create a general allowance for doubtful debts in addition to the specific allowance. The general allowance may be calculated on the basis of past experience concerning recoverability of debts.

The practice of creating general provisions is on the decline after revisions in the International Financial Reporting Standards (IFRS). Specifically, IAS 39 prohibits creation of general provisions on the basis of past experience due to the subjectivity involved in creating such an estimate. Instead, reporting entity is required to carry out impairment review to determine the recoverability of the receivables and any associated allowance.

Coupons

A discount, either of a certain specified amount or a percentage to the holder of a voucher, usually with certain terms. Commonly, the terms involve the terms of other discounts on this page, such as being valid only if a certain quantity is bought or only if the customer is older than a specified age. Coupons are often printed in newspapers, brochures, and magazines, or can be downloaded and printed from Worldwide Web pages that can be accessed via the Internet.

Rebates

A refund of part of sometimes the full price of the product following purchase, though some rebates are offered at the time of purchase. A particular case is the promise of a refund in full if applied for in a restricted date range some years in the future; the hope is that the promise will lure customers and increase sales, but that the majority will fail to meet the conditions for a valid claim.

QUESTIONNAIRE

1. Explain the importance of room selling technique in hotel industry?
2. What are the elements of marketing in room selling techniques?
3. How pricing strategies does plays a vital role in room selling techniques?
4. How does competitions influences the room selling techniques of a hotel?
5. Define personal selling?
6. As front office personnel how would you recognize customer motive for buying?
7. Explain the phenomenon of "pregnant pause"?
8. Explain 3 various front office room selling tips?
9. What is the role of sales and marketing department in room selling?
10. Explain the concept of up selling with a suitable example

13
ARRIVALS

- INTRODUCTION
- GUEST CYCLE
- FRONT OFFICE SYSTEMS.
- GUEST CYCLE UNDER THREE DIFFERENT SYSTEMS
- FRONT OFFICE FORMS
- FRONT OFFICE FUNCTIONAL ORGANISATION
- FRONT OFFICE EQUIPMENTS

INTRODUCTION

It includes registration & rooming functions. The front desk staff should determine the guest's reservation status before beginning the registration process. Guests with reservations may have already undergone pre-registration activities. Guests without reservations or walk-in guests present an opportunity for front office staff to sell guest rooms. To sell successfully, the front desk must be very familiar with the hotel's room types & guest services & be able to describe them in a positive way. A registration record should include information about the guest's intended method of payment, the planned length of stay, & any special guest needs. It should also include the guest's billing address, telephone number & the guest's signature. Gathering all these details at registration enhances the front office's ability to meet special guest needs, forecast room occupancies & settle accounts properly. At check out, the guest's registration card may also become the primary source for creating a guest history record.

A guest history record is a record of personal & financial information about a hotel guest which can help the hotel in its marketing & sales efforts & can be helpful in registering & serving the guest if the guest returns. The front desk staff uses registration information to assign a room & possibly a room rate for each guest. The guest may be given a room key & a map of the property & allowed to proceed to the room without assistance. When the guest arrives at the room & accepts it, the occupancy stage of the guest cycle begins.

I-Guest Cycle

- The guest cycle describes the activities that each guest passes by from the moment he/she calls to communicate a reservation inquiry till he/she departs from the hotel. In fact, the guest cycle encompasses 4 different stages, which are depicted in the underneath diagram:

Pre-Arrival ⇒ Arrival ⇒ Occupancy ⇒ Departure

- Each stage of the guest cycle is associated guest service, and guest accounting activity(ies).

1. Guest services:

Reservation ⇒ Registration ⇒ Occupancy services ⇒ Check-out and history

2. Guest Accounting:

Establishment of credits ⇒ Posting charges ⇒ Night auditing ⇒ settlement of accounts

- Below is a description of the activities undertaken at each stage of the guest cycle:

1. Pre-arrival

- At the pre-arrival stage, the hotel must create for every potential guest a reservation Record. Doing this initiates the hotel guest cycle. Moreover, reservation records help personalize guest services and appropriately *schedule needed staff and facilities.*
- The reservation department should, then, complete all the pre-registration activities and prepare guest folios (applicable only for automated systems). Doing so will eventually maximize room sales by *accurately* monitoring room availability and forecasting room revenues:

WELCOME CARD/KEY
HOTEL ABC
THE MALL, DELHI

PHONE NO. .... FAX NO. ....

(FRONT SIDE)

ROOM NO. ....

NAME ....

RATE......................... PLAN .... NO. OF PAX ....

BILLING INSTRUCTIONS...

CREDIT CARD.................................. NO. ....

DATE OF ISSUE................................ EXPIRY DATE...............................

DATE AND TIME OF ARRIVAL..

DATE AND TIME OF DEPARTURE..

CHECK OUT TIME 12 NOON

GUEST's SIGNATURE SR. RECEPTIONIST SIGNATURE

(BACK SIDE)

RESTAURANT A OPENS FROM 12 NOON TO 3 P.M. AND FROM 8 P.M. TO 12 MID NIGHT AND SERVES INDIAN FOOD

RESTAURANT B OPENS FROM 7 P.M. TILL 2 A.M. AND SERVES CHINESE FOOD WITH LIVE BAND

24 HOURS RUNNING HOT AND COLD WATER

24 HOURS COFFEE SHOP

24 HOURS ROOM SERVICE'

24 HOURS MONEY CHANGER

TRAVEL COUNTER

SECRETARIAT SERVICE

2. Arrival

- At the arrival stage, registration and rooming functions takes place and the hotel establishes a business relation-ship with the guest.
- The check-in clerk should determine the guest's reservation status (i.e. pre-registered guests *versus* walk-ins). Later, he/she shall prepare a registration record or make the guest sign the already-printed pre-registration record (under some of the semi-automated and all fully automated systems).
- The registration records shall include the following *personal* and *financial* items:

  a) Personal information:

    1. Name and Surname of the guest along with billing address, telephone number, and any other coordinates
    2. Passport number, birth certificate, and/or driving license number (whatever applicable)
    3. Any special needs or requests
    4. Guest Signature

'C' FORM
(RULE 10 & 14)
HOTEL ABC
THE MALL, DELHI

NO. ....

THE REGISTRATION OF FOREIGNER's RULE, 1939

1. NAME OF THE HOTEL ....
2. NAME OF FOREIGNER..
3. NO. OF PERSONS IN THE FAMILY...
4. NATIONALITY..
5. NO. OF PASSPORT..
6. DATE OF ISSUE..
7. PLACE OF ISSUE..
8. REGISTRATION NO. ....
9. PLACE OF REGISTRATION...
10. DATE OF ARRIVAL IN THE HOTEL............ TIME..............................
11. DATE AND PLACE OF ARRIVAL IN INDIA...
12. ARRIVED FROM ....
13. PROCEEDING TO ....
14. MODE OF TRANSPORT USED...
15. ADDRESS IN INDIA...
16. PURPOSE OF VISIT..
17. DATE OF DEPARTURE FROM HOTEL..
18. NO. OF DATE AND PLACE OF ISSUE OF VISA AND ITS VALIDITY........
19. PERMANENT HOME ADDRESS...

MANAGER's SIGNATURE

b) Financial information:

1. Date of arrival
2. Expected date of departure or length of stay depending on how the system in the hotel is designed
3. Assigned room number
4. Assigned room rate
5. Guest's intended method of payment

- Registration records can be used for various purposes:
  a) Satisfy guest needs
  b) Forecast room occupancies
  c) Settle *properly* guest accounts
  d) Establish guest history records at check-out [personal & financial information]
  e) Assign a room type and a room rate for each guest
  f) Determine long-run availability [i.e. reservation information] versus short-run availability [i.e. room status]
  g) Satisfy special categories of guests such as disabled people through barrier-free designs.

GUEST REGISTRATION CARD

HOTEL ABC

THE MALL, DELHI

No. ....

NAME...

(Surname) (First name)

NATIONALITY............... DATE OF BIRTH..................

DESIGNATION........... DATE OF MARRIAGE ANNIVERSARY....

ADDRESS...

ARRIVED FROM............... PROCEDDING TO ....

TYPE OF ACCOMMODATION.....SS.....DS.....SR......DR.......

NUMBER OF PAX.......... PURPOSE OF VISIT..................

DATE AND TIME OF ARRIVAL.................................

EXPECTED DATE AND TIME OF DEPARTURE.........................

RATE.............. PLAN ....

MODE OF PAYMENT......CASH...... CREDIT CARD..... OTHER...

CREDIT CARD NAME................ NUMBER......................

DATE OF EXPIRY...................

BILL TO......................

FOR FOREIGNER's ONLY **FOR OFFICE USE**

PASSPORT NO. ....

DATE AND PLACE OF ISSUE.....................

DATE IF EXPIRY..........................

DATE OF ARRIVAL IN INDIA.............

DATE OF STAY IN INDIA....................

TYPE OF VISA ....

VISA NO. ....

DATE OF ISSUE.................

PLACE OF ISSUE........................

VALID UP TO ....

WHETHER EMPLOYED IN INDIA YES/NO

IF YES:

REGISTRATION NO. IN INDIA...................

PLACE OF REGISTRATION.......................

DATE OF REGISTRATION........................

ADDRESS IN INDIA (IF ANY).....................................

I AGREE TO RELEASE MY ROOM(S) BY 12 NOON ON THE DATE OF DEPARTURE. SHOULD I FAIL TO CHECK OUT, I AUTHORISE THE MANAGEMENT TO PACK AND REMOVE MY BELONGINGS TP THE HOTEL LUGGAGE LEFT ROOM SO THAT MY ROOMS WILL BE AVAILABLE FOR INCOMING GUESTS WITH CONFIRMED RESERVATIONS.

GUEST's SIGNATURE SIGNATURE

CHECK OUT TIME 12 NOON

3. Occupancy

- At the occupancy stage, the front office department shall coordinate guest services *in a timely and accurate manner*.

  Moreover, front office clerks should encourage repeat guests by paying *a great attention* to guest complaints. This is ensured by placing complaint and/or suggestion cards in every public place and revenue centers in the hotel.

  Moreover, the hotel shall, at least on a daily basis, collect comment cards, proceed with their analysis, and provide positive feedback to guest as soon as possible.

- In addition, shall design effective procedures in order to protect the funds and valuables of guests. This might be ensured through guest key control, property surveillance, safe deposit boxes, and well designed emergency panels and exits...
- Another activity at occupancy is to process posting of guest charges [i.e. post room rates, F&B charges, additional expenses, and taxes...] to various guest folios, master Folios... While doing so, front office clerks shall continuously check for deviations from the house limit, and take corrective measures as to change the status of the guest to Paid-in-advance. Finally, front office clerks shall *periodically* review Account Balances in coordination with the night auditor.

BILL FOLIO

FOLIO NO. ....

ROOM NO. .... TYPE OF ACCOMMODATION.........

NAME..................... NO. OF PAX.....................

DESIGNATION..

ADDRESS.....................................

PHONE NO. ....FAX NO. ....EMAIL..........

CREDIT CARD...

CREDIT CARD NO. ....N DATE OF EXPIRY............

BILLING INSTRUCTIONS ....

RATE............................... PLAN.................................

DATE AND TIME OF ARRIVAL....................................

DATE AND TIME OF DEPARTURE...............................

DATE	Reference	PREVIOUS BALANCE PICK UP	CREDIT	BALANCE
			LAST BALANCE AMOUNT DUE	

GUEST's SIGNATURE **CASHIER's SIGNATURE**

5. Departure

- At the departure stage, the guest shall be walked out of the hotel. Moreover, front office clerks shall create guest history record. Finally, cashiers shall settle guest account outstanding balances [i.e.: balance the Guest account to **0**]
- In general, a proper checkout occurs when the guest:
  a) Vacates the room
  b) Receives an *accurate* settlement of the guest account
  c) Returns room keys
  d) Leaves the hotel
- At departure, checkout personnel should encourage guests to consider returning to the hotel on any future date. That's why cashiers should act like a true sales person, and might eventually accept guest future reservations. That way, the stages of the guest cycle become really a cycle (i.e. start from where it ends).
- If at departure, the guest account is not fully settled, then late charges accumulates. In such an undesired case, the responsibility of collection lies within the accounting department, however the front office department shall provide all necessary types of information to make this collection easier, quicker, and feasible.

Post Departure

This is phase which takes place after the guest leaves the hotel. After this stage guest is away from the hotel, but the intention of the hotel is to maintain relations with the guest so that he gives repeat business.

A thank you card is sent to the guest for using guest services.

Feedback on the hotels services is sought from the guest.

II- Front Office Systems

- Until the 1960's, nearly all hotels were operating under the manual system. At late 70's, with the introduction of computers, hotels shifted to semi-automated systems. Nowadays, most of the five-star hotels operate under the fully automated system. Below is a brief description of the three different systems under which hotels might operate.

1. Non-automated [manual] systems: This very system is the one characterized by the sole usage of hands. In fact, all formats, procedures, and different kinds of calculations are done manually.
2. Semi-automated [Electro-mechanical] systems: This system gets use of some Electro-mechanical equipment. In fact, under the semi-automated system, each department might have its own computer system under which it handles all its operations.
3. Fully automated [computer based] systems: That's the best system ever used in the hotel industry. In fact, it is characterized by the excessive use of departmental software package programs integrated and connected to a main frame or terminal situated at the front office department.

III. Guest Cycle under Three Different Systems

- At this stage, it is essential to notice that the following stages of the guest cycle under the three different systems do not conflict with each other. In fact, the only differences are due to the nature of the system use. Therefore, what will be discussed above is not the repetition of the sequence; rather only differences will be highlighted.

1. Non-automated systems:

A. Pre-arrival activities

- At the pre-arrival stage, reservation requests should be introduced in a loose-leaf notebook or index card. Moreover, only reservations up to 6 months horizons shall be honored. Lastly, it is not practical, under this very system, to issue reservation confirmation numbers, initiate pre-registration activities (at the exception of VIP and groups) and prepare occupancy forecasts. The reason is, time and money loss along with insufficient labor force to manually conduct all the above mentioned activities.

B. Arrival activities:

- At the arrival stage, guests shall either sign a page in the registration book or fill manually a registration record. Under this very system, the most widely used front office equipment is the room rack, in which registration records are inserted to serve as room rack slips. Moreover, registration books and records shall be time stamped as an internal control proving when the guest exactly came, who registered him/her...Lastly, guest folios shall be opened for each registered guest.

C. Occupancy activities:

- Under the occupancy activities, registration records shall be prepared with multi-copies. In fact, one copy shall be distributed to room rack, another stamped to the guest folio, another given to switchboard operators, and a final copy handed to the uniformed service personnel. Lastly, guests with charge privileges charges and payments shall be posted to respective guest folios.

D. Departure activities:

- At departure stage, cashiers should settle each guest account's outstanding balance and get room keys back from guests. Moreover, cashiers shall notify the housekeeping department that the room is no more occupied (i.e. room status change) to let this very department clean the room and prepare it for new arrivals. In addition, cashiers shall remove room rack slips from room racks to indicate departure. Lastly, these very rack slips of departed guests shall be filed in a cardboard box to serve as a guest history record.

GUEST'S HISTORY CARD

Name of the guest: Mr./Ms. ....

Family name Name

Middle Name

Nationality..

Residence Address ....

T. No.................................... Mobile No. ....

E. Mail... Fax No. ....

Office Address ....

T. No. ....

E. Mail .... Fax no. ....

Date of birth..................... Marriage Anniversary date................................

Religion..

Likings... Remarks...

Passport No. .... Date of issue ....

Place of issue......................... Date of expiry ....

Credit Card .... Numbers ....

Date of expiry ....

HISTORY OF PREVIOUS STAY

S NO.	DATE CHECKED-IN	DATE CHECKED-OUT	ROOM NO.	TARIFF	REMARKS	SR. RECEPTIONIST SIGNATURE

Lobby Manager's Signature

2. Semi-automated Systems

- This very system is less common in small and middle size hotels. For, these very hotels, financially wise, might not afford the huge investments associated with the installation of different hardware and software.
- The main advantage of this very system over manual system is that various reports can *automatically* be generated. However, the major disadvantages associated with this system are various complexities of operating and controlling devices due to the fact that these equipment are not integrated with other systems and are subject to frequent maintenance problems.

A. Pre-arrival activities

- At this very stage, guests can either call a national reservation network or directly contact the hotel. Moreover, reservation clerks can prepare pre-registration records, guest folios, and information rack slips.

B. Arrival activities:

- At this very stage, already reserved guests shall verify their pre-registration forms and have only to sign it. On the other hand, walk-ins shall complete a multiple copy registration record from the beginning.

C. Occupancy activities:

- At the occupancy stage, in order to track the different guest charge expenditures and all other possible guest transactions, hotels get an intensive use of various kinds of vouchers. Moreover, the most widely used equipment, under this very stage, is the mechanical cash registers and front office posting machines. Lastly, under this very stage, night auditor shall continuously resolve any discrepancy in guest accounts and efficiently reconcile guest folios.

D. Departure activities:

- At this very stage, cashiers shall relay room status information to the housekeeping department. Moreover, they should place registration records of departed guests in property's guest history files.

4. Fully automated systems

A. Pre-arrival activities:

- Under this stage, the reservation department is equipped with a software package, which is *interfaced and connected* with one or more central reservation office(s). Moreover, the reservation department can automatically generate letters of confirmation, produce requests for guest deposits and handle pre-registration activities for all types of guests and generate daily expected arrival lists, occupancy and revenue forecast lists...

B. Arrival activities:

- At this stage, various reservation records can be transferred to front office department. Moreover, hotels might be equipped with an on-line credit authorization terminals *for timely Credit Card Approval*, self check-in / check-out terminals. Lastly, all guest charges and payments are saved in electronic guest folios.
- As far as walk-ins are concerned, all registration activities should be initiated from the very beginning.

C. Occupancy activities:

- Under this very stage, guest purchases at different revenue outlets are electronically transferred and posted to appropriate guest accounts. Moreover, the front office department can run and process continuous trial balances and, therefore, eliminate the tedious work for the Night Auditor.

D. Departure activities:

- At this very stage, cashiers can automatically produce bills to be sent to various guests with direct billing privileges and create electronic guest history records.

IV. Front Office Forms

- At different stages of the guest cycle different forms are used depending on which operating system a hotel chooses. Below are some of the common forms used:

1. Pre-arrival activities:
    a) Reservation record or a reservation file
    b) Letter of confirmation
    c) Reservation rack and reservation rack slips
2. Arrival activities:
    a) Registration card (or record) or registration file
    b) Room rack and room rack slips
3. Occupancy activities:
    a) Guest folio: shall be of duplicate forms and pre-numbered for cross-indexing control purposes
    b) Vouchers: support documents detailing facts of a transaction, but does not replace the source document (i.e. the invoice). Examples of vouchers might include charge vouchers, allowance vouchers, paid-out voucher, and correction vouchers...
    c) Information rack slips
4. Departure activities:
    a) Credit card vouchers
    b) Cash vouchers
    c) Personal check vouchers
    d) Transfer vouchers
    e) Guest history records

V. Front Office Functional Organization

- Whatsoever system and setting the hotel might use, it should reflect easy access to the equipment, forms, and supplies necessary. Moreover, the setting shall reflect position flexibility. Moreover, nowadays trend shows that traditional mail, message, and key racks are unnecessary at the Front Desk. Rather, they shall be stored in drawers or slots located under or away from the Front Desk. For, this would ensure security and safety of guests.

1. Front Desk designed alternatives:
    a) Circular or semi-circular structure: this very structure provides an effective service to more guests and appears more modern and innovative

but since guests will approach the Front Desk from all angles, more staff is needed.

b) Traditional straight desk: Under this very design, fewer staff is needed, but fewer guests can be served at the same time.

c) Deskless environment: Under this design, there is no Front Desk at all. This is usually replaced by a hostess, or steward welcoming the guest, seating him or her on a chair/sofa, and conduct registration activities there while, for example, having a cocktail or a drink.

VI. Front Office Equipment:

1. Room rack
2. Mail, message, and key racks
3. Reservation racks
4. Information racks
5. Folio trays or folio buckets
6. Account posting machine
7. Voucher racks
8. Cash registers
9. Telephone equipment

QUESTIONNAIRE

1. List and explain the various steps in the registration process?
2. What is Pre-Registration Activity? Explain in detail with its advantages.
3. Give step-by-step procedure of handling group arrivals.
4. What is the procedure of handling FIT arrival?
5. Explain the following:
   a) Bill folio
   b) Pre registration
   c) Guest history card
   d) 'C' form.
6. Distinguish between the following:
   a) Key card and card key

b) Registration card and Registration register

c) Walk-in and walking a guest

7. What is Guest Cycle? What are different types of systems used in guest cycle?
8. What are different steps used in the pre-arrival activities?
9. What are the different equipments used in Front Office?
10. Draw the formats of the following:

a) Guest registration card.

b) Guest registration Register.

c) Bill folio

d) Welcome key card

e) 'c' form

14

DURING THE STAY ACTIVITIES

- INFORMATION SERVICES
- MESSAGE AND MAIL HANDLING
- KEY HANDLING
- ROOM SELLING TECHNIQUE
- HOSPITALITY DESK
- COMPLAINTS HANDLING
- GUEST HISTORY
- QUESTIONNAIRE

INFORMATION SERVICES

Front office staff must know the following points:

Hotel Product Check List

- Room number and location of each room: floor and access.
- Type of accommodation available: single, double, twin, etc. extra bed etc.
- Additional facilities: Terrace, private balcony, Jacuzzi, etc.
- Room facilities: Telephone, mini bar, channel music, fax machine, etc.
- State of furnishings: Newly redecorated, good, poor, old fashioned, etc.
- Fire emergency drill.
- Hotel rates: per person, per day, per room, etc.
- Details of tariff: Half board, full board, B.P., etc.
- Special tariffs: High / mid / low season, festival season, discount rates.

Standing Arrangements:

- Service charges.
- Reservation deposit policy.
- Price and service times of all meals in the restaurant.
- Room and floor service facilities & charges.
- Policy for pets and dogs.
- Car parking, garage, petrol, car repairs facilities.
- Telephone call charges.
- Corkage charges.
- Liquor, cigarettes and snacks service time and charges.
- Cheque, traveler's cheque and personal cheque policies.
- Credit card policy
- Travel agents and company business policy.

Hotel Facilities:

- Number and position of public cloak room, staircases, elevators, etc.
- Position and amenities of lounge, TV room or reading room, restaurants, etc.
- Opening and closing hours of bar, games room, health club, swimming pool, etc.
- Provision for packed food, early dinner, late supper.
- Banqueting and conference facilities.
- Theater tickets, taxi hire, car hire, laundry, dry cleaning, etc.

Business Centre

This section of the front office provides for all secretarial needs of the guest such as photocopies, faxes, binding, web browsing, etc. A small meeting/ conference room may also be the part of the business centre for use of the guests. This is manned round the clock and is easily accessible to the guest.

MESSAGE & MAIL HANDLING

Message Handling

Receiving messages for in-house guests in their absence, recording them and communicating them to the guests as soon as possible are an important function of the front desk staff. The efficiency and professionalism of the hotel and the attitude of the staff is reflected by the way this function is carried out by the staff. Usually when a guest goes out of his room he would leave his room key at the counter where the information clerk would put it in the appropriate pigeon hole of his room in the mail and key rack. The guest my leave a filled "Location Form" indicating where he will be for the next few hours.

There are only two ways that a person can contact an in-house guest.

(1) In case of a phone call the telephone operator will connect it to the room of the guest. Since the guest is not in the room the call comes back to the operator who connects it to the Information Section of the Front Desk. After checking that the guest has left his key at the desk (as confirmed by the key being in the "Mail and Key Rack") the telephone call is transferred to the "Message Desk". The message clerk prepares the message slip in triplicate. It is important to read back the message to the caller and confirm the details before signing off. The top two copies are given to the Information Clerk who puts it the room no on the forms (from the Information Rack). The Top Copy is sent to the room to be slipped under the door. The Second Copy is put in the appropriate room no pigeon hole of the Mail and Key Rack. In addition, for further safety, an "attention card" or a "mail and message advice card" is put on the door knob of the room or "message light" is activated in those hotels which use electronic systems. The message details may also be fed into the computer and the guest may view it on the screen of the T.V. in his room.

(2) In case of the visitor coming to the hotel, he is asked to first try the house telephones to contact the guest. When he finds the guest is not in his room he comes to the Information Desk and fills in the message slip in triplicate as given above.

MESSAGE SLIP

To ______________________ Room No ____________

Date _____________ Time _____________

DURING YOUR ABSENCE

Mr. / Mrs. / Ms ____________________________________

Of ____

Tel No ______________________

Called by Telephone

Please call him/her

Came to see you

Will return

Wants to see you

Urgent

MESSAGE ____

____

____

____

Received by ____

MAIL HANDLING

Importance

Mail handling procedure is a very important function which the Front Office staff has to handle in a hotel. A receptionist in a hotel has to be very careful that all the mail receives due attention and are attended to without any delay to avoid embarrassment.

Types of mail - Incoming & Outgoing, Ordinary & Registered:

Basically while discussing there are two types of mail. Incoming & Outgoing.

Incoming Mail

Various types of mail may be received in a hotel, like mail for Hotel Management and Hotel staff and mail for guests. In addition the mail may be an ordinary mail or registered/recorded mail etc.

Staff has to be extra careful about recorded mail. All incoming mail must be DATE AND TIME STAMPED. A proper record of all the recorded mail is kept as per requirement i.e., the entries are made in either registered letter book, parcels book or telegram book etc. No such record is maintained for ordinary mail. After having date and time marked the mail, it is sorted and classified under 3 main categories.

1. **HOTEL MAIL** is identified by the designation of a senior manager of the hotel egg General Manager, Banquet Manager Etc. This mail is delivered to the office of the managers concerned.
2. **STAFF MAIL** is identified by the presence of the name of employee, designation and department mentioned in the address. This is usually sorted and delivered through the Time Office.
3. **GUEST MAIL** : Any mail that is left is supposed to be guest mail

Guest Mail may belong to any one of the following categories:

1. Present Guest Mail
2. Past Guest Mail
3. Future guest Mail
4. Wrongly Addressed Mail

PRESENT GUEST MAIL

The guest mail is first arranged in ALPHABETICAL ORDER and then checked against the INFORMATION RACK to identify the PRESENT GUESTS. Wherever applicable the room no is entered in pencil on the letters and then they are put in the appropriate room no pigeon hole in the MAIL AND KEY RACK to be handed to the guests when they come to deposit or collect their keys

Any mail that is left still belongs to guests who have already departed (past guest) or to guests who have still to arrive (future guests)

PAST GUEST MAIL

Sometime the hotel receives mail for the guests who have already departed from the hotel after having stayed for some period. The hotel to avoid any embarrassment as to what to do with such mail and how to hand it over to the person quickly, ask the departing guest to leave their forwarding address and for how long they would want their mail to be redirected to that address. A special program called "Mail Forwarding Card" is used for this. Many hotels keep these cards in the stationery folder in the room while others keep these slips at the Front Desk and give them to the guest at the time of departure. This card contains the address to which and the dates/ period till by which the guest would like all the mail received by the hotel after his departure to be forwarded. These cards are filed alphabetically and when the expiry date is reached they are cleared out systematically. Any letter received after the expiry date is either returned back to the sender or in case the permanent address of the guest is available, is redirected to him at his permanent address.

FUTURE GUEST MAIL

General Mail for guests yet to arrive is kept in the back office in pigeon holes marked alphabetically. An indication is made in the reservation record about this awaited mail i.e., in case of Whitney system the words "Awaited Mail" is written on the Whitney slip. In case of diary system it is recorded in the diary against his name in remarks column and in case of Computer system it is updated in the computer. Later this mail is sent to the Front Desk and is kept with the receptionist in special slot on the day of arrival of the guest and when the guest arrives the receptionist hands over the mail to the guest at the time of registration.

If there is any mail that is delivered within thirty days after it has been received, it is marked "Addressee Unknown" and sent back to the Post Office which will send them to the Dead Letter Office.

KEY HANDLING

Key Card

While key card locks on guest rooms are quickly becoming the standard, some hotels still don't take advantage of the added safety provided to guests.

Guest room locking systems these days include punch and magnetic key cards which have locks with flash memory and other productivity linked functions. The system can directly be linked with PMS.

Key Control

A control system by which it is ensured that room keys are always at the proper place i.e. if the room is occupied and the guest is in the room then the key is with him, and if the guest is not in the room or the room is unsold then the room key is in its proper pigeon hole of key and mail rack. A lack of proper system result in loss of revenue as a room which is vacant may be shown occupied and may also cause confusion and chaos as an occupied room maybe accessed by an unauthorized guest.

Two locking systems are using in hotels:

- HARD KEY SYSTEM (metallic keys)
- ELECTRONIC KEY SYSTEM

Process of Key Control

The process of key control in case of hard keys is done by receptionist who prepares a key control sheet at around midnight or 1.00a.m through night receptionist report which contains details such as room not be assigned, vacant, occupied double lock,etc.

The keys of vacant room should be at the key and mail rack in the appropriate pigeon hole and if it is not there and also if the bill is settled, then departure is shown in the various registers as per bills and housekeeping.

The missing keys of the vacant rooms are tried to be located which could be with housekeeping or bell desk. It is checked, and if not found, is entered in the report.

Details of missing key list is made. It could be that the guest did a self departure and mistakenly took away the key. Such room numbers are noted. Name of the guest, his check out date and time is also noted. His address is taken from the registration card.

ROOM SELLING TECHNIQUES

The sales function has become an important and vital part of front office work. with more and more companies entering the hotel and catering field, the public now have a much wider choice, so it is essential for an establishment to present and attractive and economic product.

The consumer must be persuaded to buy the product and this factor of front office work has influenced the training and selection of the reception staff. The receptionist must be capable of making a sale, since front office efficiency is judged on selling success. Sales techniques can be learned, although without a doubt some people will; have more flair for work.

Although the marketing strategy will usually be devised by senior personnel, it is the reception staff who will implement it. So it is importance that front office staff should be aware of main objectives of marketing a hotel.

To plan for a point of sale front office, a front office staff must promote other profit centers of the hotel. This planning includes setting objectives, brainstorming areas of promotion, evaluating alternatives, drawing up budgets, and developing an evaluation tool for feedback.

Upselling

Upselling is a valuable technique for increasing a hotel's growth and profitability. However, it's not just a tool for increasing profits, but also a means of increasing customer satisfaction because you are suggesting additional products or services that will enhance their stay. Upselling is particularly effective when you have established trusting relationships with existing clients. Because these customers know and trust your business practices and service level, there's an expectation of quality. These techniques can be both simple and profitable.

Hospitality Desk

The Hospitality Desk is located at the entrance of the Lobby of Hotel

The Guest Service Associates are ready to answer any of your questions about the hotel specials and services such as the latest dining and room promos, ongoing and upcoming events and many other facilities.

One can also learn from our Guest Service Associates some additional information on the many ways to enjoy the best where to shop, native items and delicacies, nature and cultural touring etc.

This desk would provide assistance to the guests as follows:

- Hand over name badges and welcome packs
- Advise the various halls where the meetings/sessions are taking place
- Arrange luncheons/dinners for the delegates
- Coordinate AM/PM tea/coffee breaks + lunches
- Hotel Room booking
- Air ticket re-confirmations
- Arrange cars
- Coordinate/assist the transport schedule
- All other services to make the delegate and the staff stay comfortable

GUEST COMPLAINT HANDLING

How to handle complaints:

1. Listen carefully when a guest complaints do not interrupt, listen carefully. Because a guest who is complaining. Do not interrupt and

give excuses. The guest is angry and to lessen the anger, let him tell you the entire problem.

2. Clarify if you are in doubt about the specific problem of your guest then do not guess his problem but, clarify it by asking questions and understanding the nature of problem.
3. Think about your guest wants when guest complaints he might tell you so many things along with the actual problem. But you have to try and the important message from the complaint, i.e. find out the root cause.
4. Think how you can help considering the nature of the problem and the complaint; decide the plan of action quickly.
5. Act immediately take immediate action and take the action in front of the guest so that he feels that he is taken care of.
6. Follow-up merely taking action is not sufficient, so follow-up with the other departments, if the complaint has been handled.
7. No false promises it is very dangerous to make false promise. If you can't solve a particular problem do not promise, otherwise you may lose not only one customer but many.
8. Ask senior if you feel you can't solve a certain problem or you are not authorized to take a decision, ask you're senior to help you.

Guest History

The front office is the first touch point for a guest staying at a hotel. A repeat guest is always pleasantly surprised when he is making a reservation for the second time at the property, and the front desk operator tells him about his special request preferences, non-smoking room, low floor, etc, before they can make these requests to the front desk operator. For instance, guest history notes on special diets go to F&B or room service, and a special request of a particular type of bedding will go to the Housekeeping department.

The front office plays an important role in developing relationships with the guest, and since guest recognition is an important aspect of that relationship, the one question that a front desk operator cannot afford to ask a guest is, "Have you stayed with us before?" However, recognizing a guest isn't an easy task. Part of the trick is to recognize whether someone making a booking is a repeat guest, whether he is doing so by phone, calling the toll free reservations number or booking over the Internet. This isn't always easy. Most people usually visit a hotel in just one capacity. However, there are some guests who may quite easily come in different roles — convention attendee, family vacationer, meeting planner, or just one of the boys on a golf outing — with different room and package preferences for each visit. Name changes due to marriages and divorces are also an obvious recognition challenge.

GUEST HISTORY CARD

WELCOME! We hope you enjoy your visit.
You feedback is extremely valuable to us and
we thank you for completing this guest survey.

PLEASE PRINT

Name: ______________________________

Address: ______________________________

City: ____________ **State/Prov:** ________ **Postal Code:** __________

Email Address: ______________________________

Primary Telephone: ( ) -

Alternate Telephone: ( ) -

Facsimile: ( ) -

Is this your first visit? ☐ **YES** ☐ **NO**

How long have you been looking at new homes? ______________

What price range are you considering? ______________

When are planning to move? ______________

Your current residence is: ☐ **House** ☐ **House-Lease/Rent** ☐ **Condominium** ☐ **Townhome** ☐ **Apartment** ☐ **Other**

Will you be selling your present home? ☐ **YES** ☐ **NO**

If yes, is it presently on the market? ☐ **YES** ☐ **NO**

What price range are you considering? ______________

How did you hear about us? ______________

Primary reason for visit today? ______________

If Accompanied and registered by a Real Estate Agent/Realtor

Realtor Name: ______________

Realtor Telephone: ______________

Realtor Email Address: ______________

May we help you with other information? ______________

Comments: ______________

QUESTIONNAIRE

1. What do you understand by information services?
2. Discuss in detail mail handling and message handling?
3. How will you control guest complaints in a hotel?
4. Discuss the key control process in brief?
5. Mention the importance of hospitality desk?
6. Give the importance of guest history
7. Draw the format of guest history card
8. What do you understand by upselling?

15

COORDINATION WITH OTHER DEPARTMENTS

- COORDINATION WITH OTHER DEPARTMENTS OF HOTEL

INTRODUCTION

The front office staffs interacts with all departments of the hotel including housekeeping, Marketing and Sales, Food and Beverage, Banquet, Controller, Maintenance, Security, and Human Resources. These departments view the front office as a communication liaison in providing guest services. Each of the departments has a unique Inter-departmental communication to create effective communication with other departments in a hotel.

Interdepartmental Communication

Marketing and Sales

1. Provide data on guest histories to marketing and sales - details concerning each guest's visit – to be used for marketing for marketing campaigns, develop promotions, prepare mailing labels, and select appropriate advertising media
2. Process requests for reservations for sleeping rooms from marketing and sales
3. Offer good first impression to the public

4. Relay messages to marketing and sales
5. Meet information requests of guests for meetings, seminars

Housekeeping

1. Receive housekeeping room status from each other
2. Report potential house count (a report of the number of guests registered in the hotel) to each other
3. Relay guest requests for amenities and supplies to housekeeping
4. Report room sales projections
5. Relay accurate housekeeping status
6. Relay security concerns to front office

Food and Beverage

1. Record accurate information on
2. Relaying messages to food and beverage vouchers and subsequent postings
3. Reporting predicted house counts to food and beverage so that F&B can schedule employees and predict sales
4. Processing requests for paid-outs from food and beverage personnel
5. Inter-face with point-of-sale terminals

Banquets

1. Relay information to guests about scheduled events for banquet department
2. Process payment of guest charges for scheduled events for banquet department
3. Prepare daily announcement board and marquee for banquet department

Maintenance

1. Provide room status to maintenance
2. Relay information on requests for guest room maintenance

Security

1. Maintain guest security – fire safety, emergency communication systems, and routine investigation of guest security
2. Alert for people who don't belong in the lobby and impel front office staff to report inconsistencies with the security department.

Controller

The controller relies on the front office staff to provide a daily summary of financial transactions through a well - prepared night audit. This information is also used to measure management ability to meet budget targets. Since the front office provides the controller with financial data for billing and maintenance of credit - card ledgers, these two departments must relay payments and charges through the posting machine or property management system.

- The front desk provides daily summary of the financial transaction after night auditing to the finance controller.
- The information by the front desk helps the finance controller to make budgets and allocate resources for the current financial period.
- Front desk provides the controller with the financial data for keeping record and for the maintenance of the credit card ledger

Human Resource Management

1. Rely upon front office staff to do initial screening of candidates
   a. Distribute application forms
   b. Directions to personnel office

QUESTIONNAIRE

1. Write notes on inter-departmental co-operation of front office with the following departments:
   a) Housekeeping
   b) Food & Beverage Service
   c) Engineering
   d) Sales & Marketing
   e) Room Service
   f) Public Relations
2. Explain the importance & purpose of Co-ordination of front office with other departments?
3. How inter-departmental co-operation can help the hotel to improve the sales? Explain with suitable Examples.
4. List the departments with which the front office department co-ordinates in a five-star hotel?

GLOSSARY

A

A.A.U.I: Automobile Association of Upper India

A.H.M.A: American Hotel and Motel Association It publishes a booklet called Red book. Now AHMA is called AHLA (American, hotels and lodging association).

A.I.I: Antemeridian (before noon).

AIDA: A management term referring to marketing management and the abbreviation stands for Attention, Interest, desire, and action.

ADA: American with disabilities act which protects people with disabilities from being discriminated against when seeking accommodations and employment.

A.D.P: Automatic data processing.

A.P.C: All payments cash

A.S.T.A: American society of Travel agents. The largest worldwide trade association of retail and wholesale travel agent and allied industry service its headquarters are in New York.

A'la carte: It is a type of menu which lists all the dishes available in the restaurant and each dish is priced individually.

Access Time: The time interval between when data are called for or requested to be stored in storage device and data goes to storage after use. Read and write time.

Account aging: A method for tracking past due from guests accounts according to the date the charges originated.

Account payable transaction: A financial procedure in which goods and services are received by the hotel before the hotel makes payment for them.

Account posting machine: A device used to post, monitor and balance charges and credits to guest account.

Ageing statement: A statement which shows how old the unpaid account has become.

Account receivable load: Out of the total sales, that proportion of sales that are charged to accounts, and which are to be collected on later dates.

Account receivable transaction: A financial procedure in which goods and services are provided to the consumer for which the payment shall be received in future. The consumer may be an individual or a company or an organization.

Account settlement: The payment of outstanding balance on the folio or city account by the consumer, either by cash or by credit (i.e. an agreement of the amount of outstanding bill at a later date).

Accountancy cycle : A period (can be daily, weekly, monthly, or yearly) from which a financial transaction occurs to the time it is reconciled and is shown on the financial report of the company.

Accounting system: A system of accounting for recording, analyzing and summarizing the financial transactions of the company.

Accounts receivable ledger: A ledger of the aggregate of individual account receivable records

Account : The way of first classifying and then summarizing of money transactions within the framework of an accounting system is called account.

Accounting equation: Liabilities and owner's equity is called Assets.

Arrival/departure report: A list of all the check -ins and check -outs of a day.

Adds: Last minute reservations added to the list of expected arrivals on the day of arrival.

Adjacent Rooms: Rooms close to each other, such as across the corridor.

Adjoining rooms: Two rooms adjacent to each other and with a door in the common wall, may be used for a family if the inside connecting doorway is opened or for two different guests if that door is closed Also called connecting rooms, and interleading rooms.

Advance deposit: An amount of money that is sent by the prospective guest in advance generally deposited in the guest account also called as deposit reservation. This cash is in anticipation to cover the estimated use of hotel services/product and is also known as "anticipated Usage Amount".

Advances: Any money disbursed for guests such as loans or payments made on behalf of the guests. This amount is charged to the account like other charges also called as cash paid out or cash disbursement.

Affiliate reservation network: A hotel chains reservation system in which all participating properties are contractually related.

Affiliated hotel: A hotel which is usually on franchise or referral system of another group or chain

After departure: also called as late charge and refers to any credit purchase money voucher which reaches the bills section after the guest has settled his bill and checked out. This requires late charge billing.

Agent: Does not stock and sells the goods on commission basis.

Agency ledger: That section of the city ledger where the travel agency transactions/accounts are recorded

Alphabetical Rack/Alpha Rack/Alphabetical Index: A Whitney rack which is arranged in alphabetical order and to arrange on the reception counter this is also called as Information rack.

Allocatable expenses: All those expenditure that can be classified or shared amongst various departments of the company.

Allowance: An accounts term which refers to the amount which is reduced from the guest folio as an adjustment against improper, unsatisfactory or no service to the guest it may also be due to a posting error and also called as account allowance.

Allowance voucher: A voucher used to support an account allowance.

American plan: also called as en-pension, or full pension or a full board meal and bed and board plan. Here the room tariff includes the room charges and full meals i.e. English breakfast, lunch and dinner (table d'hôte) charges. It may also include early morning tea and evening tea charges.

Arranging: A data processing function whereby data are sorted in a predetermined sequence.

All suite hotels: A hotel which usually have all suite rooms

Arrival date: A date when a prospective guest is expected to arrive in the hotel

Arrival time: The expected time of arrival of a prospective guest

Arrival, departure and change sheet: A consolidated document prepared and maintained by the front desk staff recording all the arrivals, departures and change of rooms. In some hotels three separate sheets are maintained for each of these activities.

Assets: Items that have monetary value.

Attitude: An attitude is a learned tendency to respond to a given product in a particular way. Attitude has three components the cognitive, the effective and the behavioral.

Atrium concept: A design in which guest rooms overlook the lobby from the first floor to the roof

Audit: The review, test and verification of financial transactions in an accounting system

Audit trial: serves as documented history of transactions.

Authorization approval code: It is the authorization approval by credit card Company for the extension of credit limit facility in case the credit card holder's credit is about to exceed the assigned floor limit.

Available room: The number of rooms that the hotel has for sale out of the total number of rooms in the hotel this figure may vary each day.

Above the line: Promotional expenditure aimed at consumers, for example advertising as opposed to below the line 'expenditure, aimed at sales channels such as times to salesman.

Average rate per guest: It is the average of the revenue earned per guest by the hotel for an accounting period. For example, average rate per guest for a day will be equal to the total rooms revenue collected for the day divided by the total number of guests accommodated for that day.

Average room revenue/rate: It is the average money collected from the sale of total number of rooms by the hotel for an accounting period. For example the average daily room rate is equal to total room revenue collected for a day divided by the total number of rooms sold for that day. This average is also referred to as sales per room occupied.

B

B.A: British Airways

B.T.A: British Tourist Authority

BASIC: Beginners all purpose symbolic instruction code

Bal. : Balance.

Back office: It is that branch of the hotel which is responsible for coordinating all support services. All managerial activities and maintaining the ongoing status of the business and their activities are called back office functions. Department that usually don't come in direct contact with the guest and also called as Back of the house

Back to back: A travel trade term which refers to a sequence of consecutive group departures and arrivals usually arranged by tour operators so rooms are never vacant i.e. a manner of operating tourists on a consistent and continuous basis. For example a flight arriving with 250 passengers would pick up another 250 passengers who have completed their stay. This eliminates ferry mileage completely or reduces it to minimum possible.

Back-of-the-house: Those areas and sections of the hotel with which normally the hotel resident guest does not come in direct contact.

Bag Delivery: The process of delivering the luggage of group members to individual group member's room after the group has check in to the room.

Bag Pull: Process of bringing down the luggage of the group members from their rooms to lobby on the day of departure of the group just before the departure.

Balance sheet: A statement of the financial position of the company at a specific time, showing the position of assets, liabilities and equity of the company

Bank: Refers to the petty cash or float/impressted money given to cashier for making day-to-day small payments such as V.P.O. etc.

Bed and breakfast-Type of meal plan also called as continental plan where the room tariff quoted includes along with room rate the continental breakfast also.

Bed board: Usually hardboard provided on the bed on special request of the guest.

Bed occupancy: A ratio of number of beds sold to number of rooms available for sale. When the ratio is multiplied by one hundred the figure obtained is bed occupancy percentage and is also called as guest occupancy.

Beliefs: It is the last stages of learning i.e. a process by which people acquire the knowledge and experience that they apply to buying and using product.

Bell captain: in charge of bell desk staff i.e. uniformed staff and also called as hall porter.

Bell desk/bell stand: The bell desk is a special desk located in the lobby from where the senior bell captain operates with his team and also called as "porters' lodge".

Bell persons/boys slip: This is a slip which is prepared to communicate to the bellboy about the room of the guest which has requested for bell service.

Bell cart: A luggage trolley used to carry luggage to and from the guest room by the bell boy and also called "Bell Hop trolley".

Bench mark: A test or set of tests for assessing the performance of a computer programmer

Breakeven point: A point at which neither a profit nor loss is incurred nor the revenue is just sufficient to meet the total of fixed and variable costs

Bermuda plan: A type of meal plan where the room tariff includes along with room rate the American breakfast rates

Bill to account: This situation refers to the case when the unpaid bill or guest's account is transferred to a non-guest ledger for billing (of course approval of both parties is necessary).

Bin card: A stock card used in storekeeping which is attached to a bin, container or shelf. On it are recorded receipts, issues and a running total of the particular item stored in the bin, container or on the shelf.

Black-listed guest: A list of unwanted guests those guest who make a lot of fuss and create problems for the hotel (non payment of bill, damage to hotel property, misbehave with its staff and/or other guests of the hotel etc.) FHRAI is usually informed about such guests.

Blanket reservation: A block of rooms held for a particular group with individual members requesting assignments from that block i.e. a unit that has been reserved for a specific arrival date but not for a specific guest, also referred to as blocked room.

Booked room: A specific room that is reserved for a specific guest and also called as "Blocking"

Bounced reservation: Sometime due to some error in planning a guest with reservation may be refused accommodation. This situation is called bounced reservation situation, also called walking the guest.

Breakage: If an individual guest or a group does not avail of some services or amenities such as meals/food included in the package then the gain which accrues to the hotel is called breakage.

Break Even analysis: An analysis of the relationships among costs, revenue and sale volume allowing hotel to determine the revenue required to cover all costs.

Break Even point: Total sale required to cover the total cost, the point of sale where hotel makes neither profit nor loss.

Brochures: Printed stationary, containing brief description of the services and facilities in the form of colored photographs and nicely phrased text that the hotel is offering to its prospective guests. Generally given free to various travel agents, tourist bureaus, etc. for further distribution to prospective guests and an advertisement material in the form of folders, booklet, pamphlets, etc

Brunch: A meal served between breakfast and lunch and usually served in place of these two meals.

Broker: Represents both parties the Buyer and the Seller and gets commission from both the parties and they are different from agent.

Bucket: It is a specially designed collapsible rack which is normally kept on the cashier's counter top for holding the guest folio. It is also called as 'cashier's well' and 'folio tray' and the 'tub'.

Budget: A statement of expected/projected expenditure constructed from anticipated/ projected revenue and available financial resources for a period of time, usually one year and the process of preparing budget is called budgeting.

Bundling: Making a package of two or more hotel products/services to be offered to a guest at a package rate.

Bumped reservation: Refusal of accommodation to a guest holding confirmed reservation and subsequently putting him in some other hotel

Buyer confidence: A guest's predetermined desire to book a room at a hotel at almost any cost.

Brain storming: Any number of ideas is following out quickly. Then short listing them by collect a group, explain the rules, display the role and practice.

Brand loyalty: The institutionalized/preferences of a customer for a product/ service based on a brand name or logo.

C

CCTV: Closed circuit TV

C.I.P: Commercially Important person a person who has influence over a large number of prospective buyers

COBOL: Common Business Oriented Language.

C.R.T: Cathode Ray Tube

CPU: Central processing unit

CP: Continental plan

Coy: Company

Crib: Baby's cot/bed

Captive audience: Those guests of the hotel who are suggested to use facilities/services other than room of the hotel either for convenience or lack of other options

Cabana: A room on the beach or near the swimming pool of a hotel, away from the main building

Call sheet: A sheet which records list of room numbers, and times of the guests requiring to be called and also called as wake-call-sheet. This also contains details such as newspaper, early morning tea or breakfast required by the guest.

Cancellation: A process of cancelling the reservations by guest before the date of expected arrival, made previously by him.

Cancellation code: A code number assigned to cancelled reservation to future references and a document listing all such cancellation codes is called cancellation record and also a record or list of all guests who cancelled their reservation is called cancellation report.

Card key-An electronic or magnetic small plastic card used in electronic locking system that operates through a master control console at front desk which is wired to every guest room door and also called as magnetic or electronic card.

Cash discount: An allowance offered by a creditor or debtor to encourage prompt payment.

Cash flow: It is the time period between the goods or service sold to a customer to the period actual cash for that sale is received.

Cash payout transaction: A cash transaction in which the hotel makes cash advance to a guest or non-guest account.

Cash register: A device used to record and maintain cash balance and the device may be mechanical, semi-automatic or automatic or electronic.

Cash sheet: A document in report form prepared by cashier, carrying all transactions against folio accounts, cash payouts, and departmental cash sales. This document serves as a primary cross-reference document in the hotel's audit.

Cash transaction: An exchange of goods or services for cash

Casino hotel: A hotel with gambling facilities

Centralized Electronic Locking System: An electronic locking system that operates through a master control at the front office which is wired to every guest room door the front office can lock any guest room through centralized electronic locking system.

Cathexis: An effective bond between a consumer and a product Consumers are often thought to be matching self image with the product image in an act of purchase.

Catharsis: Spelling out of the emotions when things go wrong feelings must be expressed.

Chain hotel: A hotel owned by chain hotel or affiliated to a hotel chain.

Chamber maid: A housekeeping staff normally responsible for cleaning of rooms and bed making

Chance guest: A guest who comes without reservation and requests for a room

Chance trade: Business done usually for cash with chance guests

Change: Moving a guest from one room to another for various reasons.

Charge back: Sometimes the credit card company refuses the payment of a voucher signed by the customer who is sent by the hotel and this situation is called charge back.

Charge Voucher: It is also called debit voucher or account receivable voucher, all signed bills and VPO are also called charge voucher.

Chartered flight: This is a special arrangement in which the airlines book a flight from one destination to another for the exclusive use of a group of persons who normally belong to the same organization or by a travel agent for his group. These are normally much cheaper to regularly scheduled flight and are usually in supplement to the regular flight.

Check-in: Procedure of receiving the guest, assigning and allocation of room and registering of a guest in the hotel.

Cognitive Dissonance: Customers experience some anxiety over the choice which they have made that perhaps one of the constructions, offering might have been a better choice. A conflict between two internally held values "I am a sensible person but I have made a foolish purchase".

Check-out: The procedure involved (baggage handling, bill settlement etc.) at departure time.

Check-out time/hours: It is the time by which the guest should check out otherwise next day's charges will be charged. Usually it is 12.00 noon.

City account: Basically an account receivable for someone other than a registered guest

City ledger: A collection of city, or non guest, receivable account balances.

Close of the day: An arbitrary hour fixed by the hotel which separates the record of one day from the next day.

Cleaners: Members of housekeeping department who clean public areas such as corridors.

Closed: Dates for which a reservation system will not accept additional reservation.

Closet bed: A standard size bed that swings into a wall or cabinet in the form of a closet can accommodate one or two persons and simple removal from floor area as they are built into a closed wall.

Commercial hotels: A hotel which is mainly patronized by businessmen and situated downtown usually

Commercial rate: Special discounted rate offered to a frequently visiting hotel guest.

Commission: Amount payable to travel agents for arranging groups stay in the hotel and an amount payable to an agent usually based on business given to hotel.

Commissionaire: Member of uniformed staff whose place of duty is outside the main entrance of hotel and also called door man, link man and carriage attendant.

Core Competency: Refers to the strengths of the hotel

Commissioned sales: Materialized business given to the hotel by a third party such as travel agent for which the hotel has to pay commission to the third party.

Competitive price: Construction of room tariff based on the rates of the competitor In this case the rate fixation is based on external rate structure criterions, rather than the inter-rate structure criterions.

Conversion Ratio: The number of transient booking made versus the number of calls received.

Complimentary: Usually accommodation given to a guest free and generally an abbreviated form "comp" is used. A business promotional or goodwill activity, complimentary rooms are given by the hotel.

Computer system: An electronic system which comprises of an input-output device, a central processing unit and a memory unit called as hardware or the physical components and the programmer and the instructions used called as software. This total system is used to either problem solving and or data processing functions.

Concessionaire: Abbreviated as concession sometimes refers to the shops providing services and amenities and facilities etc to the resident guest.

Generally they are not operated by the hotel, and are rented to experts. These are also called as rentals.

Conducted Tour: It is a group tour in which right from the beginning of the tour to the end there is a conductor who accompanies the group and looks after the ground and other arrangements which are incident during the tour. Also called as escorted tour and managed tour.

Compression of demand: The theory that the need for hotel rooms in a city or geographical area will remain constant in spite of what the occupancy level is. If one part of the area is sold out the demand for rooms will compress in such a way as to drive those looking for rooms elsewhere.

Concierge: A person usually found in American hotels responsible for providing guest services and needs etc. In some hotels concierge provides information service to guest also.

Cold calls: Sales calls on customers with no previously identified interest in a product.

Customers profile: This summarizes the characteristics of Hotel guest. This is used to assist in product formulation and in directing advertising and sales promotion.

Confirmation notification: Also called as acknowledgement letter. Sometimes means the letter or other mode of communication such as phone, letter, etc. by which the prospective guest (who has requested for room reservation) is informed of the acceptance of his request.

Connecting rooms: It is also called interconnected rooms and in these two rooms situated side by side and also have a door between both the rooms. In case both the rooms are hired by a family they may open the door in between both the rooms with the help of housekeeping.

Construction cost: A sum total of all the initial/pre-opening expenses of a property this is an important factor to be considered while calculating the room tariff.

Continental breakfast: It includes small glass of canned juice, breakfast rolls/toast, butter, preserves (jam, honey, marmalade) and tea/coffee.

Contribution margin: It refers to the difference between the sales and total variable costs of any item or group of items.

Configuration: A group of amenities which are interconnected and are programmed to operate as a system.

Contribution to profitability: It refers to the difference between contribution margin and fixed expenses or sales (variable cost and fixed expenses).

Control folio: Also called as master folio sometime, refers to some folio.

Convertible bed: A sofa which can be converted into a single or double bed the bed is also called sofa convertible into bed.

Corkage: Refers to charges made by a licensed establishment for providing service equipment and bottle openers, soda, etc. to customers who bring their own alcoholic beverage for consumption in the hotel.

Corner room: An outside room, i.e. a room on the corner of perimeter of the building facing outward with two exposures

Cost benefit: It is financial analysis to determine if the benefits of the system are more as compared to the cost of the system or not.

Cost center: Also called as non-revenue departments of hotel and refers to all those operating departments of hotels which are non-revenue producing. These departments simply incur cost and have very little or no contact with the guests.

Cost effective: A system in which the benefits overweigh the costs. It is also called 'Justified'. Also called as 'Price Performance Ratio'

Cot: in American terminology refers to an extra bed and in English terminology refers to child's bed. Sometimes Rollaway beds are also called cot.

Credit Risk: Credit extended to an individual or company that may be unable to pay.

Coupons: These are documents issued by airlines or travel agents to their passengers or travelers respectively, to be produced by the hotels and specify the various services and facilities etc. which the guest can get on the basis of these vouchers and used by guests to settle their hotel accounts.

Credit: An account term which means that the transaction will reduce the accounts receivable

Credit Authorization: This is the maximum credit limit which a credit card company authorizes to its card holders and it varies from card to card for example a silver card and gold card etc.

Credit card voucher: The forms supplied by card issuing authority and are used for imprinting a credit card and recording the amount charged and also called as credit card invoice.

Credit card volume: That proportion of total sales which is on credit this figure is an indicator of cash flow positions of the hotel.

Credit limit: This is the limit of amount of money up to which the guest is allowed credit facility. After the limit is reached the hotel requests the guest to clear his bill either partly or fully.

Credit or credit entry: Writing of financial transaction of the right hand side of a "T" account. This transaction increases liabilities and revenue account while decreasing asset and expense account.

Cut-off-date: That date by which the confirmations should come otherwise after this date the block of rooms is released for general sale.

Cut-off-time/hour: It is the specified hour/time at which the unclaimed reservations are released and can be sold to any walk-in, i.e. if the guest who had booked the room comes after this hour, he may be refused accommodation.

D

D.G.C.A: Director General of Civil Aviation

D.N.A: Stands for did not arrive and refers to the guest who has made a confirmed/guaranteed reservation but does not check in on the expected date of arrival is treated as did not arrive. These guests are treated as no shows and are charged retention charge.

D.N.S-Did not stay

DSS: Decision Support System

D.O.T: Department of Tourism

D.P: Date processing

D.D.P: Distributed Data Processing

DNA: Did Not Arrive

Daily report of operations: After the daily audit a report is prepared which included operating statistics, bank activity, revenue activity, transaction activity, etc.

Data processing cycle: Refers to time and procedures involved in the handling of data in a data processing operation.

Data processing: Input-process-output operation of data to achieve results

Data: Raw, unevaluated fact that alone has no relevance but as a group can be used to draw conclusions.

Data base system: A non redundant collection of data items process able by one of more application. Minimizing storage and summarizing data relationship.

Date and time punching machine: equipment this is used for printing date and time on documents.

Date Roll: A certain point in the night to establish a change in date.

Day rate: Room tariff offered to a guest who stays only during daytime and also called as 'Day use rate'.

Day use room: A status indicating that the room will be used for day only

Debit card: Plastic magnetic strip coated card can directly debit the card holder's bank account for purchase of goods and services.

Debit/debit entry: Recording of financial transactions on the left hand side of 'T' account. These entries increase assets and expenses account and reduce liabilities and revenue accounts.

Delinquent account: The resident's guest accounts which are not settled in cash at the time of check out are transferred to city ledger. The city ledger account that is not settled within a reasonable time is called delinquent account.

Demi pension: Also called half pension or modified American plan, which means the room tariff, includes room rate, English breakfast and one major meal i.e. either lunch or dinner.

Deep clean: Process of completely cleaning a room

Departure date: The scheduled date of the check out of a guest

Departure notification slip: A notification slip prepared at check-out time and circulated to all departments informing about the departure of the guest.

Difference returnable: Also called 'due back' or 'due bank' and exchange and refers to the excess turn-in over net receipts. The difference is returnable to front office cashier.

Direct expenses: An expense which is incurred only when goods or services are sold and would cease when the service or goods is no more sold for example expense or cost of food to a restaurant.

Director/Manager Grounds: An in charge of landscaping and surrounding area of the hotel

Direct Bills: These are the bills of those guests who have checked out without setting their bills because the instruction about them is that their bill is to be forwarded to companies, etc.

Disbursement Docket: It is a voucher which is made when the hotel pays an amount for an operating department.

Discretionary income: Surplus income, after meeting the basic needs, such as food, clothing, and shelter and taxes which the guest can spend as he wants for example say the Gross income is 1000 rupees and says disposable or net income is 800 rupees and say out of these 500 rupees is for basic needs. The 300 rupees which is left is Discretionary Income.

Director loss prevention: Security and safety manager

Dispense bar: A bar from where drinks are obtained by hotel staff for serving to guests.

Diversity Training: Training the employees that they must understand and appreciate the differences in people.

Double occupancy: When a room is occupied by two persons it is called double occupancy.

Driving rate: When demand dictates a hotel, a hotel may never ever begin selling on discounted rates, and thus have them restricted from the start this practice attempt to maximize revenue when demand is known to be forthcoming.

Double Bed: This is a bed which accommodates two persons.

Double up: When a room is occupied by two unrelated guests it is called as double up. For each of these two a separate Whitney slip is kept in the rack.

Discrepant Code: Also called discrepancy report.

Double-double: Also called twin double a room with two double beds i.e. sleeping accommodation for four persons.

Down grade: Moving the guest's reservation to a lower quality room is called downgrade.

Due Back: Situation when a guest is to be returned money at the time of check out as he has deposited more than due to him and the money is returned and a visitor paid out is signed.

Due out: Room that is expected to become vacant after the following day's checkout time

Dunning letters: From time to time the outstanding bills statements sent by the hotel to former guests with delinquent accounts.

Duplex: A costly suite where the two rooms situated on successive floors are connected through an internal staircase.

E

ECO: Express check out.

EPBAX: Electronic Private automatic Branch/Box Exchange.

ECR: Stands for electronic cash register and it is an electronic cash control device.

E.D.P: Electronic Data Processing

Enhanced configuration: The term is used to mean when more services/ amenities are included in the guest room as compared to a standard room.

Early arrival: A guest who arrives before his expected/scheduled date/time of arrival

Eco-Tourists: Tourists who plan vacations to understand tne culture, environment, ecology, flora and fauna of a particular area.

Efficiency accommodation: Accommodation that includes kitchen facilities

Efficiency rate: Measurement of performance designed to measure variance between a desired standard and actual condition.

Electronic folio: The making and maintenance of guest folio in computer memory a soft copy record.

Electronic Key: A plastic key with electronic codes embedded on a magnetic strip and can open the guest room and it is also called card key.

Electronic fund transfer: The method of payment of goods or services in which the transfer of actual cash between two accounts is performed electronically

Empowerment: Ability and authority to satisfy guest complaints/request with in the policies

Employee Handbook: A book containing conduct rules and general information for the employees

Equity: is the claim on business by the owners of the business. If the business is owned by one person the equity is called capital and earned surplus. A partnership will show the claim of each owner listed separately. A corporation will list its ownership claims as capital stock.

Equivalent occupancy: If the management plans a change in ARR(higher/ lower) then the occupancy percentage needed to achieve the same net revenue as was achieved earlier by old price and occupancy percentage.

Euro: The accepted currency for some Europeans countries Belgium, Germany, Spain, France, Ireland, Italy, Luxembourg, the Netherlands, Austria, Portugal, Finland and Greece.

Early: It is also called as under stays.

Early Bird: A term used in automatic system of Night Auditing and referring to mainly creating and distribution of reports and it is also called as "Flash".

E.P: European plan and in this the tariff is only for the room rent and guest is required to pay for all meals ordered separately.

Evening shift: The duty starting from usually 3 P.M to 11 P.M

Executive Floor: The floor is specially designed to look after the world class services. The floor may have secretariat services, a small conference room, fax, computers; etc .The guest is expected to pay for these services if used. It is also called tower concept.

Expected arrival list: Room reservation department sends a day before the expected arrival date, a list containing the names of guests along with all information received at the time of reservation to reception.

Expected departure list: Receptionist prepares a daily report showing the numbers and names of guests expected to depart. It also contains the list of stayovers.

Express check out: An activity which involves compilation and early morning distribution of guest folio to all those guests who are expected to check out that morning.

Extended Stay: It attracts long-term guests and provides light homemade food and also provides kitchen, bedrooms, sitting room, dining room, etc.

F

F.E.R.A: Foreign Exchange Regulation Act

F.F.I.T: foreign free independent traveler

F.H.R.A.I: Federation of Hotels and Restaurant Association of India

F.I.T: Free independent traveler (any individual who is not in a group) or a non-affiliated group member also called as free individual traveler

F, F&E: Furniture, Fixture and Equipment

F form: The loose leaf used for the guests registration is also called F form.

Family plan rate: A special discounted rate for families where children staying in the same room and it is offered to encourage families to travel together

Farm out: In case of a full house, assignment of guests with reservation to other units of chain or other properties

Financial transaction: The sale of goods or services for cash, or deferred cash payments

Fixed cost: All those expenses which are not dependent on sales volume and also called as "Fixed overheads"

Fixed room rate: A room tariff which is fixed and does not change with the number of guests in the room and also referred to as flat rate or "Run of the house rate"

Flextime: An employee is required to report in between 8 a.m to 10 a.m and is expected to work for nine hours. The flextime is usually allowed in the departments which do not have much of public dealing.

Float: Impress money given to cashier to return balance to guest

Floor limit: The credit limit that the hotel allows to a guest and also called as house limit in some hotels

Floor porter: Male members of housekeeping staff whose duty is lifting and moving of heavy articles within the department and also called "floor Porters"

Folio header: Upper portion of folio showing columns such as room number and personal details like date of arrival, date of departure, room tariff etc.

Folio/Guest folio: A statement of guest account, shows the balance of guest's financial obligation to hotel and also called as guest bill or account card.

Forecast: A future projection of estimated business and it is also called budgeted sale or occupancy forecast in front office.

Forecasted guest load: Forecasted occupancy for any given time of the hotel

Forfeited deposit: The amount that the guest has paid as advance for booking a room, may be forfeited in case of his 'no show' and is called as retention charges in that case.

Franchise: A hotel owner who has access to a national/international reservation system and receives the benefits of the corporation's management expertise, financial assistance, marketing facilities and group handling

Franking Machine: A machine used for printing postage stamp value on the envelope.

Free sale: Term used when rooms are available for sale.

Front: an American term which refers to the next bellboy available for rooming a guest

Front of the house: Those parts of the hotel with which the guest comes in direct contact

Front office cashier: Cashier who is responsible for all cash transactions at front office

Full day: It is a way of measuring a chargeable day for accounting purpose for a guest. For example, it will be three meals for an American plan hotel and no meals and only overnight stay for European hotels

Follow: A continuation bill made for a guest staying in the hotel after seven days (in case he does not pay his weekly bill) and the outstanding amount of previous bill is transferred to this bill.

Full house: A situation of 100% room occupancy in the hotel

Fully automated: Refers to computerized electronic data processing (EDP) system in which data is handled automatically.

Flow chart: A system analysis or a tool to graphically present a procedure in which symbols are used to designate the logic of how the problem is solved

G

G.I.T: Group Inclusive Tour

G.O.I: Government of India

GIGO: Garbage-in Garbage-out (a computer term)

G.D.S: Global Distribution System

Garni hotels: A hotel which has no food and beverage service facility

General cashier: The chief cashier of the hotel with whom deposits of all cashiers are made and who also issues floats

Go Green: Eco friendly hotels/area; preserve our ecology and flora fauna.

Graveyard shift: A work shift which begins from midnight

Group base: The measurement of how many group rooms are "one the books" on a given night

Green fees: An amount to be paid by guests using golf course

Gate Way City: A city located in an area that makes them the first practical stop for an International Flight coming in to a country

Grandmaster key: This key can open all the rooms of the hotel even if they are double locked and it is the key of general manager or executive housekeeper. This key is used to open the room in case of emergency and in the presence of security officer, executive housekeeper, general manager or their representatives.

Group plan rate: A special discounted rate offered to groups as an incentive to attract large number of guests and hence sell more rooms

Guaranteed reservation: Where the hotel is sure to get room rate whether the guest who has made a booking comes or not

Guest accounting-A process by which a guest's financial transaction can be monitored and controlled

Guest: an individual client who has registered with the hotel

Guest check: The voucher that are presented to a guest when he avails of services/facilities at various outlets such as restaurant, bar, etc. of the hotel

Guest cycle: The concept of the guest movement to, through and from the hotel for the purpose of writing and monitoring guest and hotel transaction(pre-sale, point of sale and post-sale phases) and involves activities before the arrival, at arrival, during stay, at the time of departure and after departure for a guest by the hotel

Guest day/night: Stay of one guest for one night also called as room night and bed night

Guest history card: A card which is maintained for regular and VIP guests and the personal details such as his liking and disliking, birthdays, marriage anniversary etc. are recorded in this card. Any complaints, suggestions and number of visits are also recorded in it.

Guest ledger: The accounts of registered guests are recorded in it and it is also called as 'Room ledger' or 'Transit ledger'

Guest supply usage per occupied room: The measurement of housekeeping supplies used in a guest room averaged over time

Guest profile: It includes things such as habits, likes, dislikes, etc. of a guest. Geographic analysis, Demographic analysis and Psychographic analysis

Group Resume: A report sent to all concerned departments informing details of the group

Guest services: All the tangible and non-tangible amenities and facilities and services that the hotel offers its guests

Guest folio: The bill sheet kept up to date by the F.O cashier reading the details of charges for each individual guest of all events

Guide: An authorized and licensed person who explains the historical and other places of interest to the touring group and a tour which is accompanied by a guide is called Guide Tour

H

HOTERMAI: Hotel and Restaurant Equipment Manufacturers Association of India

H.S.M.A: Hotel Sales Management Association and it is an international organization of marketing which maintains liaison with all requests of the travel industry to discuss and implement areas of mutual interest and its headquarters are in New York.

HAI: Hotel Association of India

H&RA: Hotel and Restaurant Association

HRAWI: Hotel and Restaurant Association of Western India

Half day rate: A room rate based on length of guest stay it is more common in airport hotels.

Handicap room: room with specially designed features for handicapped guests

Hard copy: A print out of information generated by computer system

Hard Goods: Items such as T.V, and Fridge etc. in a room which are expensive to replace

Hardware: Physical computer device and equipment such as magnetic, electrical and electronic device

High balance: Means when the guest's outstanding bill is near or over the credit limit balance set by hotel, and such guests are called high risk guests

Hollywood bed: When two twin beds are joined together with one common head board to make one bed it is called Hollywood bed

Hospitality services industry: All businesses involved in accommodation, food, entertainment, transportation, healthcare etc. to the guest

Hybrid Market: Combined target markets

Hot list: A list of lost/stolen credit card sent by the credit card company to the hotel and this is also called "Stop Bulleting" and "Cancellation Bulleting".

Hotel Information System (H.I.S): An orderly arrangement of hotel data procedures and decision making criteria designed to increase managerial effectiveness through the proper handling and flow of information

House count: Total number of guest staying in the hotel at a particular time

House phone: Telephone usually in the lobby of the hotel from where the visitor can contact the guest in the room

Housekeeper's Caddie: A handheld carrying case that can be easily brought in to a guest room. The caddie consists of glass cleaner, bathroom cleaner, multipurpose cleaner, and bath amenities, etc.

House profit: The gross profit earned before deducting taxes

House limit: The credit limit set by the hotel for its guests

House use: A room used by the hotel staff free of cost

Housekeeper's report: A report prepared by the housekeeper of the status of rooms

Housing bureau: A reservation office like central reservation office

Hubbart formula: A formula developed by Ray Hubbart for determining room rate keeping in consideration operating expenses, room sales, and a pre-desired return on investment(R.O.I)

Human engineering: It is a new concept of replacing human resources by automated systems so that the human resource may be freed to provide more personalized service to the guest

Human resource audit: An inventory of human power, i.e. how many were appointed, how many left and how many are still there and this also refers to 'Succession Built Up'.

I

I.A.A.I: International Airports Authority of India

I.A.C: Indian Airlines Corporation

I.A.T.A: International Air Transport Association/International Association of Travel Agents

I.A.T.O-Indian Association of Tour Operation

IR: Instant Reservation

I.C.A.O: International Civil Aviation Organization

I.D.D: International Direct Dialing

I.H.A: International Hotel Association

IH& RA: International Hotel and Restaurant Associates

I.L.O: International Labour Organization

I.M.F: International Monetary Fund

I.S.D: International Subscriber Dialing

I.U.O.T.O: International Union of Official Travel Organization

I.Y.H.F: International Youth Hostel Federation

IDP: Integrated Data processing

Ideal average rate: Point at which room are sold at the best rate possible

Idle time: also called hidden rest and this is the period that must be allowed during duty when a person does not work

Imprinter: A special device/machine used for taking the impression of credit card on vouchers

Incidental account: Charges which are guests own responsibility and not paid by a company or travel agent.

Inclusive Tour: A tour in which the prices for various services and product are all inclusive in a flat rate and the guest has to pay only for those services and products which are not included in the package.

Independent: An individual property not affiliated or a part of a chain

Induction: Familiarization tour of new employees/recruits of the hotel and staff

Information dissemination: Flow of communication and documents throughout a department or unit

Information rack: A rack which has Whitney slips arranged in alphabetical order of all the guest staying in the hotel

Information: This is which adds to what is known and it communicates knowledge, provides feedback and reduces uncertainty.

In-house guest: Refers to a guest who is registered and not checked-out

Incidentals: Non Room and Tax charges

Input data: Raw data which is to processed by computer system

Input: The first phase of a data processing or computer system

Input unit: This part of computer system through which data/information are entered

Input/output device (I/O) : The components of a computer system through which instruction/data are entered

In-season rate: This is the maximum rack rate that is announced by a resort hotel in season as the demand of rooms is heaviest during this period

Inside call: An intra hotel telephone call (call within the hotel only)

Inside room: A guest room that faces and inner courtyard of the hotel

Integrated Circuit (I.C) : A solid state electronic component of a computer system also called as chip

Inter sell agency: A reservation system that handles reservation for many products such as airlines, car rentals and hotels etc.

Interference: A shared boundary defined by common physical connection characteristics single characteristics and measuring of individual/singles (connection link between two otherwise different bodies)

Individual Market Potential: The number of rooms a hotel has for sales within a given time frame

Interface: Designing the ability of one computer to communicate with another

Intermediary: Person or entity that acts as a liaison between a guest and the hotel

Internal control: Verification of documentation of financial transaction

Intuitive pricing: The pricing of accommodation or services of hotel done on the basis of what people are willing to pay and whatever the market will bear

Itinerary: It is a tour programmed which details the dates, times and other services such as sightseeing etc. for the tour from the beginning to the end of the tour. It also includes the details such as flight number, train number and their departure time, etc. It is usually made by the travel agent in consultation with the tour leader/organizer.

J

J.A.L: Japan Airlines

J.T.P: Joint Tourism Promotion

Journal: A date-wise record of financial transaction showing the result of various debit and credit entries

Junior suite/petite suite/mini suite: A large room with partition for making separate bed room and sitting room

K

K.L.M: Koninklijke Luchtvaart Maatschappij NV (Royal Dutch Airlines)

Key and mail rack: A pigeon hole type rack used in old hotels for keeping the keys of guest room and the mail of in-house guest when he is not in the room

Key card: A sort of an identification card given to guest by the receptionist at the time of check in usually contains general information facility; catering outlets, location of hotel, etc. should be produced when asked by the hotel staff and also called as Room Key Card

Kind size bed: An extra long, extra wide double bed and it is an American term

Keying: Coding system in an advertisement to identify the response from the media

L

LPM: Lines per minute

Lanai room: A room from the balcony of which a waterfall or a water body can be seen

Late arrival: A guest with reservation who intimate in advance to the hotel about the late arrival i.e. after cut off time

Late check out: A guest who with the permission of the hotel checks out of the hotel after the check out time, without extra charge

Late charges-The amount of any purchase informed by any P.OS cashier to the main cashier after the departure of a guest and which remains outstanding or the charges which a hotel charges to a guest who does not leave at check-out time and wants to stay for a few hours extra

Lead time: The time between when a reservation is made and when the guest is due to arrive

Lead maid: An experienced maid who may compliment a Housekeeper's job on a floor

Letter of confirmation: A letter of confirmation sent to guest in response to guest's request for room reservation.

Liabilities: Debts or financial obligations by the firm to a creditor

Light baggage: Also called scanty baggage when the guest arrives with no or little baggage usually advance is taken from such guest and the departments should be informed not to give credit to him

Lightning call: Most urgent telephone calls

Line of authority: Hierarchy of administrative responsibility

Lock out: When a guest in not allowed access to the room usually due to an unpaid bill

Log book: A book/register which is used to record activities and to communicate to the next shift and also called as record of happenings.

Late Hold: A room reservation where the guest is expected to arrive late and then the normal check-in time and the room is to be held late.

Loss leader: A product which is priced below the break-even point price

Lost and Found: An area where all items found by the staff is stored

Luggage pass: An authority for the guest luggage to be removed from hotel

M

MAS: Malaysian Airlines System

MLS: Stands for Minimum length of stay and it refers to a restriction than mandates that all new reservations stay at the hotel for a minimum number of nights

MIS: Management Information System

MAP: Modified American plan and also called as Demi Pension. The tariff is inclusive of room rent, continental breakfast and lunch or dinner and in case guests want both the major meals then he is charged extra.

M.O.D: Manager on Duty

MOCI: Ministry of Commerce and Industries

M.C.O: Miscellaneous charge order and this is a voucher which authorizes the holder to get accommodation from the hotel for which he has already prepaid

Market Segments: A segment of the actual or potential business mix at any given hotel

Machine-assisted: A hotel information system which is totally machine based.

Mail forward book: It contains the name and addresses of those guests who have checked out and are to be re-directed their mail.

Mail shots: Direct mail to a specific person with a specific offer is called Mail shot

Management contract property: A hotel that is operated by a consultant that provides operational and marketing expertise and a professional staff

Marginal cost: It is the cost only incurred if the room is sold to the guest and is also called operational/variable cost.

Media schedule: Allocation of expenditure between different forms of promotion such as posters, T.V, advertising, Newspaper advertising, etc. usually lists specific amounts allocated to individual media giving advertising frequency.

Managerial reports: All documents providing feedback on financial status, productivity, and overall effectiveness of business operation.

Media: Vehicles of communication such as T.V, Radio, Press, Magazine, etc.

Market mix: The distribution (percentage wise) of the hotel guests into various categories such as conventioneer, tourist and businessman, etc

Master key: A key that unlocks all the rooms on a particular floor of the hotel

Marketing Plan: A plan report that summarizes departmental goals, advertising schedules, financial targets and market conditions for the coming year sometimes also called as Master Budget.

Market penetration: Going more and more into the market already achieved i.e. more and more exploring the area which has already given business.

Marketing myopia: Understanding what business one is in a term coined by "Theodore Lofit"

Management Process: Process concerned with creating an environment in which a balance between concern for production and concern for people is maintained as well as guide to decision taking is provided (creating an environment).

Market share: Represents that share of market (in terms of revenue, number of guest, or any other index), which the hotel captures out of the total market

Merchant: Basically who buys, possesses and then sells the goods to consumer

Minus: The list of expected arrival is more than the rooms available.

Marketing: marketing is looking at business from customer point of view and from function point of view it is identifying, anticipating and satisfying the customer's need for a profit.

Motel: It is located at highways guests travelling by their own vehicles patronize these hotels.

Multiple occupancy: When the hotel room is occupied by more than one person it is called as multiple occupancy

Multitasking: Training the employees so that they learn to perform various jobs in the hotel also called "Cross Training".

Murphy bed: A bed which is hinged at the base of the headboard and swings up into the wall for storage and can be used during night to sleep

Marketing Mix: It is a combination of controllable factors such as product/ service, price, Promotion and Place, they are called 4P's. The hospitality industry however recognizes people, physical Evidence and process also as Marketing Mix.

Materialization: Those reservations where a guest actually arrives

Merchandising: Advertising and promotion which takes place within the process and maximizing the opportunities to sell

N

N.A.A: National Airport Authorities

N.C.R: National Cash Register

N.T.A: Note to be allowed

Net Profit (Before Taxes): Department profit fixed expenses(overhead costs such as G.M, Accounts department, sales department, Heat, Light and Power, Insurances, Security and Personnel,etc.

Need Analysis: This is a process by which the management determines the required scope of a potential large purchase

Net Profit-Taxes: What we take home.

Net Rate: Net rate chargeable to guest after making all deductions/discounts

Needs: A felt discrepancies between the actual state and derived state of mind of a person in other words Need is the state in which you are deprived on some thing

Night audit: An activity performed by night auditor in the night to check that whatever has been done during the day is correct or not

No post status: A term used to indicate a guest who is not allowed to charge purchases to his room account

No Information Guest: A guest who wants that information about his staying in the hotel should not be given to anyone hence no slip is put in information.

Notification Slip: Typed slips containing the names of all arrivals is sent to housekeeping, telephone department and room service to notify about their arrival.

No show: A guest who does not arrive on the schedule date of arrival after making a confirmed reservation is called "no show". Another term is DNA (did not arrive) for this type of guest

O

Out of Order (O.O.O) : A room which is not ready for sale due to planned or unexpected shut down

Occupancy driven: A policy where the management may forgo a higher average rate for greater occupancy levels

Opportunity Cost: The situation when the hotel is not able to sell the rooms on a particular day and looses revenue from that for ever

Outsourcing: Utilizing the services of an outside vendor for product or services

Over Selling: A situation when more room, than actually available are sold by the hotel

Objective and policy: Objective is 'what to do' and policy is 'how to do it'.

Occupancy load: Refers to occupancy percentage i.e. the ratio of hotel rooms sold to the number of hotel rooms available for sale

Occupancy Report: Night receptionist prepares occupancy report. This includes occupancy ratio, expected departures list, VIP, groups, airlines crews in the house.

Occupancy mix: Also referred to as profile of occupancy which means percentage break up of sold rooms on single, double and annual occupancy

Occupancy: Sale of room and its occupancy status for a guest

OFF: Means that the room is off the list of rooms available for sale due to some reason and also called as 'Red Slip Room'.

Off-season rate: A special reduced rate offered by the hotels during off-season such as by hill resorts etc.

Operating System: Software that controls the operation of a data processing system

Omission error: By mistake omitting an important transaction

On change: A term used when guest has checked out but the room is not cleared by the housekeeping for the next check in.

On-the house: The term refers to complementary i.e. no charge.

Open: Date for the guest for which a reservation system can still accept reservation

Opinion leader: A person who can influence the community

Option Date: It is the designated date by which the prospective guest is required to confirm his booking

On line system: Access to computer in which the input data enters the computer directly from the point of origin or in which the output data is transmitted directly to where it is used

Outside laundry valet: A contracted laundry service (not operated by hotel).

Outside room: Room facing outside of the hotel with an exposure to the city.

Overbooking: A situation in which hotel books more room than available

Overstay: A situation in which the guest does not leave on the day of scheduled departure and continues staying in the hotel

P

P.P.P.N: Per Person per Night

P.A.T.A: Pacific Asia Travel Association

P.R.P.N: Per room Per Night

P.I.A: Pakistan International Airline

P.S.O: Passengers Service Order

PAX: Number of Persons

PPM: Pages per minute it refers to the printing speed capability of printer.

PMS: Property management system the software system developed to undertake the various jobs at front office.

P.B.X: Private Branch/Box Exchange

PMBX: Private Manual Branch/Box Exchange

PABX: Private Automatic Branch/Box Exchange

P.O.S: Point of sales it refers to the guest can avail various services and facilities at various outlets like restaurants, bar, swimming pool, health club, beauty parlor, etc.

Package tour: usually refers to consolidated charges for services such as accommodation, transfers, meals and transport, etc. Given to groups normally

Prospecting: Searching out, finding and screening new business

PIA: Where the guest is required to pay the room rent in advance i.e. at the time of arrival

Pass on log: It is a log book (other than front office log book) through which various issues and problems of hotels which may affect the Front Office operation are communicated.

Perceptions: How a person observes a thing by five senses sound, sight, smell, touch and taste is called perception. It can also be defined as Reception ad Interpretation of sensory stimuli.

Parcels book: A document where the record of parcels received and subsequently delivered to in-house guest is maintained.

Profitability Index: Also called Desirability Index obtained by dividing the present value of the net benefits by the percent value of cash outlays.

Parlor: The living room part of the studio and the European term for this is 'salon' and it is also called as sitting room.

Payback period: Total time required to recover the cost like fixed cost, operational cost, etc. for example hotel wants to install computers in front office, total fixed cost and the cost of training staff and other operational cost will be calculated and compared with the savings and benefits derived from computers. The time required to recover the computerization cost will be payback period.

Perfect sell: A hypothetical situation in which all rooms of hotels are occupied and no guest has been 'walked'.

Penthouse: Luxury suite on the terrace of the hotel

Playing the cards: It is the process of transferring the number of the reservation card of a guest to his G.R. card and vice versa and this is done at the time of arrival of the guest

Plus position: When rooms available exceed guest arrivals

Pleasure Transient: It refers to transient guest market of the hotel that comes for pleasure tourism

Point of Sale/purchase: It refers to time and location of consumer's purchase during his stay at the hotel from hotel's point of view it is called point of sales (POS) and from guest perspective it is called point of purchase.

POS terminal: A computer term for input equipment immediately accessible to the place of sale.

Prime selling time: That period of the day when maximum requests for room reservation are received usually

Position: Status of number of rooms available for sale

Posting: The process of debiting and crediting charges and payments to a guest bill

Potential average rate: A statistics that combines the potential average single and double rates multiple occupancy percentage and rate spread to produce the average rate that would be achieved if all rooms were sold at their full rack rates.

Pre-arrival: That phase which is before the arrival of the guest and after the booking has been done activities during this period are called pre arrival activities.

Pre-assignment: Assignment of room to a prospective guest even before his arrival

Pre-registration: An activity before the arrival of the guest where the guest's registration card is filled with all the information which is already available about the guest, i.e. registration before arrival further when the guest is pre assigned a room then the process is called "Pre Key" and further when the key of such pre-assigned room is kept in a key envelope to be delivered to guest then this is called the "Key Pack".

Profession: A Systematized body of knowledge and it has a code of ethics and there is no end to knowledge.

Product life cycle: Concept which says that all products have a point of growth, maturity and decline due to change and competition

Promotional rate: A special room rate offered to promote future business and this is also called discounted tariff.

P&L statement: A statement which shows changes in ownership Equity

Procedure narrative: Description or statement of what is to be done

Procedure analysis: Study of the flow of work

Package: A programme or set of programmes written from general use in a specified application

Psychological pricing: A system of pricing where the main consideration of costing is not the costs but the expectation of the customer's willingness to pay

Peripheral Devices: External devices performing tasks such as input, output, etc

Q

Quad: A room occupied by four persons

Queen bed: An American term referring to a double bed and second largest bed in hotel

R

R.S.V.P: Respondez Sil Vous plait (Reply if you please).

R.A.M: Random Access Memory

RNA: Room not assigned

RNAC: Royal Nepal Airlines Corporation

R.O.M: Read only memory

Rack rate: This is the normal published room rate mentioned on tariff card and also written on the slip in the room rack and also called as "Top Retail Rate".

Rack slip: A paper slip which is adjusted in racks such as reservation rack, room rack and information rack.

Rate cutting: Reducing room tariff to attract more business

Rate driven: A policy of the hotel that may forgo occupancy level for higher average rate

Real time: A computer term which means very fast processing of data where there is practically no time gap between input and output and also processing of transactions as they occur rather than batching them.

Release Time: Most hotels operate on the basis that unless previously notified, accommodation will be released if the guest fails to arrive by 6 P.M.

Reservation map: A device used to determine what type of rooms is available and when they are available.

Red book: A publication of AHMA of the member hotels, describing their facilities and tariff etc

Red spread: The difference between single and double occupancy rate

Refusal report: A report made by some hotels of the names of guests who were refused accommodation due to non-availability to know the excess demand.

Rate trigger: A provision in computer based reservation system by which computer can change the rate based on preset criteria

Registration: A process of completion of check-in and the guest signing a registration card or arrival register.

Rate structure: Combination of all the rates offered at a hotel

Registration card: A document where a checking-in guest writes details such as name, address, passport details, nationality, date of arrival, date of departure, purpose of visit, etc. and signs sometimes called as "Reg. card" and "G.R card".

Reminder-o-timer: A special alarm clock used for wake-up calls it can be set forty eight times at fifteen minutes interval.

Receptive customer: A guest who is more likely to be interested in a product/ service than general guest, because of his personal interest or need

Reservation avenue: A mean by which a guest is able to make a reservation at hotel.

Reservation activity fee: The amount of money paid as commission to various agencies such as travel agents for giving business to the hotel.

Reservation: An activity of booking room in advance for a prospective guest on his request and mutual agreement whereby the hotel is bound to provide the guest accommodation on the scheduled day of arrival of the guest and the guest is bound to take it.

Reservation form: A document where all the detailed information about the guest is recorded at the time of booking request

Reservation horizon: The planning period throughout which the hotel will be willing to accept and confirm inquiries for available rooms i.e. the period up to which the booking for future can be accepted and also called booking lead time.

Release date: Rooms may be allocated to agents for sale who may deal with them without reference to the hotel. The release date is the point at which the control of the sale rests to the hotel usually 24 or 48 hrs. Before each sale date

Reservation rack: A part of Whitney system, where all the information of the prospective guest received from him is recorded. The slips are kept in alphabetical order and the racks are filled chronologically by arrival date order

Resident manager: Usually responsible for the front of the house, and may act as hotel manager in the absence of GM.

Room cost: Calculation of fixed cost a hotel incurs in preparing a room for sale

Residential hotel: A hotel where long term guest on special terms and conditions stay guests are generally required to sign a lease bond.

Resort hotel: A hotel situated at resort places such as bills, beaches, winter sports, etc. Generally a centre of recreational activities

Retention charges: These are the changes which may be collected from a guest/agency for making a confirmed booking in the hotel and when does not come on the scheduled date due to reasons best known to him. In case the guest/agency has made any advance payment, the same may be Forfeited as Retention charges.

Routing: The process where credits/debits incurred by one account are manually or automatically transferred to another account.

Room night: One room occupied for one night

Role-Playing: Mock working before doing the actual work.

Revenue centre: All those sections of the hotel which generate revenue. The front office, restaurants, bars, health club, swimming pool, beauty parlor, etc. are the revenue centers in a hotel.

Revenue forecast report: Expected future revenue calculated by multiplying forecasted occupancy by current room rate.

Room assignment: Allotting a specific room to a check-in guest

Room availability: Those rooms which are available for letting

Room count: The number of occupied rooms

Room discrepancy report: A report showing the discrepancy as per housekeeping and front desk in occupancy status

Room index: Room index is a chronological system of dates records of the occupancy of each bedroom and suite

Room inspection report: A report of the inspection of room prepared by the floor supervisor after she inspects a room which has been readied by the chambermaid

Room rack: A rack which is a part of Whitney system in which slips are arranged room number wise the rack shows the room occupancy status also called as Room Index and Numerical Rack and Numerical Index.

Room rack slip: A paper slip used to display room status and guests assignments in the room rack

Room rate variance report: A report listing rooms which have not been sold at rack rate

Room revenue: The sum total of money generated by the sale of rooms for a given period of time and also called as room sales.

Room service: Service of food and beverages in the room and part of food and beverage department

Room type: Various grouping of rooms such as standard, suites, etc

Rooming: A procedure of directing a guest and installation of his luggage to room at check-in time

Rooming a guest: The procedure of escorting the guest and carrying of his luggage to the assigned room by the bellboy

Rooming list: A list sent by the travel agent to the hotel of the names, nationality and other details of the group members in advance.

Rule of the thumb: A method of fixing room tariff here for each Rs. one thousand investment, one rupee per day will be room rate.

Ryokan: A term referring to a traditional Japanese inn

S

S.A.T.C: South Asia Travel Commission

S.A.S: Scandinavian Airlines System

S.I.T.S: Special Interest Tours (people who normally visit a place once only)

S.T.D: Subscriber Trunk Dialing and by obtaining the correct code from the S.T.D booklet, subscriber may dial to almost all places without having to ask the operator to connect call.

S.O.P: Standard Operating Procedures

S.T.B: State Tourism Board

SPATT: A special attention guest, for example, a guest needing a wheel chair.

Safe deposit boxes: Individual lockers like bank vaults allotted to guests for keeping their valuables and documents etc.

Sales journal: A permanent summarized record of today's business

Sales Obstacles: Various factors when effects the buying behaviors of a person negatively are called sales obstacles

Sample room: A room used to merchandise only.

Scanty Baggage: A guest with light baggage these guests if unknown and a walk in are requested to pay room rent in advance and are also requested to settle all bill in cash.

Self check-out: Computerized system to allow the guest to review his folio and settle the account to credit card used at check in and also called as Express check out.

Self registering kiosk: A freestanding machine capable of registering a guest and dispensing a room key

Self registration: A system that automatically registers a guest and dispenses a key, based on guest's reservation and credit card information.

Self registration/check out terminal/kiosk: A computer terminal located in the lobby like a teller machine

Sell up/up selling: Convincing a prospective guest to take a higher priced room'

Sells position: Refers to the room's availability status.

Service charge: A certain percentage of bill amounts added to the bill to the guest. This amount is distributed to service staff in place of tips.

Service elevator: Back elevator used by hotel staff and for transportation of commodities of food to different floors

Shoulder period-A mid-price period between full season and off season.

Siberia: A term normally used for inferior quality rooms, such as near the staircase etc. Guest must be informed about its situation and condition before selling it.

Single bed: it can accommodate one person usually

Single room: Meant for one persons sleeping

Six P.M release: Means that the room for a guest with reservation will be held only up to 6 pm and released after that time usually done in case where there is no guaranteed reservation, (credit card guarantee or company or any other guarantee) or deposit reservation. Also called as time-cancelled reservation

Segmentation Market: Splitting the overall market into certain clusters each of which represents a group wanting a specific kind of product or some which differentiate them from other segments.

Skipper: A guest who leaves the hotel without settling his bill

Sleep out: A sold room where the guest did not stay during the night.

Sleeper: Room available for sale but not sold out.

Sleeper: The American meaning of the term is that the room appears to be occupied although it is vacant due to the negligence of front desk staff and as per the English terminology the term means the guest staying in the hotel

Skunks: People who are more concerned with achieving results, than about following rules and procedures but who operate within the confines' of a larger organizations.

Sleepers list: A list of all occupants of sleeping accommodation in the hotel on any given night

Slide: The transportation error caused by a misplaced decimal, for example 30.50 is written as 3.050

Sofa convertible bed: Usually a sofa where the back can be unfolded in to the same level as that of seat to make a bed usually meant for one person only.

Soft copy: Display on the computer screen

Software: A stored set of instructions (programmers) which govern the operation of computer system.

Slippage: The term used when analyzing the group room performance it is the difference between what is contracted and what actually arrives.

Sold out: Rooms not available

Sofacum bed: A sofa which unfolds to form a full size bed for one or two persons depending upon its width and usually designed with a fixed back

Split folio: Folio in which guest's charges are separated into two or more folios

Spoilage: This term refers to the "Room going unoccupied".

Star reservation: Means room is reserved for a VIP.

Soft goods: Those items of room which can be easily and without much expense replaced for example bed sheets, draperies, etc.

Statistics: Collection of quantitative data for analytical and interpretive purpose.

Stay over: A hotel guest who does not leave and continues staying in the hotel.

Stop over guest: Also called as layover guest and this refers to the guest who en route from one destination to another stops in between on a third destination and breaks his journey this is generally on airlines expenses.

Storage: A function in which the data are placed in a select area of the system for future access and retrieval

Strategy: It may be defined as "the scheme whereby a firm's resources and advantages are managed or developed in order to achieve that objective, exploit an opportunity or surpass a completer strategy connects a broad set of guidelines that would direct the entire planning and operating process".

Studio bed/sofa cum bed: A bed usually without head board and foot board which can also be used as sofa during the day

Suite: A combination of two or more rooms out of which at least one is used as sitting room and other as bedroom

Suite Hotel: A hotel with suites and no normal room is called suite hotel.

State of exception: A room status code that describes reasons why guest rooms are not available for sale for example out of order rooms

Swot Analysis: A management term meaning understanding the "strength" "weakness" "opportunities" and "Threats" of a product, property or a person.

Supper: A term referring to a late night meal

Swing: A work shift between the day shift and grave yard shift (4 pm: 12 nights).

Synergy: A combined action where the total production of the combined parts exceeds by far from the contribution of individual parts composing the whole.

System: An orderly arrangement of components in an inter-related series and the whole is more than the mere simulation of its parts.

Systems analyst: A person responsible for overall design of the system

T

T.Q.M: Total Quality Management it refers to establish one behavior for a specific period of time such as "Smile" and maintain it, observe the results, for low cost of operation don't reduce the quality, quantity, etc. but remove mistake. Quality should be in relation to the expectation to the guests. Specific, Measurable attainable, and Time driven standards should be established

T.A.A.I: Travel Agents Association of India

T.W.A: Trans World Airlines

TIPS: To Insure Prompt Service

TQM: Total quality management it refers to a management technique that encourages managers to look at processes used to produce products and services with a critical eye.

Tariff: The published room rate list

Telex: a 24 hour's teleprinter service which provides for instantaneous transmission of message in print

Target rate: An average rate goal a hotel sets to achieve for a certain day or market segment

Three Quarter Bed: It can accommodate one person may be used for a lady can child

Target market: Market segment the hotel wants to penetrate.

Time lead: A coordinator of a team of maids of a particular floor to introduce team spirit, competitive spirit and sharing of tasks

Time sharing: A method of operation in which a resource of computer facility is shared by several users via terminals for different purposes at approximately the same time

Time-shared hotel: A relatively new concept where an investor buys a unit which is shared by other users to whom it may be rented out when not in use by the investor and also called condominium.

Top Down: A sales method that involves offering most expensive room first

Total market potential: The total number of available rooms within the competitive set

Time-sharing: Use of computer to process multiple requests by users

Trace: A remark about reservation which requires action at a specified date by staff e.g. a specified department such as housekeeping, etc

Trade discount: A reduction made on the list or advertised selling price to others usually in same line of business

Traffic sheet: A telephone department control sheet usually used for long distance calls

Transcript: A form which is used by the night auditor whereby he separates the day's charges by rooms and departments

Transfer and transfer folio: A procedure of moving one figure from one form to another (carried over from first form and brought forward to another form) Generally used in case of guest folio amount when at the end of the week the outstanding figure is transferred to a new unnumbered folio, usually when the first folio is full.

Transfer: It refers to the process of transferring the amount of a guest account to some other guest account (who agrees to this arrangement) and another term used for this is "accounting transfer".

Transfer slip: It means a notification slip made when a guest changes the room also called "Move notification slip" and "Removal notification slip".

Transformation error: Incorrect handling of a data procedure due to misconception or misunderstanding

Transient hotel: A hotel catering to short stay guest i.e. a transient guest who stops en route to another destination

Transportation error: Also called as transcription error and is caused by wrong recording of sequence of digits for example 289 written as 298.

Travel agent: An entrepreneur who coordinates various contracted services (such as hotel, food and beverage, transportation, etc.) provided by various contractors to the travelers who needs them at various stages of his tour for providing these services he gets commission form hotels and other contractors.

Trial balance: A list of all accounts in a ledger

Triple Room: A room for three persons sleeping accommodation

Turnaround time: Time from when data was entered into a system until available as output information

Turn away: To refuse accommodation to walk-in guest, because the rooms are not available also called as "Displacement".

Turn down: An evening service provided by housekeeper where the prepares the bed for night use.

Turn in: The cash deposited by departmental cashier with general cashier at the end of the day.

Twin Bed: When two twin beds are joined together with a single Head Board then the combination is called as "Hollywood Twin".

Tipsy guest: A drunkard guest who may misbehave with staff

U

UNESCO: United Nations Educational, Scientific and Cultural Organization

UNICEF: United Nations International Children's Emergency Fund

UFTAA: Universal Federation of Travel Agent Association

UPS: Un-interrupted Power Supply

U.S.P: The special feature or benefits and features that differentiate our product from the competitors and becomes the basis of promotion of sale (Unique Sales Proposition)/A special point of competitive differential in a product and hotel feature that are unique to the property are also called "signature attractions".

Under booking: An erroneous belief that all the rooms are sold while in fact they are not.

Under stay: A guest who checks out before his scheduled date of departure

Upgrade: To move a reservation or staying guest to a better accommodation or class of service

Up-Sell: To try to sell higher priced room than originally anticipated.

V

V.I.P: Very Important Person

V.P.O: Visitors paid out if petty payments such as taxi fare, cinema tickets, postage, etc. are made by front desk on behalf of the guest, then a V.P.O voucher is prepared which is signed by the guest and debited to his account where the amount is entered into guest folio. These slips are also called as "Paid out slips".

V.P.P: Value Payable Post

V.D.U: Visual Display Unit.

V.T.I: Also called the "Tab", is ledger in tabular form used for recording all transactions with guests staying in the hotel.

Vacant and ready: Room status term indicating that the room has been cleaned and inspected and is ready for new arrival

Variable cost: Costs that vary in direct proportion to sales(for example, housekeeping costs with rooms sales and food and beverage costs with restaurant sales).

Voice mail box: A device used for storing, recording and playing back messages through telephone system.

Voucher: The forms used by various departments such as food and beverage selling services to guests and signed by guests, transferred to front office bills section.

W

WATA: World Association of Travel Agents

WTTC: World Travel and Tourism Council.

W.A.T.S: Wide Area Telephone Services

W.H.O: World Health Organization

W.T.O: World Tourism Organization also World Trade Organization

Wants: Is your wish and desire for something

Wait-listed: Guest who could not be given confirmed reservation because of full booking, also called stand by reservations.

Wake up device: A specially designed clock attached to telephone device and can be used to give wake up calls to guests.

Walk out: A guest who leaves the hotels without warning i.e. without settling his bill also called as Skipper

Walk through: A thorough examination/inspection by a hotel executive of the whole property.

Walk-in: A guest who comes to the hotel without prior reservation also called as "Chance guest" and "Off-the-street guest".

Walking a guest: Due to lack of availability of rooms, to refuse accommodation to a guest who is holding confirmed reservation, also called "Bounced Reservation"

Washed down: In this the hotel delete the name in guest group for any reason.

Wash factor: Deletions of unnecessary group rooms from a group block.

White Space: Unprinted areas of an advertisement

World Processing: The transformation of ideas and information into a readable form of communication through management of procedures, equipment and personnel

Watch: Another term for work shift

Watch down: Blocking fewer rooms than the number requested by a group, based on previous group history.

Watch list: A list prepared by the night manager of people showing unusual behavior such as suddenly placing large orders.

Whitney system: A proprietary system designed by the Whitney Duplicating and Check Company of New York for front office operations and records keeping

Who: An unidentified guest in a room that is vacant as per front desk record

Wholesaler: An entrepreneur who conceives finances and services group and package tour and provides to the general public through retail travel agent

Y

Y.H.A.I: Youth Hostel Association of India

Y.M.C.A: Youth Men's Christian Association

YWCA: Young Women Christians Association

Yield management: A technique based on supply and demand used to maximize revenue by lowering prices to increase sales during periods of low demand and by raising prices during periods of high demands and also called as revenue management in some cases

Yield: The ratio of actual revenue to potential revenue

Youth hostel: A budget accommodation with limited services generally catering to shoestring budget traveler (students etc. travelling on bicycle or hitch hiking)

Z

Z-bed: A folding and portable bed

Zeroing out: At the time of departure to bring the account balance to zero debits and credit offsetting one another.

SECTION 2

16

PROPERTY MANAGEMENT SYSTEM

- INTRODUCTION
- PROPERTY MANAGEMENT SYSTEM(PMS)
- CENTRALIZED RESERVATION SYSTEM(CRS)
- GLOBAL DISTRIBUTION SYSTEM(GDS)
- SELECTION OF PMS
- PMS APPLICATIONS
- EXAMPLES OF PMS
- TOP 10 PMS USED
- QUESTIONS

INTRODUCTION

In the hospitality industry a property management system also known as a PMS is a comprehensive software application used to cover some basic objectives such as coordinating the operational functions of front office, sales and planning etc. Automate hotel functions like guest bookings, guest details, online reservations, point of sale, telephone, accounts receivable, sales and marketing, banquets, food and beverage costing, materials management, HR and payroll, maintenance management, quality management and other amenities. Hotel property management systems may interface with central reservation systems and revenue or yield management systems, front office, back office, point of sale, door-locking, housekeeping optimization, pay-TV, energy management, payment card authorization and channel management systems.

Computer System

It consists of 3 interrelated and interdependent components namely:

- Hardware
- Software
- Users.

Computer Application in Front Office Operations – Replacing manual, mechanical work or use of electric devices.

PROPERTY MANAGEMENT SYSTEM (PMS)

It is a generic term used to describe the application of computer hardware and software in managing the Interface of various departments of a hotel.

Examples of PMS:

1. Fidelio
2. PMS
3. IDS
4. Inn front
5. Visual Oui
6. Opera

Interface with other software's –

1. Energy Management System (EMS)
2. Human Resource System (HRS)
3. Material Management System (MMS)
4. Accounting System
5. Point Of Sale System.

CENTRALISED RESERVATION SYSTEM (CRS)

It is a computerized reservation system for a chain or group of hotels to enable them to sell their rooms effectively.

- The hotels, their sales offices and Central Reservation offices are linked through a CRS for an effective and real time management of room inventory.
- It is primarily a Wide Area Network.

Examples of CRS:

1. Opera
2. MARSHA
3. Taj Central Reservation System
4. Leading Hotels of the World
5. Utell
6. Best Western Hotels
7. Welcomnet
8. Holiday Inn Worldwide GLOBAL DISTRIBUTION SYSTEM (GDS)

Global Distribution System (GDS)

- It is a computer-based systems linked globally through satellites, which are used for hotel reservations, airline reservations and other travel arrangements.
- Usually, the GDS terminals are with travel Agents. The travel agents may be linked to the GDS through a dial-up mode or a lease line.
- All the GDS mentioned below are linked to one-another through a parent satellite.

Examples of GDS:

1. Apollo
2. Gemini
3. Galileo
4. Sabre
5. System One
6. Worldspan
7. Amadeus
8. Axess
9. Abacus
10. Infini
11. Fantasia

SELECTION OF PMS

The steps involved in selection of a Property Management System are:

Step 1: Identification of Need

Firstly an analysis is done to determine whether there is a need of computerized system or not.

The following steps are followed in this process:

a. Selection of a team comprising the representation from all the departments at all levels from all the shifts to analyze the needs.

b. Analyze the flow of guests through the visit to the hotel i.e. an analysis of the guest cycle.

c. Analyze the flow of information from other departments to the front office e.g. billing information, room status information etc.

d. Analyze the administrative paper work produced in other departments.

e. Evaluate the needs that have been identified in terms of importance.

f. Combine the needs to determine the desired applications.

Step 2: Software Selection

- Today, software is available in modules to cater to different areas in a hotel.

- It is based on requirement, as deduced from the needs analysis in step 1, a hotel may go in for the entire PMS or parts thereof.
- Proper software selection is very important, as it involves a, heavy investment.
- Configured or customized as per the need of the hotel.

Step 3: Hardware Selection

- The hardware should be selected to run the needed software.
- The basic factors to consider here are the Processor speed, Disc drives, I/O Port for connecting peripheral devices & for networking, Monitors/ touch screens, Keyboards, Printers, Modems and Supplies: paper, forms, ribbons, ink, toner, cartridge, floppies, DAT, CD-RW etc.

  The other factors to be kept on mind while selecting the hardware are:

  a. **Positioning of hardware**: based on the workflow analysis done during needs analysis.

  b. How does it benefit the guest, who will operate it, who all will require access to the system at that position?

  c. **Climatic condition**: whether air-conditioning required/not esp. in back-of-the-house areas.

  d. **Ergonomics**: psychological & physiological effect of computers on people.

Step 4: OTHER CONSIDERATIONS

1. **Vendor Claims**: Claims made by the supplier. One must inquire about the product from the current users of the same; whether they are satisfied using the system, problems faced by them in using the system.
2. **Installation plans**: Proper planning of installation is essential for maintaining guest services & employee morale. One must have a complete plan laid out for installation of hardware & cabling in different areas of the hotel; also, who shall be installing the hardware & who shall be installing cables.
3. **Training**: Classroom & on-the-job training provided by vendor or not. If yes, charged or inclusive.
4. **Back-up power sources**: Provision of UPS.

5. **Maintenance agreement**: The cost of repair & replacement of hardware & software.

Step 5: Financial Considerations

- The decision regarding purchase or rental of a PMS since heavy investment can tie-up the cash flow of an organization.
- Also, if cost benefits are not realistically projected, profits may be difficult to come by.
- Analyze the savings in terms of overtime paid to the employees, losses due to late charges, cost of marketing database collection, wastage of energy.
- Advantages of outright purchase, discount for full payment in cash, finance charges, depreciation.
- Advantages of lease: continuance of cash flow, application of lease payments to purchase price, tax advantages of leasing etc.

PMS APPLICATIONS:

The modules of an ideal PMS are as follows:

Reservations:

1. Guest data
2. Room inventory
3. Deposits
4. Special requests
5. Blocking
6. Arrivals
7. Departures
8. VIP
9. Projected occupancy
10. Travel agents
11. Guest messages
12. Reports

Registration:

1. Reservations
2. Guest Data
3. Room inventory
4. Room status
5. Security
6. Reports
7. Self check-in

Room Status:

1. Room inventory
2. Availability
3. Reports

Posting:

1. Point of sale
2. Room
3. Tax
4. Transfer
5. Adjustments
6. Paid out
7. Miscellaneous charges
8. Phone
9. Display folio
10. Reports

Call Accounting:

1. Guest information
2. Employee information
3. Post charges
4. Messages

5. Wake-up calls
6. Reports

Checkout:

1. Folio
2. Adjustments
3. Cashier
4. Back office transfer
5. Reports
6. Guest History

Night Audit:

1. Guest charges
2. Department totals
3. City ledger
4. Cashier
5. Financial reports
6. Housekeeping

Inquiries! Reports:

1. Reservations
2. Registrations
3. Checkouts
4. Housekeeping
5. Credit balances

Back Office:

1. Accounts payable
2. Accounts receivable
3. Payroll
4. Budgets

5. General ledger
6. Reports

Housekeeping:

1. Room availability
2. Personnel assignments
3. Analysis4. Housekeeper's report
5. Equipment supplies inventory
6. Maintenance requests

Food and Beverage:

1. Point of sale
2. Posting
3. Cashier reports
4. Food/beverage inventory
5. Recipes
6. Sales control
7. Sales production analysis
8. Labor analysis

Maintenance:

1. Review work order
2. Status
3. Cost/ labor analysis
4. Inventory
5. Repair cost analysis
6. Energy usage analysis
7. Guest room power start

Security:

1. Keys

2. Fire alarm
3. Burglar alarm
4. Security code transactions

Marketing and Sales:

1. Guest history
2. Word-processing
3. Client file
4. Banquet files
5. Desktop publishing
6. Reports
7. Travel agencies

Personnel:

1. Employee file
2. Job control list
3. Word processing
4. Analysis
5. Reports

Electronic Mail

1. Security codes
2. Mail
3. Hard copy

Examples of PMS:

- The ShawMan PMS is an integrated Front Office Management Software that can host multiple properties and handle guest reservations simultaneously across many units including an integrated web-based reservation agent and auto confirmation manager.
    1. ShawMan's PMS plugs into an Integrated Telephone Call management System that supports a host of EPABX interfaces and also seamlessly

connects to ShawMan POS, MMS and CRM Systems to complete the application needs of the boarding & lodging Industry.

2. The ShawMan Hotel Centre is a unique and powerful interface design that handles registration, cashiering, and night audit functions, treating guests and rooms as two manageable objects and supports right click quick task launch of forms and reports, undo and redo, eraser and task history to effortlessly customize the desktop for each user and department to manage a slew of jobs undertaken daily by the attendants, supervisors and managers both at the Front Desk and back office.
3. A three tier client middle server architecture allows business processes and rules to be easily defined and modified such as customer profiles, multiple rate codes, meal plans, guest history, room inventory, housekeeping and more.

FIDELIO

It is one of the world's best selling front office systems, and it is the system of choice for Hilton International, Inter Continental, Mandarin Oriental, Forte, CIGA and many other chains and independents around the globe.

1. Fidelio created the original electronic room rack. Complete, graphical plan illustrations of each floor allow your front office staff to monitor and control the occupancy of every room in the building. Using a system of twelve different color codes, the status of each room is visible at a glance – either currently, or at some future date. Yellow indicates a room is "clean and vacant", blue is "dirty and arrival expected", and so on.
2. Reservations data can also be shown in tabulated form to give an overall occupancy picture for any specified day.
3. For group bookings, from the most complex convention to airline allotments, the group and block management functions handle it all. Master billing, split rates, staggered arrivals, package plans, group history, room type control, block forecasts and traces – they all help to optimize group business, without the time consuming paperwork.
4. As well as handling room management, FIDELIO Front Office maintains all guests' accounts, and offers numerous other facilities such

QUESTIONNAIRE

1. What is a PMS? How would you select a PMS suitable for a hotel?
2. Explain applications of a PMS suitable for a hotel?
3. Explain briefly about Fidelio, Shaw man and IDS?
4. Write in detail about the advantages of using PMS in front office?
5. What are the selection factors for appropriate PMS for a hotel?
6. Give the names of any top ten property management system and their functions?
7. Explain the features that are essential in Room Management Software for effective reporting?
8. List and explain the steps involved in selection of a Property Management System?

17

FRONT OFFICE ACCOUNTING

- FRONT OFFICE ACCOUNTING
- TYPES OF ACCOUNT
- BASIC PRINCIPLES OF ACCOUNTING
- VOUCHERS ,FOLIOS, LEDGER
- FRONT OFFICE ACCOUNTING SYSTEM

INTRODUCTION

An account may be imagined as a bin or container in which the results of various business transactions are stored. The increases and decreases in an account are calculated and the resulting monetary amount is called as account balance. Any financial transaction that occurs in the hotel may affect several accounts. Front office accounts are recordkeeping devices to store information about guest and non-guest financial transactions.

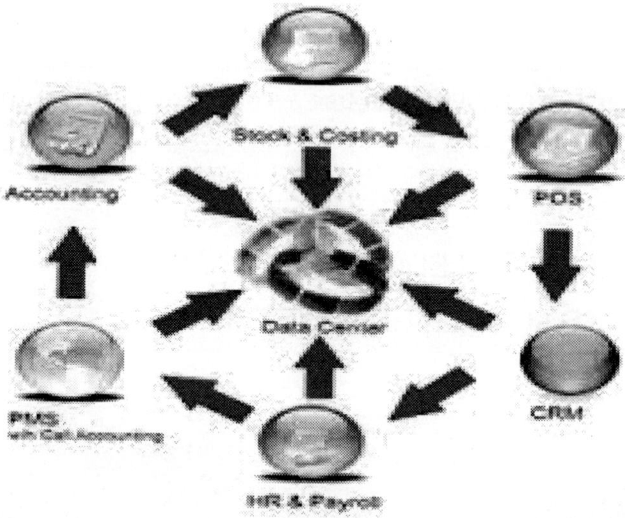

The simplest form of writing an account is the "T" form {as it resembles the letter T}

Charges	**Account**	**Payments**

Types of guest accounts at front desk:

- Guest accounts
- Non guest accounts

Guest Accounts

A guest account is a record of financial transactions which occur between a guest and the hotel. Guest accounts are created when guests guarantee their reservations or when they register at the front desk. During occupancy, the front office is responsible for and records all transactions affecting the balance of a guest account. The front office usually seeks payment for any outstanding guest account balance during the settlement stage of the guest cycle. Certain circumstances may require the guest to make a partial or full payment at other times during the guest cycle.

Non Guest Accounts

A hotel may extend in-house charge privileges to local businesses or agencies as a means of promotion, or to groups sponsoring meetings at the hotel. The front office creates non-guest accounts to track these transactions. These accounts may also be called house accounts or city accounts.

Voucher

A voucher details a single transaction to be posted to a front office account. This document lists detailed transaction information gathered at the source of the transaction. The voucher is then sent to the front office for posting onto the guest folio. Usually any service or goods brought on credit by the guest has to be supported by a voucher.

ALLOWANCE VOUCHER

No:__________

Date: __________

Name:_______________ Room A/C No :________

Detailed explanation	Amount	
	Rs.	Rs.
Rupees in words Total Rs.		

Types of Voucher

- Charge vouchers such as restaurant/bar check
- Cash advance paid out voucher
- Allowance vouchers and Correction vouchers
- Cash vouchers
- Transfer vouchers

BASIC PRINCIPLES OF ACCOUNTING

- Any amount paid by the guest to the hotel is posted in the debit column. A debit {dr.} therefore is moneys owed by the guest to the hotel
- Any money received from the guest is posted in the credit column. A credit therefore is any money paid by the guest towards settling his/her bill including advance deposits.
- The balance column reflects a progressive difference between debits and credits calculated on basis of the formula:

  "Previous balance + debits – credits = net outstanding balance"

Folios

- A folio is a statement of all transactions (i.e. debits & credits) affecting the balance of a single account. At Checkout, any guest folio should be balanced to 0 through full cash payment, credit card transfer, personal check transfer, special program transfer, and direct billing transfer...The correct way of maintaining folios starts with proper posting, which is the process of recording transactions on a folio (i.e. proper folio, proper location and proper amount).Under the manual, semi automated and fully automated systems, folios are called hand-written folios, machine-posted folios, and computer-based electronic folios respectively. Moreover, all folios shall have a unique serial number for internal control and storing purposes.

  In the front office department, there are four common types of folios used:

  a) Guest folios: accounts assigned to individual persons or guestrooms

  b) Master Folios: accounts assigned to more than one person or guest room; usually reserved for guest groups

  c) Non-Guest (or semi-permanent) folios: accounts assigned to non-guest businesses or agencies with hotel charge purchase privileges

  d) Employee Folios: accounts assigned to employees with charge purchase privileges

GUEST FOLIO			
HOTEL ABC TEL NO.		Mr./Mrs..______ address	Room No.______
		Bill No.	A/C No.
1			
2			
3			
4			
5			
6			
7			
8			
9			
10	WELCOME BACK		
11	REGISTRATION NO.		
12	NATIONALITY		
13	NO. OF PAX		
14	ARR. DATE..... DEP. TIME....		
15	ARR. TIME..... DEP. TIME....		
16	telephone reading		
17	TO		
18	FROM		
19	T. CALLS		
TARIFF AND PLAN	ROOM NO.		
CHARGED TO--			
BOOKED BY--			
RECEPTION	MANAGER	CASHIER	DEP. DATE: DEP. TIME:
BILLS ARE DUE ON PRESENTATION		signature of the guest.........................	

POINTS TO REMEMBER WITH REGARD TO A FOLIO

1. A folio is raised as soon as the guest checks in.
2. The initial outstanding balance {when it is opened} of the folio is zero
3. Details on a folio: Guest name, Room Number, date of arrival, date of departure, Room rate, address, billing instructions. Each folio has a serial no. which will help keep a control on folios for the purpose of audit.
4. The cashier is responsible for the guest folio till the guest departs.

Ledgers

- The front office ledger is the collection of front office account folios, which usually include guest ledgers (i.e. charges and payments of all guests staying at the hotel). At any moment in time, the account receivable includes the addition of guest ledger and non-guest ledger (or city ledger) which refers to charges and payments of all non-guests.

There are two main types of ledger used at the front desk:

1. **Guest ledger {Transient ledger/front office ledger and room ledger}**

   Guest ledger is the total set of all account folios of guests registered in the hotel {in-house guest} hence any debit entry to the guest folio will not only increase the guests balance but will also increase the net outstanding balance of the guest ledger.

2. **City ledger {Non-Guest Ledger}**

   City ledger records all accounts that do not belong to resident guests. At the time of check out if the resident guests outstanding balance is not brought to zero, the same is transferred from the guest ledger to the city ledger.

Accounts which are included in city ledger:

- Credit card payment accounts
- Direct billing accounts {guests' whose bill will be settled by the company}
- Airlines
- Travel agencies
- Skipper's account
- Bad cheques account {Bounced cheques of guests}
- Disputed bills account
- Retention charges account from DNA guests

Hotel ABC **Guest Ledger High Balance Report**			
Date____________			
Auditor____________		Reviewed by____________	
Room No.	Guest Name	Amount	Action Taken
103	Ms Sonia	8000/-	Contacted, paid Rs. 400 address & credit verified

122	Mr Amit Prakash	5000/-	Left 3 messages No contact action necessary
301	Mr. Vaseem	7000/-	Direct billing

Front Office Accounting System

- The front office accounting system is responsible for:
  a) Creating and maintaining an accurate accounting record for each guest or non-guest in the hotel
  b) Tracking all financial transactions throughout the guest cycle
  c) Ensuring internal control over cash and non-cash transactions
  d) Recording settlement for all goods & services provided

General Concepts of Front Office Accounting

- Below is a brief description of some accounting terminologies used frequently in the front office department
- The front office accounting system shall be customized and tailored to track each hotel's needs. Therefore, no two hotels have exactly the same front office accounting systems.

Account Aging

Most of the city ledger accounts are settled within 30 days of billing which is generally satisfactory. However there will be some which will take longer than 30 days to collect. The hotel should establish methods for tracking past due accounts which may be based on the date the charges were incurred. This practice of scheduled billings is normally referred to as account aging. At large properties the accounting division monitors account aging while at smaller properties the night auditor may assume this role. An account age analysis sheet identifies which account receivables are 30, 60, 90 or more days old. Accounts lesser than 30 days old are considered current. The accounts over 30 days are considered overdue and the ones above 90 days are delinquent. The front office should maintain a list of accounts over 90 days due.

account ageing report							
Aged Accounts receivables as on :						Sr. No.	
					Outstanding {in days}		
Name	**Balance**	**Current**	**Upto 30**	**31-60**	**61-90**	**91-120**	**120+**
Mr. J	6488.60		6488.60				
Mr. B	15365.00						15365.00
Mr. C	9575.00	4000.00	5575.00				
Total outstanding	31428.60	4000.00	12063.60				15365.00

Points of sale [i.e. POS]:

- A point of sale is the location at which goods or services are purchased; sometimes called a revenue center. Moreover, due to technology breakthrough, some non-traditional point of sales emerged such as in-room movie & in-room vending service systems.
- Since charges are usually incurred at remote points of sale, and guest and non-guest folios are maintained at the front office department, posting of different guest and non-guest charges shall be performed. An electronic transfer ensures this, under the fully automated system. Under manual and semi automated systems posting shall be done by a physical submission of different vouchers to the front office department.
- When posting charges, the following items shall be considered:
  a) Amount of the charge
  b) Name of the point of sales outlet
  c) Room number & name of the guest
  d) Brief description of the charge
  e) Guest signature & employee identification

Creation and Maintenance of Guest Accounts

- All guest folios shall be created during the pre-arrival or arrival stage of the guest cycle. Moreover, folios might be either placed in front desk folio tray [i.e. posting tray, folio well, or bucket] or stored as an electronic guest folios in fully automated systems.
- As far as walk-ins are concerned, all their guest folios are created at the arrival stage!

1. Record keeping systems

a) Non- automated systems: Ensured through a series of columns listing individual debit and credit entries accumulated during the occupancy stage after which and establishment of an ending outstanding balance is needed.

b) Semi-automated systems: Under this very system, all guest transactions should be printed sequentially on a machine-posted folio. Later, the front office clerk needs to come up with the folio outstanding balance. It is extremely important here to mention that, under this very system, each account's previous balance shall be re-entered each time a transaction is posted to the folio.

c) Fully-automated systems: All guest charges are automatically posted to an electronic folio

2. Guest charge privileges

- Potential guests who would like to have guest charge privileges shall present an imprint of an acceptable credit card or direct billing authorization at registration. Failing to do so, guests would have to pay, in full, all their charges through cash, hence called Paid-in-Advance [PIA] guests and have, hence, have no post status.

3. Credit monitoring:

- In order to monitor and control charge privileges, the front office clerk should check whether the total net purchases are less than the minimum of floor Limit (i.e.: credit card company's limit) and house limit (i.e. hotel's limit). At least, each day, lists of guests with high risk or high balance accounts shall be communicated to all point of sale outlets. This is vital since, failing to do so, will let point of sales outlets continue giving charge privileges to a point that eventually the credit card company refuses to pay the amount of money exceeding its limit. This will cause very serious financial losses to the hotel.

4. Account maintenance:

- Whatsoever system hotels operate, maintenance of guest and non-guest accounts is ensured by the following formula:

Net outstanding balance = Previous balance + Debits - Credits NOB = PB + DR - CR

Tracking Transactions

- Under the manual and semi-automated systems, tracking transactions is ensured through an intensive use of vouchers. On the other hand, under fully automated systems, tracking transactions is ensured through on-line electronic transfer of transactional information from remote points of sale to the front office main frame terminal.
- In accounting, a transaction is an exchange of goods and services for cash or a promise to pay. Under this very assumption, "nothing happens until a transaction occurs". This means that front office clerks shall first of all have a transaction, its supporting documents (i.e. vouchers, invoices...) to be able later to debit or credit certain accounts!
- In hotels transactions might have the form of:
  a) Cash payment
  b) Charge purchase
  c) Account correction
  d) Account allowance
  e) Current transfer
  f) Cash Advance

1. Cash payment:

- In this very transaction, front office clerks shall post cash payment as a credit in the guest folio. Moreover, cash vouchers shall be used as a transaction-supporting document.

2. Charge purchase:

- Charge purchases represent deferred payment transactions that increase the outstanding balance of a folio account. In this transaction type, front office clerks shall use charge vouchers as a transaction-supporting document.

3. Account correction:

- Account correction is used to resolve a posting error in a folio detected at the day the error is made (i.e. before the closing of the business day). In this transaction, front office clerks shall use correction vouchers as a transaction-supporting document.

4. Account allowance:

- Account allowances occur because of two reasons:
  a) Either as compensation of poor service or as rebates for coupon discounts. That way, guest outstanding balance decreases.
  b) As to correct a posting error detected after the closing of the business day.
- For both reasons, front office clerks shall prepare an allowance voucher as a transaction supporting document.

V. Internal Control

- In the hotel industry, the main purpose of internal control is to track transaction documentation, verify account entries and account balances, and to identify vulnerabilities in the accounting system. The keyword to internal control is auditing, which is the process of verifying front office accounting records for accuracy and completeness.
- Below are some forms that are of extreme importance to internally control, one of the most vital assets in the hotel (i.e. cash):

1. Front office cash sheet:

- The front office cash sheet lists each cash receipt or disbursement in order to reconcile cash on hand at the end of a cashier's shift with the documented transaction that occurred during the same shift.

2. Cash, house banks or petty cash:

- Petty cash is the amount of cash assigned to a cashier so that he/she can handle the various transactions that occur in a particular work shift.
- At the beginning of each shift, all cashiers must sign their cash banks and at the end of the shift, shall deposit all cash, checks, and other negotiable instruments in the general cashier's safe deposit box. Moreover, at the end of each shift, cashiers should watch out for cash discrepancies (i.e. any difference between front office cash sheet and the actual amounts in their

cash drawers). Cash discrepancies might have the form of cash overages, shortages, or due backs.

- Lastly, cashiers might come up with the net cash receipt, which is: Amount of all cash, checks, and other negotiable instruments in cashier's drawer – amount of the initial cash bank + all paid outs

3. Audit control:

- Along with the fact that hotels might employ internal control auditors, at least once in a year, (especially for hotels traded in the stock market) to get use of external certified public accountants responsible for approving hotel's accounts.

Settlement of Accounts

- One of the responsibilities of front office clerks is to settle guest accounts, which means the eventual collection of payment for outstanding account balances (i.e.: bringing account balances to 0]. This is usually ensured either by full cash payment, transfer to an approved credit card, personal check, special program, or direct billing account...

DAILY REPORT OF EXPATATION										
DATE										
EXPECTED ARRIVALS							EXPECTED DEPARTURES			
ROOM	NAME	NO OF PERSONS		TIME OF ARRIVAL	STAYING UP TO	REMARKS	ROOM NO.	NAME	TIME OF DEPARTURE	REMARKS
		ADULT	CHILD							
	VIPs expectd groups in next three days									
front office manager lobby manager cashier f&b department house keeper				REMARKS total room occupied total no. of guests in house % room occupancy % guest occupancy signature receptionist						

QUESTIONAIRE

1. What is an account?
2. What are guest accounts?
3. What are non-guest accounts?
4. What is a voucher?
5. What are the different types of voucher?
6. What is a folio?
7. What are the different types of folios used in a hotel?
8. Write in detail about the fundamental principles of accounting?
9. What is audit control and how it is done?
10. Define ledger and its different types?
11. What is an account ageing?
12. Differentiate between Account Correction & Account Allowance.

18

CONTROL OF CASH & CREDIT

CONTROL OF CASH AND CREDIT

The hotel industry is the only business where the guest enjoy the benefit of credit facility right from the time he comes to the hotel and where the business man whose primary objective is to collect revenue when the transaction is over is deprived of that and gets benefit only on or after the departure of the guest and that too sometimes after a period of 30-40 days in normal course. This results in the blocking of money and hence creates a situation of greater risk and this demands higher investment and hence it is important that the hotel takes some definite and concrete steps to ensure that the guest accounts will be settled in full at the agreed time therefore protecting the hotel from bankruptcy due to bad debts. The hotel should control the credit of its guest to also insure a healthy cash flow. Cash flow means the money which moves in and out of the business. The term credit control refers to the various measures taken by the hotel to ensure that the guest settle their account in full either themselves or someone else on their behalf {which may be a credit card company, airline company, corporate office, a travel agent or person}within a specified period of time.

Various steps are to be taken by different front office personnel at different stages of the guest cycle that will help in credit control.

Credit control procedures used for different guests at the front desk during check-in:

Guest paying by credit card

- Guest is required at the time of check-in to present his credit card
- Credit card is imprinted
- Name on the card is tallied with the name on registration card
- Check expiry date of the card
- Check the hotlist to check that it is not blacklisted
- Check that the hotel accepts the type of credit card presented by the guest

Guest paying by travel agent voucher:

- Guest presents travel agents voucher at the time of check in
- These are prepaid vouchers
- These are then tallied with the record copy the travel agent has sent the hotel in advance at the time of reservation
- The receptionist will then attach this voucher to the guest registration card and then sends it to the cashier who will open the folio and mark the instruction as required on the folio

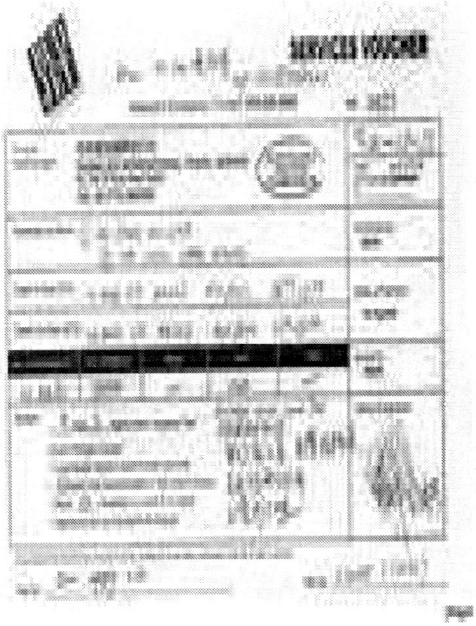

Guest checking in with tour groups

- Groups are usually prearranged and pre registered and the credit procedure is established between the tour operator and the hotel much prior to arrival.
- The cashier in such a case will open a master folio in case of group charges.
- The POS cashiers are informed not to make any credit sales transactions to any group member for their personal incidentals/expenses and charge cash for the same.

Guests from Airlines:

There are two types of guests sent by the airlines:

Stayover guests: These guests are provided with PSO {Passenger Service Order} or MAO {Meal and Accommodation Order} which detail the services and facilities that will be provided by the hotel to such guests and the airline will pay for the same. The folio in this case will be signed by the guest at check out and the bill is forwarded to the airline company for payment

Crew: These guests have to sign their bills on checkout which are forwarded to the airline for payment. Services and facilities which are provided by the hotel and paid for by the airline are mentioned in the contract which the airline makes with the hotel

AIR INDIA	INDIAN AIRLINES	JET AIRWAYS
JETLITE	INDIGO AIRLINES	SPICE JET
DECCAN	KINGFISHER AIRLINES	GO AIR

Guests having all their charges billed:

- Look through the billing instructions given at the time of reservation to check what charges are covered by guests and what charges are paid by the company.

- If the room charges are to be billed to company and other incidentals are paid by the guest himself such as laundry, food etc. confirm with the guest at the time of check in itself how he will pay his incidentals and the same instruction must be marked on the folio.
- Examples of such guests are members of FHRAI and TAAI. In such cases a split folio is used where charges are charges are distributed into two {between company/organization and individuals} one for rooms and the other for incidentals.

Guest with scanty baggage:

- These guests are not allowed to purchase anything on credit. All payments are to be settled in cash unless well known to the hotel.
- An advance/deposit is taken from them at the time of check-in to be adjusted against room and incidental charges.
- The registration cards, folio and arrival notification slips will have APC {All payments cash}.
- A credit limit is also fixed in case of well known guests with scanty baggage and the moment his outstanding balance reaches the limit the night auditor prepares a slip which tells the guest to deposit some cash before making any new credit transactions.

Walk-in/chance guests

- To avoid any possibility of a skipper and hence loss of revenue, the hotel will usually ask for an advance payment or deposit at the time of check-in.
- The deposit should be enough to cover the room charges and incidental charges.

CREDIT FACILITY FOR COMPANIES/CORPORATIONS

Hotels have to check the solvency status of the company first and also cross check with the company's banker before listing the company on the list of credit approved companies of the hotel.

The account department maintains this list and is sent to the other departments of the hotel such as reservations, front desk, bills, sales etc.

Different limits are set for different companies, depending on the size of the company, volume of business provided and the reputation of the company. For example a company with reputation of prompt payment shall get a higher credit limit rather than a newer and smaller company

CREDIT CONTROL DURING STAY OF A GUEST

A credit limit is set for the guest depending on his credit profile and then in turn must be marked on his folios. The front office must monitor guest and non-guest accounts to ensure they remain within acceptable credit limits. Typically, a line of credit is set for guests who establish charge privileges during the reservations or registration process. Guests who present an acceptable credit card at registration may be extended a line of credit equal to the floor limit {credit limit set by the issuing credit card company}. Guest and non-guest accounts with other approved credit arrangements are subject to limitations established by the front office. These internal credit restrictions are called house limits.

HAVE YOU DEPOSITED YOUR ROOM KEY AND THE SAFE DEPOSIT LOCKER KEY

Folio No 202	Status
Room No.	Tariff-Rs. 10500
Locker No.	

Name : **Mr. Khanna**

Designation : **CEO**

Address : **Roopa Exports**
Chennai

Mode of Payment: **Bill to company**

PKG. PL. GRP. MST.

Arrival Date	Time	Pax	Dep.
1.06.07	12.45 p.m.	01	4.06.07

Date	Reference	Description	Base Charge	VAT	Misc. Charges	LT	ST	Dr.	Cr.	Total Bal.
1.06.07		Bar	1200					1200		
		Dinner	1500					2700		
		Room Charges	10500	1260				15460		
2.04.07		Telephone	560					16020		
		Room Charges	10500	1260				27780		
3.04.07		Break fast	750					28530		
		Spa	825					29355		
		Banquet dinner	24000		2400			55755		
		Room Charges	10500	1260				67515		
4.04.07		Break fast	750					68265		68265.00

I agree to pay the full amount of these charges, I also agree that all Charges in this account are correct. BALANCE DUE

CASHIER'S SIGNATURE__________ GUEST'S SIGNATURE__________

Front office management may need to be notified when a front office account approaches the house limit. Such accounts are called high risk or high balance accounts. The front office auditor, or night auditor, is primarily responsible for identifying accounts which have reached or exceeded predetermined credit limits. Front office management may request the guest to make a partial payment to reduce the outstanding account balance.

AFTER DEPARTURE ACTIVITIES

If the guest settles his bill through credit card or airlines voucher or travel agents voucher or through a corporate company account his room account is zeroed out at the time of check out and the outstanding balance is transferred to the city ledger.

At the end of a specified period the hotel accounting department sends the bills statement to the concerned company for making the payment and it is expected out of the companies that they will make the payment promptly.

If they are late in doing so a follow up measure will be taken by the hotel requesting them to speed up the payment in case of further failure a strong reminder will be sent and if all these measures don't produce any results a legal notice through a lawyer will be sent.

Hotels must ensure that the guests who are given credit facility from the hotel are able to pay their bill in full within the scheduled period of time and only then the hotel should fix a house limit. Usually the hotel's credit policy allows credit to:

1. Guaranteed payment reservation guests
2. Company guarantee payment guests
3. Credit card guarantee guests
4. Deposit/advance payment reservation guests

PROBLEMS IN CREDIT CONTROL MAY ARISE IF:

1. Guest is not explained clearly as to which credit cards/foreign currencies are accepted by the hotel.
2. The guest is not informed that if his bill exceeds the house limit he will have to pay the balance in cash
3. Communication gap between accounts department and cashier or night auditor and cashier
4. Negligence by the staff to look at the black list

CASH CONTROL:

- All cash must be kept under lock and key and under the supervision of the cashier.
- The cash bank/float given to the cashier is also controlled and a check is kept on the same
- The cashier should take proper precautions when dealing with foreign currency
- Whenever the guest pays in cash the cashier has to make a cash receipt and hand it over to the guest.
- The cash collected everyday should be sent to the bank for deposit.

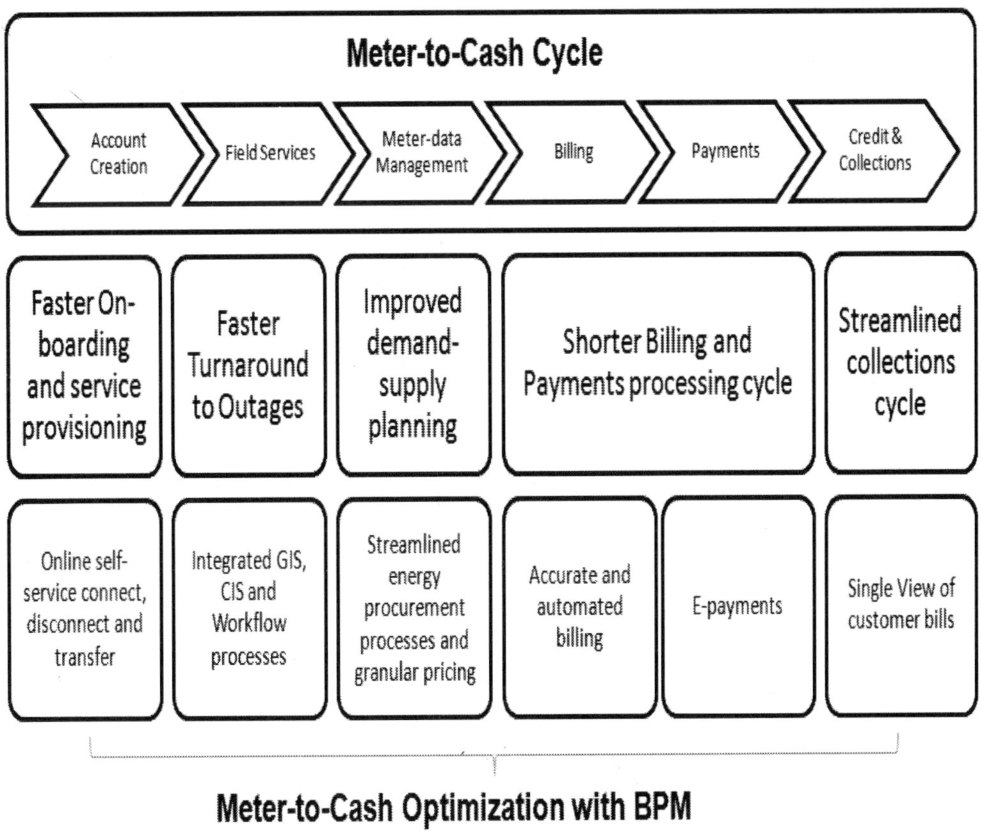

Cash control is important from the point of view of hotel as credit sales are usually discouraged.

PROTECTION OF HOTEL FUNDS:

- Cashiers should make frequent money drops to have minimum cash in hand.
- Cash drawers should be accessible to only one cashier at a time and should be kept closed when not in use.
- Alarm systems should be installed in all areas of the hotel where cash transactions take place.
- A consistent system for handling bank deposits and money pickup should be developed and followed.
- Staff handling money like the cashier, security etc should be appointed only after strict scrutiny and cross checking with their previous employers. They should be rotated from time to time and a new combination of staff should be used.
- They must also be trained to react in emergency situations.

QUESTIONNAIRE

1. What can be done by hotel management to obtain control in hotel operations?
2. What are the problems arise in credit control?
3. What is the credit facilities provided to company?
4. What are the after departure activities take place?
5. How to deal guest with scanty baggage?
6. What are the steps to be taken for the protection of hotel funds?

19

NIGHT AUDITING

- FUNCTIONS
- AUDIT PROCEDURES (NON AUTOMATED, SEMI AUTOMATED AND FULLY AUTOMATED

THE NIGHT AUDIT

- Hotels operate 24×7 so Front Office regularly review and verify the accounts.
- Audit is a daily review of guest account transactions at Front Office against revenue centre

Transactions

- Audit is performed to ensure **accuracy, reliability & thoroughness** of accounting system.
- Audit of active non-guest accounts also.
- Audit results in balanced guest & non-guest accounts, accurate account statements, credit monitoring and reports generation.

Why is it called Night Audit?

It is called Night Audit because it is performed at Night. In olden days, manual system was followed and

Nighttimes was the most appropriate period for auditing due to very little business and movement.

FUNCTIONS OF THE NIGHT AUDIT

MAIN PURPOSE: To verify the accuracy and completeness of guest and non-guest accounts.

SPECIFIC FUNCTIONS

- Verifying posted entries to guest and non-guest accounts.
- Balancing all Front Office accounts.
- Resolving room status and rate discrepancies.
- Maintaining guest credit limits.
- Producing operational and managerial reports.

THE ROLE OF THE NIGHT AUDITOR

ATTENTION needs to be paid to:

1. Accounting details, Procedural controls, Guest credit restrictions.
2. Nature of cash transactions.
3. Tracking room reservation and related statistics.

4. Daily summary of cash and credit activities at front desk.
5. Reporting results of operation to the management.

ESTABLISHING AN END OF THE DAY

Generally night shifts are from 11pm to 7am. End of the day is the closing time of the majority revenue outlets.

CROSS-REFERENCING

- For internal control purposes, an accounting system should provide independent supporting documentation (e.g. a coffee shop guest check and a front office guest folio) to verify each transaction for cross-referencing.
- Guest and non-guest accounts are compared with source documents from revenue centers to prove individual transaction entries and account totals.

GUEST CREDIT MONITORING

- Establishing lines of credit or Credit limit depends upon many factors such as house limit, floor limit, guest's status & reputation etc..
- It determines the potential credit risk of guest. It is reflected through High Balance Report.

AUDIT POSTING FORMULA

Previous Balance + Debits - Credits = Net Outstanding Balance

PB + DR - CR = NOB

DAILY AND SUPPLEMENTAL TRANSCRIPTS

- A **Daily Transcript** is a detailed report of all guest accounts that indicates each charge transaction affecting a guest account for the day
- A **Supplemental Transcript** is a detailed report of all non-guest accounts that indicates each charge transaction that affected a non-guest account that day.
- Used as the worksheets to detect posting errors.
- Used in non and semi automated systems.
- Consists of revenue center, transaction type and transaction total.

OPERATING MODES FOR NIGHT AUDIT

1. Non Automated (manually)
2. Semi Automated (mechanically)
3. Automated (electronically)

Non – Automated

- Four common night audit forms are used:
    a. Daily & Supplemental Transcript (either VTL is directly used or it is copied on to format from Folios—columns are summarized or totaled)
    b. Guest and Non-Guest Folios
    c. Front Office Cash Sheets/ Cash Books
    d. Audit Recapitulation Sheet (A complete summary of Front Office accounting for the day).

Drawbacks:

- Not feasible for large hotels.
- Prone to errors due to volume of data.
- Tedious
- May prove costly.

Semi – Automated

- Accounting Posting Machines are the basis for mechanical auditing. It is most important development in the history of Front Office Accounting.
- Posting machines are of two types:
    – Electromechanical and Electronic.

    Functions of both the machines are same except that:

    - Electromechanical machine can store limited no. of department totals.
    - Electromechanical machine cannot retain total balances.
    - Electromechanical machine cannot be combined with other equipment (at POS).

On the other hand, electronic machines are as good as a PC, in terms of cost. In fact, they are the foundation for modern day PMS.

Steps in Machine Posting

1. Locating the folio.
2. Take folio out of the bucket.
3. Place folio along with the check in the posting machine.
4. Enter previous closing balance.
5. Post the check amount with department code.
6. Machine balances the folio.
7. Folio is refiled in bucket.

Simultaneously, the following occurs:

1. The voucher is imprinted with the same information as posted to the accounts folios (this acts as a verification that the voucher has been posted).
2. Identical information printed on an Internal Machine Paper Tape (known as Audit Trail).
3. Amount of each charge is added to or subtracted from the running departmental total.

Forms/ Formats used in Auditing

1. FO Cash Report
2. D-Report (Night Auditor's Report/ D-Card): It mentions the total opening balance, debits, credits & net outstanding balances. Used for reconciliation with departmental summaries.

Fully – Automated

- There is complete computer interfacing. The computer in a fraction of time performs all Audit Functions (Guest Ledger & Non Guest Ledger compared with daily departmental reports to locate errors).
- Computer guides the auditor/ user through the stages in auditing. It asks for certain data inputs before beginning with the audit process.
- Computer performs all the vertical checks. It Organizes, Compiles & Prints the records. System Updates are run at the end of the day.

NIGHT AUDIT PROCESS

- Focus is on Two Areas:

1. Discovery and Correction of accounting errors.
2. Creation of accounting and management reports.

- The degree of audit scrutiny depends on:
    1. Frequency of errors – relates the quality of Front Office work.
    2. No. of Transactions to be reviewed- correlates with the size and complexity of the hotel.

Steps

1. Complete outstanding postings.
2. Reconcile room status discrepancies.
3. Verify Room Rates.
4. Balance all departmental accounts.
5. Verify No-Show reservations.
6. Post Room Rates & Taxes.
7. Prepare required Reports.
8. Prepare Cash receipts for deposit.
9. Clear or Back up the system.
10. Distribute Reports.

Complete outstanding postings

- Ensuring proper posting of all transactions affecting non-guest and guest accounts.
- Transactions are supposed to be posted to accounts as they are received. Night Auditor has to ensure that all vouchers are posted.
- Further he has to verify (even in computerized system) the postings. This he does by matching reports from interfaces with reports from Front Office system in a computerized environment.

Reconcile Room Status Discrepancies

- Discrepancies cause loss of revenue, omissions and confusion.
- First housekeeper's report is reconciled with room rack.
- Then, room rack is tallied with folios.

- The evening shift does this work to save time and resolve guest problems.

Verify Room Rates

- Verify discounts/ complimentary etc.
- If rate charged are less than Rack Rates, then:
    a) Are the rates discounted? Is the Discount correct?
    b) Are there two guests on sharing basis? Is there a second folio?
    c) Is the complimentary room correctly authorized?

Balance all Departments

- First balance all departments and then look for individual errors (within an out of balance department).
- Revenue center provides source documents and Front Office Accounts provides department transaction information.
- If error is found, a detailed audit needs to be done.

Verify No-Show reasons

- Checking Reservation Racks for pending arrivals.
- Filing and posting No-show charges. One has to be careful in this case. There may be a regular guest / corporate etc. A cancellation might not have been recorded.

Post Room Rates and Taxes

- After verifying post Room Rates and Taxes.

Prepare Reports

- The following are some of the reports prepared by the auditor -
    a) Operations Reports
    b) Sales summary
    c) High Balance Reports
    d) Detailed department reports and summary (for accounts department)

Deposit Cash

- Sales summary and cash deposits of points of sale are tallied.
- Checkouts tallied with cash receipts.
- Cash is counted and tallied with cash sheet/ cash book and sealed in an envelope for deposit in accounts department.

Clear *I* Back Up System

- Clear up the total figures for the day and open fresh accounts for next day.
  a) Manual: Closing Balance of VTL is entered as Opening Balance for the next day's VTL sheet.
  b) Semi-Automated: Totals in machine are zeroed. A "Z- Card" is used to verify zero balances in the machine. It is submitted with Night Audit work.
  c) Automated: System backs up the reports on various media e.g. paper, DAT etc. Backup is Daily/ Weekly.

Distribute Reports

- Reports are selectively distributed because of their sensitive nature.

VERIFYING THE NIGHT AUDIT

- Many types of posting, mathematical, and clerical errors can be identified in night audit.
- Some of the errors are

Pickup Errors

- In manual/ semi-automated systems, previous balance is entered (picked up) incorrectly.
- Can happen whenever a posting is made to a folio.
- Difficulty to identify.

Transposition Errors

- The numbers related to transaction are reversed. (eg. Rs. 645 to Rs. 654)
- Easiest to identify.

Missing Folios

- In non or semi-automated systems,
- Folio has been filed incorrectly or removed from the folio bucket.
- May be because closing 'A' folio and not closing 'B' folio.
- When a folio is missing, the night audit will not balance.
- In automated, folios are stored electronically, no issue of missing folios.

QUESTIONNAIRE

1. Describe the duties and responsibilities of a night auditor?
2. Explain in details the procedure of night auditing
3. How can be a night audit is verified?
4. What are various forms and formats used in night audit?
5. What is night audit? What are the functions of night audit?
6. What are operating modes for night audit?
7. What are the different reports a night auditor generates?

20

FRONT OFFICE AND GUEST SAFETY AND SECURITY

- FUNCTIONS
- IMPORTANCE OF SECURITY SYSTEM
- SAFE DEPOSIT
- KEY CONTROL
- SECURITY MEASURE'S
- EMERGENCY SITUATION

IMPORTANCE OF A SECURITY SYSTEM

The guest, who comes to a particular hotel, comes with an understanding that he and his belongings both will be safe and secure during his stay at the hotel. At the same time it is also quite important that the hotel staff and assets are protected and secure. Hence it is very important to have a proper security system in place to protect staff, guests and physical resources and assets such as equipment, appliances buildings, and gardens of the hotel and also the belongings of the guest.

The management must take care that the security and safety systems cover the following areas:

- Guest: Protection from crimes such as murder, abduction and health hazards from outsiders, hotel staff, pests, food poisoning etc.
- Staff: Providing staff lockers, insurances, health schemes, provident funds etc. Protective clothing, shoes, fire fighting drills, supply of clean drinking water use of aqua guards, sanitized wash rooms etc.
- Guest luggage: Secure luggage store rooms and proper equipment such as luggage trolley and bell hop trolley should be provided.
- Hotel Equipments: Lifts, Boilers, Kitchen equipment, furniture fitting and building etc. must be protected and for these the security and safety should cover up fire safety equipment, bomb threat security system, water floods security system, earthquake security system, safe vault security system etc.
- Protection of raw materials, goods, provisions and groceries etc. for this the security system should cover proper storage and pest control systems, apart from the application of total material management system.

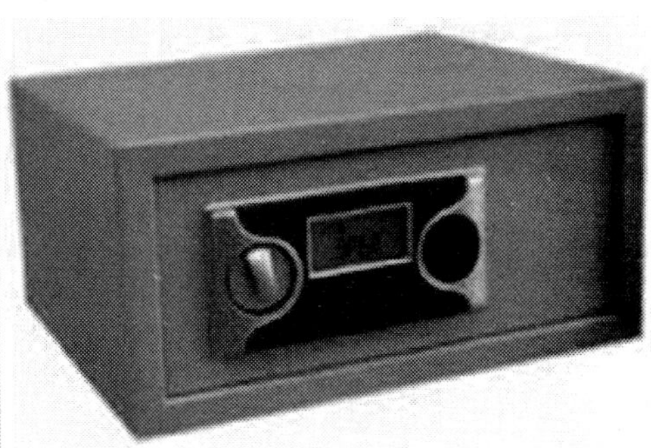

TYPES OF SECURITY

1. Physical aspect
2. Security of persons
3. Security of systems

1. Physical aspect is divided into two parts:
   a) Internal
   b) External

a) Internal security

- Against theft
- Fire safety
- Proper lighting
- Safeguarding assets
- Track unwanted guests

b) External Security

- Proper lighting outside the building
- Proper fencing of the building
- Facing of pool area to avoid accidents in the night
- Manning of service gates to restrict entry
- Fixing of closed circuit TV cameras

2) Security aspects of persons

a) Staff

- Effective recruitment and selection
- Identification of staff
- Key control
- Red tag system
- Training
- Locker inspection

b) Guests:

- Check scanty baggage guests
- Guests suspected of taking away hotel property should be charged according to hotel policy
- Guest room security:
- Provide wide angle door viewer, dead bolt locks, night torch, chains on doors etc
- Employees should be trained to not give any information about in house guests to outsiders
- While issuing a card key ask for key card if in doubt of the guest.
- Housekeeping staff should never leave keys expose on unattended carts in corridors

3) Security aspects of systems:

- Record of all losses and missing items immediately
- Inventory control should be proper
- Auditing should be done on a regular basis
- Proper system for cash disbursements should be made

The term system implies the operations of the hotel all the equipment used for operation, procedures laid down for operations and policies to be followed. Systems procedures and policies if followed properly shall safeguard the assets and increase life span of equipment as well as avoid any breakdown maintenance

This would mean the following:

Fix duties and responsibilities: Fix duties of staff members so that they don't interfere with others' work.

Make surprise checks

Staffs who has access to liquid assets should be made to sign a bond so that in case of theft the concerned person can easily be caught

Hiring of some independent security company to check the security system of the hotel

Security Issue

Security encompasses areas such as security of the property itself, company assets, employees' and customers' personal belongings and valuables, life security; personal security etc.

In all workplaces management stipulates that it is not responsible for valuables and employees personal belongings (their handbags, items kept in the personal lockers, etc.). Yet management must take all possible measures to prevent theft among employees and of employee belongings through its hiring practices and through the implementation of effective management, human resources and operational policies, such as:

- Background checks of selected applicants
- Policies related to employees' entry to, and exit from, the workplace
- Spot checks of locker rooms and lockers
- Effective supervision and control during the work cycle
- Policies related to the discovery of criminal records and wrongdoing among, and by, employees
- Control of people entering and exiting the workplace

With regard to guest valuables, management informs guests that the hotel is not responsible for valuables left in the room, advising them to secure these in safety deposit boxes provided by the hotel. Besides taking care of security issues related to the people they employ (as outlined above), management must undertake some necessary measures, among which:

- Providing "secure" (safety) deposit boxes and areas to keep valuables
- Policies and practices to ensure the security of these boxes and areas
- Management and operational policies regarding the security of guest rooms
- Management and operational policies regarding the security of public areas
- Security policies and practices for the back-of-the-house areas
- Employment and training of security personnel
- Policies and practices to minimize the "presence" and "patronage" of "shady characters" and criminals, verification of registration and

check-in personal data and documentation submitted, and curtailing free movement of unknowns on the premises, as well as direct, free flowing communication with local, national and international security authorities)

- Training of staff in guest and valuable security
- Effective supervision and control procedures.

Safe deposit facility in the hotel for security of guests' valuables:

- It is the responsibility of management to develop and maintain proper safe deposit procedures for its property.
- If this facility is available for guests, notices regarding it should be put up in various conspicuous/noticeable places in the hotel and also should be mentioned to the guest.
- Safe deposit boxes should be located in an area, in vicinity of the front desk and which has limited access. Unauthorized guests or personnel should not be permitted inside the area.
- Front office staff should be well-versed with the procedures regarding safe deposit boxes.
- Strict control should apply to the storage and issue of safe deposit keys.
- At any point of time there should be only one key issued for each safe even if more than one person is using the safe.
- Two keys are required to open a safe deposit box: one being the guest's key and the other being the control key/guard key put in by the cashier/safe deposit attendant.
- After the verification f the identity of the guest, the safe deposit attendant/ cashier should accompany the guest to the safe deposit area where in clear sight should make use of the control key and the guest's key to open the safe.

Sometimes the hotel may not be able to meet the demand for individual safe box; in that case a large box containing the belongings of more than one guest is used. Each guest's belongings are put in an envelope which is sealed. The key to this box is stored in a secure place and a log is maintained which records an entry each time the key is used to open the box

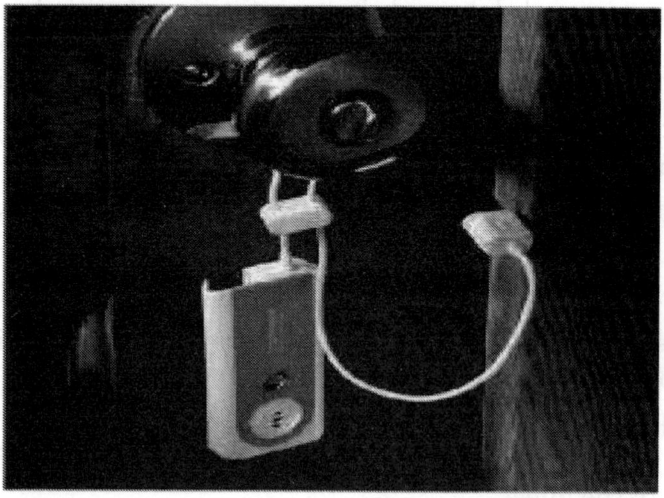

Key Card Locks

While key card locks on guest rooms are quickly becoming the standard, some hotels still don't take advantage of the added safety provided to guests.

Guest room locking systems these days include punch and magnetic key cards which have locks with flash memory and other productivity linked functions. The system can directly be linked with PMS.

KEY CONTROL

A control system by which it is ensured that room keys are always at the proper place i.e. if the room is occupied and the guest is in the room then the key is with him, and if the guest is not in the room or the room is unsold then the room key is in its proper pigeon hole of key and mail rack. A lack of proper system result in loss of revenue as a room which is vacant may be shown occupied and may also cause confusion and chaos as an occupied room maybe accessed by an unauthorized guest.

Two locking systems are using in hotels:

- HARD KEY SYSTEM (metallic keys)
- ELECTRONIC KEY SYSTEM

Process of Key Control

The process of key control in case of hard keys is done by receptionist who prepares a key control sheet at around midnight or 1.00a.m through night receptionist report which contains details such as room not be assigned, vacant, occupied double lock,etc.

The keys of vacant room should be at the key and mail rack in the appropriate pigeon hole and if it is not there and also if the bill is settled, then departure is shown in the various registers as per bills and housekeeping.

The missing keys of the vacant rooms are tried to be located which could be with housekeeping or bell desk. It is checked, and if not found, is entered in the report.

Details of missing key list are made. It could be that the guest did a self departure and mistakenly took away the key. Such room numbers are noted. Name of the guest, his check out date and time is also noted. His address is taken from the registration card.

Some other security measures taken by hotels:

Security Guards

Most hotels do not have security guards while some employ them only at night. At Best Western Sterling Inn, we have our own staff of trained security guards working 24-hours every day to provide the best in safety and security for our guests

Defibrillation Units:

A life saving device in case of heart attacks, defibrillation units are starting to be deployed among police and emergency personnel across the nation.

Security Cameras

Few Hotels have security cameras with digital technology, intelligent access central system, software interface with CCTV for matching undesirable visitors and criminals, interfacing with motion detectors, pocket lie detectors and spy cameras and use of biometric readers like hand key reader or face recognition system etc.

Fire Alarms:

While most hotels now have smoke detectors and fire alarms, Some hotels have a state of the art alarm system with smoke detectors in each guest room and throughout the entire complex that is monitored 24 hours a day, 7 days per week that pinpoints the exact point of the alarm allowing our security staff to respond immediately to the area of any alarm condition.

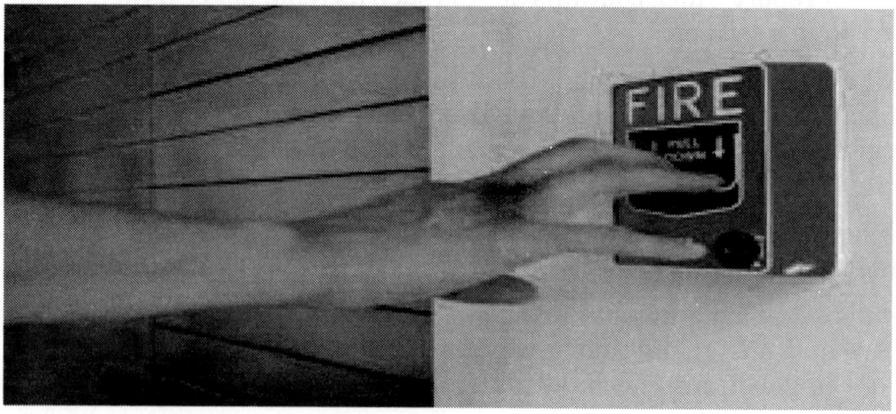

Emergency Power

Very few hotels have any provision for emergency power in case of an electrical outage while a few hotels provide limited emergency stand-by power to provide elevator service and some lighting. Some hotels have a 2-Megawatt stand-by generator that provides 100% emergency power that can provide uninterrupted guest service during a power outage.

Emergency Manual

Hotels maintain an emergency manual, detailing operations in the event of a variety of emergencies.

Employee Photo ID

For added security, some hotels have employees wearing a photo ID nametag allowing quick identification.

In-Room Safes

In addition to the safety deposit boxes offered by most hotels at the front desks, Some hotels provide in-room guest safes capable of holding a lap-top computer that use the guest's own credit card as the key.

Guest Elevators

Elevators may also be interfaced with a room electronic locking system, where swiping the room card key takes the guest to the floor on which he is staying.

Bomb threat security:

Precautions and measures that may be taken in the above case:

1. Security nets and body searches for guests not known to the staff.
2. Banqueting suites and other non-public areas should be security checked and locked after use
3. Goods received and bags should be checked and kept tidy.

4. If a bomb threat is received via telephone, the telephonist should note carefully what exactly is said, the time of the call received the accent of the caller and background noise if any. After the alert the GM should stay put in the lobby where he can be reached easily.
5. Duties and responsibility of staff during an emergency should be well-defined.
6. The hotel should work closely with the police to keep them updated.
7. Chamber maids and HK supervisors should be trained to conduct security checks in the guest rooms.

Security measures for women travelers

- Mirrored walls of the guestroom floor elevators so that you can see who is walking behind you
- Well-lit public areas such a s lobby bars
- Valet parking services to avoid the need o a woman to enter the parking lot
- Assigning rooms closer to the elevator
- If a woman traveler is not assigned a room on the special executive floor, hotels most often on request, upgrade her accommodation to that floor without an increase in room rate. The floor is staffed almost 24 hours a day with a concierge

Safety issues

When we take the same hotel as example, it is management's duty to ensure "safety" in several areas, such as:

- The structure itself
- Installations and fixtures (check electrical, plumbing, air-conditioning and other installations)
- Public and work areas (e.g. slippery floors, hazardous obstacles in traffic areas), safety of furniture, equipment, appliances, and utensils.

This is followed by:

- Health safety (nontoxic cleaning material and detergents used)
- Good quality air (what we breathe, dependent upon the type of equipment, installations and fixtures used, and regular repairs and maintenance)

- Food safety (a whole world in itself including sanitation, food quality, food spoilage, correct handling procedures, allowable and recommended temperatures, etc.), and checking and control procedures.

An important "preventive measure" is eliminating the possibility of communicating contagious diseases. Even if local regulations do not require it, it is recommended to send food and beverage handlers for a regular medical checkup. Another preventive measure is the formulation and implementation of policies and procedures related to employee accidents which may present a threat to food sanitation.

Culinary staff who cut themselves accidentally at work, as often happens while slicing food products, have to immediately stop handling food, and report to their Executive Chef and to the person in charge of First Aid in their company (Security or Human Resources Department) for preliminary treatment and handling. Healing and precautionary measures are taken before they are allowed back at their job.

There are also some basic "dress" requirements for staff involved in food and beverage preparations: e.g. Chefs' hats (to prevent hair and whatever hair contains to fall into the food), discreet earrings (non-dangling) or no earrings for women, and long hair neatly and securely tied in a bun at the back of the head.

Of no lesser importance is the safety of work tools and work procedures covering all areas, such as stable ladders, secure shelving, safety shoes, well-fitting work garments, clearly written and complete safety procedures and guidelines from management, safety training, and safety installations and equipment, e.g. fire fighting units, regular maintenance schedules for safety equipment and installations, wider traffic areas (to prevent accidents), adequate staffing, and last but not least, continuous effective training in work procedures.

All of this necessitates comprehensive planning, the creation of clear policies and work procedures, organization, implementation, training of supervisors and employees, supervision and control.

FIRES

Fires in the hotel may result in the injury and loss of life of both the guests and the staff.

Main causes of fire are:

I) Smoking:

- Smoke only where allowed.
- Put out cigarettes in the right place.
- Sufficient ash trays should be provided in eating places and in rooms, but away from curtains and draperies.
- Educate the guests about fire possibilities due to smoking.

ii) Defective wiring, faulty appliances and motor and worn out insulation

Such hazards should be immediately reported to the concerned person and such equipment should be immediately repaired

iii) Laundry Areas:

Care should be taken to see that none of the electrical equipment is left on after use

iv) Gas leaks:

Precautions should be taken against this especially in kitchen areas.

v) Combustible waste

Combustible material should never b e left near the boiler room

vi) Kitchen

All equipment such as chimneys, exhausts, ventilators, grills, and hoods etc. which collect a lot of fume vapor and catch fire easily should be cleaned regularly.

vii) Elevator shafts

These require constant check and inspection. Cigarette butts can ignite the debris and oils that gather at the bottom of elevator shafts.

Types of Fire and Fire Extinguishers

Hotel personnel are trained about the fire protection procedure and the types of fire. They must be able to recognize the various types of fire, all fire require air. Air contains O_2 which is necessary for combustion. Fire has been classified in 5 categories depending on how they can be extinguished-

Class A Fire

It is the fire of wood, paper, linen and similar dry materials. They are extinguished by cooling and quenching effect of water. The water reduces the temperature of burning substances below their combustion temperature. These are the most frequent and easiest to extinguish when there is an ample water supply and when water can be directed on the combustible material .Keeping the other combustible material wet will limit the spreading of fire

Class B Fire

These include fires of oil, gasoline, grease and other petroleum product. These fires are extinguished by blanketing the source of burning substances and eliminating the supply of O_2. Petroleum products is lighter than water and will float on water and continue to burn and spread by means of flowing water to other section of the building, hence water is never used for this category.

Class C Fire

These are the fires of pressurized gases. For e.g. L.P.G., most of the gases are lighter than air but L.P.G. is heavier than air. Water is not to be used for this class of fire.

Class D Fire

These are fire of metals having low burning temperature for e. g. Na, Mg etc. This class of fire does not exist in the hotel.

Class E Fire

These are electrical fire. The fire extinguishing agent must not conduct electrical energy which could spread the fire. Electrical fires are usually blanketed and cooled down. Water is a good cooling agent but it also conducts electricity, so it is not used to control or extinguish this class of fire. Electrical fire is usually caused by a part of circuit overheating or by short circuit. Controlling the sizes of electrical fuses and circuit breaker will often minimize this class of fire.

There are 2 systems of fire protection:

1. Portable fire extinguisher.
2. Stationary fire fighting system.

Portable Fire Extinguisher

a. **Soda acid fire extinguisher:** It is used for class A fire. The extinguishing agent is H_2O.The fire extinguisher is a cylinder type of pan in which a rubber or flexible hose is attached to the top. When it is desired to use the extinguisher, it is carried to the fire and inverted. A small bottle of acid usually H_2SO_4 is spilled when the cylinder is inverted or turn upside down. Powdered sodas, bicarbonate of soda (Baking Soda) is mixed with H2O when the tank is charge or fills with water. The chemical reaction of acid and soda water creates a pressure which forces the water out of the cylinder or tank. The hose is used to direct the flow of water to the fire. It has 2 disadvantages:

- It must be kept away from freezing
- Acid causes corrogen problem which reduce the life of the tank or cylinder. The corrogen problem has been minimized by replacing the acid with CO_2 cartridge. Upon the cylinder inversion the cartridge opens and releases CO_2 gas under high pressure. The high pressure gas than forces the water out of cylinder.

b. **$CaCl_2$ fire extinguisher:** It is also used on class A fire. . $CaCl_2$ is a salt which when added to water form brine which has very low freezing temperature. CO_2 cartridge is used as pressure agent to force H_2O and $CaCl_2$ out of the cylinder to the fire. These extinguishers are used where freezing is a potential hazard

c. **Foam type extinguisher:** It is used on class B type of fire. The extinguisher is charged with special chemical (Al_2SiO_4), the chemical spread on the burning material and the solution, blanket the fire by excluding O_2.

d. **CO_2 fire extinguisher:** It is used on C, D and E class of fire. The CO_2 types spray a chemical fog towards the fire. The fog quickly excludes the O_2 from the burning material and blanket the combustible material.

e. **D.C.P. extinguisher:** It can be used on C, D and E class of fire. The most common extinguishing agent is sodium bicarbonate or plain baking soda. The extinguisher is charged with the dry chemical and a small tank of CO_2 gas. The CO_2 gas exerts pressure on dry chemical and forces it out of a nozzle directly to the fire. The powder strict the fire and the heat from the fire breaks down the chemical which releases CO_2 gas on a large scale which helps in extinguishing the fire.

Stationary Fire Fighting System

a. **Automatic sprinklers:** It is generally mounted just below the ceiling height with a temperature detector or smoke detector, attached with each sprinkler. The temperature from the fire melts the fusible link on the detector, which opens a water valve. The water is then sprayed on the ceiling and falls on the floor, extinguishing the fire. If the fire area should spread, more sprinklers are automatically opened, thus confining the fire to a small area. The temperature detector can be purchased for different activating temperature. The high temperature detectors are often used in kitchens.

b. **Fire Hose System:** It is a semi portable system. In this system the fire hose box is permanently located but the flexible hose can be moved to various distances throughout the building. The hose used to fight fire within a building should be of linen type. The linen allows some water seepage through it which will prevent its burning when in use.

HANDLING EMERGENCY SITUATIONS

Apart from fire and bomb threat etc. the front office staff at some point of time have to handle a lot of unusual situations also. Some such situations may be death and illness of guests, theft in hotels etc and many others.

1) Death of a guest in the hotel:

- Once the information comes to the front desk it should directly be reported to the front office manager.
- The front office manager will then report it to the GM or resident manager
- The security manager should also be informed immediately
- The police is informed and the hotel doctor is summoned who will check and confirm the death
- Meanwhile the hotel will locate the residential address of the deceased and will inform the relatives.
- Once the police complete all formalities and activities and gives the permission, the dead body is fully covered and then removed from the room on a stretcher. For this purpose the service elevator and not the guest elevator is used
- A death certificate is obtained from the doctor
- A report should be prepared as to who informed of the death, time, room number and date of death. In case there is any luggage of the deceased in the room a list should be prepared and the luggage should be kept in the luggage room and the person performing this activity should sign this report
- The guest room is locked and sealed.
- After obtaining clearance from the police the room is opened and thoroughly disinfected and spring cleaned and only after permission of the police and subsequent permission of the GM or resident manager the room should be sold.

Some important facts to be kept in mind are:

- Do not enter the room alone always take the lobby manager and security officer with you
- In case you are aware that the deceased was under the treatment of a specific doctor, the same should be called instead of the hotel doctor. His physician will also be helpful in knowing and notifying the incident to the relatives and people known to him
- Do not disturb the body or touch anything before the arrival of the police as this may be a murder or suicide case.

2) Handling accident cases:

- Knowledge of first aid would come very handy in such situations. In general the following points should be taken care of :
- Remove the person who has met with accident from the site of accident {as early as possible and take him to a more comfortable area, use a stretcher in case the need be}.4
- Call the doctor and if possible give him the details of accident and gravity of the accident.
- Take someone along with you to the site of the accident as you may need help
- Keep alert you must serve the victim immediately by providing first aid
- Try to protect your establishment from any false allegations

Prepare a full report of the whole accident giving details of the date and time who reported the incident, room no., site of the accident etc. Also make your comments as to the reason of the accident and how could it have been prevented and what action is to be taken to avoid the same in the future.

The Accident Book

- An accident book is usually maintained in all organizations and the receptionist should record all details of accidents which have occurred to employees whilst carrying out their daily activities.
- The book must be kept in a place easily accessible by any injured person or a person bona fide
- Particulars of an accident may be entered here in either by the injured person himself or by a person acting on his behalf

- The accident book when filled up should be preserved for a period of three years after the date of the last entry
- Every employer is required to take steps to investigate the circumstances of the accident recorded and if there happens to be any discrepancy between the circumstances found by him and the entry made, he is required to record the circumstances so found.

3) Situation of Theft:

Theft is divided into four categories:

I. **Theft by employees of the hotel** can be avoided by:

- Work business and personal references should be checked before the employee is hired.
- A detailed record of all employees who enter the guest room such as chamber maids bellboys room boys maintenance etc
- All hotel keys should be returned to the department concerned and no employee should be allowed to take keys out of the hotel's premises.

II. **Damage of hotel property by the guest** can be avoided by:

- The hotel staff should identify the main cause for the damage.
- If the damage is appears to be done intentionally the hotel can ask the guest to pay compensation for the same. For this it is necessary that the front desk is well versed with the cost of the damaged item.

III. **Theft of hotel property by the guest:**

Can be avoided by taking the following steps:

- Installing automatic locks on the guest room doors
- Appointing a security officer who would walk and take rounds at regular intervals
- Inform guests to use the safe vault of the hotel and not to keep valuables in the guest room
- Keep a watch on walk in as their likelihood of being a thief is more as compared to a guest who has undergone a process of making a reservation in the hotel
- Avoid giving room numbers of resident guests to visitors or over the telephone callers.

- In case the guest loses his key and asks housekeeping to open the room door for them, HK should direct them to front desk
- Master key should be kept under strict supervision and control

Theft by outside visitors can be avoided by:

- Being aware of suspicious persons
- Regular and irregular schedule of vigil and rounds
- Stagger lunch and rest periods of employees so as to keep one person on duty on each floor at all times
- Instruct eh telephone operator not to connect calls to the guest room in case the request is made by the caller by room number. The receptionist should insist on knowing the name of the guest who the caller wishes to speak to.
- Guest should be informed to keep the balcony door closed to avoid anyone entering the rooms from the balcony
- Closed circuit televisions should be used

4) Situation of illness and epidemics:

- The receptionist may be called for assistance during sickness of a guest.
- Patient should be advised to consult the house physician but in case the guest has his own physician the same should be called.
- Housekeeping needs to be notified about the sickness and instructions if any
- If the case of serious sickness, the guest should be moved to a nursing home
- During epidemics all precautionary measures especially in food and beverage service area should be followed

5) Handling a drunken guest:

- The guest should be removed from the lobby as early as possible but being careful not to irritate/offend him.
- Preferably taken to the back office or to his room.
- If he behaves unruly, the hotel security must be called.

QUESTIONNAIRE

1. What is Safety and Security System? Write the importance of security system.
2. Write different types of security?
3. What is Fire? Explain main causes of fire.
4. Explain different types of fire and fire extinguishers.
5. Write some security measures taken by hotel?
6. Explain five handling emergency situations.
7. Why Key Control is important in reference to safety and security of guest.
8. Classify the staff use keys into different parts and explain to each in brief.
9. Write a short note on Electronic key card.
10. Classify the internal threats that can occur into different parts of hotels and give steps to avoid threads.
11. Write down step by step procedure which you require to follow in case of bomb threat in hotel.

21

FRENCH USED IN FRONT OFFICE OPERATION INTERMEDIATE FRENCH

- FRENCH PHRASES, GRAMMAR AND VOCABULARY
- 25 MOST USED FRENCH PHRASES
- WORDS USED IN HOTELS
- WORDS USED FOR DAILY PURPOSES
- GENERAL FRENCH TERMS USED IN HOTELS

FRENCH PHRASES, GRAMMAR AND VOCABULARY

1. S'il vous plaît **(see-voo-play)** - *please*
2. Je suis **(zheu swee)** – I am
3. Je cherche **(zheu share-sh)** – *I'm looking for*
4. Je veux **(zheu veu)** – *I want*
5. Un hôtel**(ern otell)** – *A hotel*
6. Une chambre **(une shombre)** - *A room*
7. Manger **(mon-zhay)** - *To eat*
8. Boire **(bwar)** – *to drink*
9. Payer **(pay-yeh)** – *to pay*
10. Acheter **(ash-tay)** – *to buy*
11. Petit-déjeuner **(peuti – dayzheurnay)** - *Breakfast*
12. Diner **(dee-nay)** - *Dinner*
13. Un demi **(ern deu-mee)** – *A half pint of draught beer*
14. Un verre **(ern vair)** - *a glass*
15. De l'eau **(deu-lo)** - *some water*
16. Un thé (au lait)**(ern tay olay)** - *a tea (with milk)*
17. La toilette **(lar twa-lette)** - *the washroom, toilet.*
18. Prix **(pree)** - *price*
19. Carte de crédit **(kart deu cray-dee)** - *Credit card*
20. Une banque **(une bonk)** – *A bank*
21. Des magasins **(day magga-zan)** - *Shops*
22. Un supermarché **(ern supair-mar-shay)** – *A supermarket*
23. La gare **(lar gar)** – *The train station*
24. L'aeroport**(l'aero-por)** – *the airport*
25. Une voiture **(une vwa-tiure)** – *a car.*

25 MOST USED FRENCH PHRASES

1. Bonjour. **(bon-zhour)** *Hello*
2. Merci. **(mair-see)** *Thankyou*

3. Au revoir. **(oh-reu-vwar)** *Goodbye*
4. Je ne comprends pas. **(zheu neu kompron par** *I don't understand*
5. Je ne parle pas français. **(zheu neu parl par fron-say)**
   I don't speak French
6. Pouvez vous parler plus lentement, s'il vous plait
   (poo-vay-voo par-lay ploo lontermon)
   Could you speak more slowly, please.
7. Pouvez-vous répéter, s'il vous plaît.
   (poo-vay-voo ray-pay-tay, see-voo-play)
   Could you repeat that please.
8. S'il vous plaît, je cherche......
   (see-voo-play, zheu share-sh ......)
   Please, I'm looking for (whatever you are looking for).
9. Avez-vous.... **(avay -voo)** *Do you have.... ?*
10. Avez-vous une chambre pour deux personnes?
    (avay -voo une shombre poor deuh pair-sonn)
    Do you have a room for two ?
11. A quelle heure est-ce que cela ferme ?
    (a kel eure esk slar fairme)
    When does it shut ?
12. Combien ça coûte ?
    (kom-bjanne sar coot)
    How much is it ?
13. Ou sont les toilettes, s'il vous plaît ?
    (oo son lay twar-let, see-voo-play
    Where is the toilet / washroom, please ?
14. Ou est-ce qu'on peut trouver des restaurants, s'il vous plaît?
    (oo esk on peu troo-vay day resto-ron, see-voo-play)
    Where are there some restaurants, please ?

15. Un café et un café au lait, s'il vous plaît.
    (ern caffay ay ern caffay olay, see-voo-play)
    One black coffee, and one white coffee please.
16. L'addition, s'il vous plaît.
    (lad-eesi-onsee-voo-play)
    Could I have the bill please.
17. A l'aeroport, s'il vous plaît. **(ar l'aeropor see-voo-play)**
    To the airport, please.
18. Une table pour deux / quatre personnes.
    (oon tarbleu poor deuh /cat-r pair-son)
    A table for two / for four.
19. Je ne me sens pas bien.**(zheu neu meu son par bjanne)**
    I'm not feeling very well.
20. Nous sommes perdus.**(noo som pair-dju)**
    We're lost.
21. Nous voulons aller à .... **(noo voolon allay are...)**
    We want to go to (wherever you want to go).
22. Je cherche un distributeur de billets.
    (zheu share-sh ern dee-stree-beaut-eur deu bee-ay)
    I'm looking for an ATM / cash dispenser.
23. Pouvez-vous m'appeler un taxi, s'il vous plaît ;
    (poovay voo maplay ern taxi see-voo-play)
    Could you please call me a cab.
24. Nous sommes très pressés / en retard.
    (noo som tray pressay / on retar)
    We're in a great hurry / late.
25. Quel temps va-t-il faire aujourd'hui?
    (kel tom vartil fair oh-zhour-dwee)
    What's the weather going to be like today?

WORDS USED IN HOTELS

English	French	Pronunciation
Bar	le bar	*luh bahr*
Bellhop	le bagagiste	*luh bah-gah-zheest*
Business center	le centre d'affaires	*luh sahNtr dah-fehr*
Concierge (caretaker)	le (la) concierge	*luh (lah) kohN-syehrzh*
Doorman	le portier	*luh pohr-tyay*
Elevator	l'ascenseur *m.*	*lah-sahN-suhr*
Fitness center	le club santé	*luh klewb sahN-tay*
Gift shop	la boutique	*lah boo-teek*
Maid service	la gouvernante	*lah goo-vehr-nahNt*
Restaurant	le restaurant	*luh rehs-toh-rahN*
Staircase	l'escalier *m.*	*lehs-kahl-yay*
Swimming pool	la piscine	*lah pee-seen*
Valet parking	l'attendance du garage *f.*	*lah-tahN-dahNs dew gah-rahzh*

WORDS USED FOR DAILY PURPOSES

If you need something to make your stay more enjoyable, don't be afraid to speak up. Here are a few items you might want or need:

I would like ...	Je voudrais ...	*zhuh voo-dreh*
I need ...	Il me faut ...	*eel muh foh*
I need ...	J'ai besoin de (d') ...	*zhay buh zwaN duh*
Please send me ...	Veuillez m'envoyer ...	*vuh-yay mahN-vwah-yay*
There isn't (aren't) ...	Il n'y a pas de ...	*eel nyah pah duh*

Don't forget to show good manners by using the following phrases:

Please	s'il vous plaît	*seel voo pleh*
thank you very much	merci beaucoup	*mehr-see bo-koo*
you're welcome	de rien	*duh ryaN*
you're welcome	pas de quoi	*pahd kwah*
don't mention it	Je vous en prie	*zhuh voo zahN pree*

GENERAL FRENCH TERMS USED IN HOTELS

English	French	Pronunciation
air conditioning	la climatisation	*lah klee-mah-tee-zah-syohN*
an ashtray	un cendrier	*uhN sahN-dree-yay*
a balcony	un balcon	*uhN bahl-kohN*
a bar of soap	une savonnette	*ewn sah-voh-neht*
a bathroom	une salle de bains	*ewn sahl duh baN*
a blanket	une couverture	*ewn koo-vehr-tewr*
a hair dryer	un sèche-cheveux	*uhN sehsh shuh-vuh*
Hangers	des cintres	*day saNtr*
a key	une clé	*ewn klay*
ice cubes	des glaçons	*deh glah-sohN*
some mineral water	de l'eau minérale	*duh lo mee-nay-rahl*
a pillow	un oreiller	*uhN noh-reh-yay*
a safe (deposit box)	un coffre	*uhN kohfr*
a shower	une douche	*ewn doosh*
a single (double) room	une chambre à un (deux) lit(s)	*ewn shahNbr ah uhN (duh) lee*
on the courtyard	côté cour	*koh-tay koor*
on the garden	côté jardin	*koh-tay zhahr-daN*
on the sea	côté mer	*koh-tay mehra*
Telephone	un téléphone	*uhN tay-lay-fohn*
a television	une télévision	*ewn tay-lay-vee-zyohN*
(color)	(en couleurs)	*(ahN koo-luhr)*
(flat screen)	(écran plat)	*(ay-krahN plah)*
(large screen)	(grand écran)	*(grahN tay-krahN)*
Tissues	des mouchoirs en papier	*day moo-shwahr ahN pah-pyay*
toilet paper (roll)	un rouleau de papier hygiénique	*uhN roo-lo duh pah-pyay ee-zhyay-neek*
a towel	une serviette	*ewn sehr-vyeht*
a beach towel	un drap de bain	*uhN drah duh baN*
a transformer	un transformateur	*uhN trahNz-fohr-mah-tuhr*

SECTION 3

22

PLANNING & EVALUATING FRONT OFFICE OPERATION

- FRENCH PHRASES, GRAMMAR AND VOCABULARY
- INTRODUCTION
- MANAGEMENT FUNCTIONS
- FORECASTING TECHNIQUES
- BENEFITS OF FORECASTING
- FORECASTING ROOM AVAILABILITY
- FORECASTING DATA
- PERCENTAGE OF NO-SHOWS
- PERCENTAGE OF WALK-INS
- PERCENTAGE OF OVER-STAYS
- PERCENTAGE OF UNDER-STAYS
- FORECAST FORMULA
- SAMPLE FORECAST FORMS
- TEN DAY FORECAST
- THREE DAY FORECAST

INTRODUCTION

According to experts planning and evaluation depends upon on manager's experience and knowledge of the organization and a particular departments. The managers collect data from the past experience which helps manager in planning and evaluation for future. The data is in the form of reports, information, etc. And managers evaluate these data in the form of reports, charts, diagram, curves, line, pie chart etc. According to me perfect planning depends upon the collection of data and its evaluation etc. The comparison can be made in form of percentage figures graphs curves pie chart line etc. The use of historic data to determine the direction of future trends. Forecasting is used by companies to determine how to allocate their budgets for an upcoming period of time. This is typically based on demand for the goods and services it offers, compared to the cost of producing them. Investors utilize forecasting to determine if events affecting a company, such as sales expectations, will increase or decrease the price of shares in that company. Forecasting also provides an important benchmark for firms which have a long-term perspective of operations.

A planning tool that helps management in its attempts to cope with the uncertainty of the future, relying mainly on data from the past and present and analysis of trends. Forecasting starts with certain assumptions based on the management's experience, knowledge, and judgment. These estimates are projected into the coming months or years using one or more techniques such as Box-Jenkins models, Delphi method, exponential smoothing, moving averages, regression analysis, and trend projection.

MANAGEMENT FUNCTIONS

The 4 basic management functions that make up the management process are described in the following sections:

1. PLANNING
2. ORGANIZING
3. INFLUENCING
4. CONTROLLING.

PLANNING

Planning involves choosing tasks that must be performed to attain organizational goals, outlining how the tasks must be performed, and indicating when they should be performed. Planning activity focuses on attaining **goals.**

Managers outline exactly what organizations should do to be successful. Planning is concerned with the success of the organization in the short term as well as in the long term.

ORGANIZING

Organizing can be thought of as assigning the tasks developed in the planning stages, to various individuals or groups within the organization. Organizing is to create a mechanism to put plans into action. People within the organization are given work assignments that contribute to the company's goals. Tasks are organized so that the output of each individual contributes to the success of departments, which, in turn, contributes to the success of divisions, which ultimately contributes to the success of the organization.

INFLUENCING

Influencing is also referred to as motivating, Leading or directing. Influencing can be defined as guiding the activities of organization members in he direction that helps the organization move towards the fulfillment of the goals. The purpose of influencing is to increase productivity. Human-oriented work situations usual generate higher levels of production over the long term than do task oriented work situations because people find the latter type distasteful.

CONTROLLING

Controlling is the following roles played by the manager:

1. Gather information that measures performance
2. Compare present performance to pre established performance norms.
3. Determine the next action plan and modifications for meeting the desired performance parameters.

Controlling is an ongoing process.

A. Forecasting Techniques

Forecasting means to say what will probably happen in the future. Thus forecasting is the predication of future happenings based on the precise analysis of the data available for the past rather than guess work. Forecasting plays a very important role in the Short Term Planning.

B. Benefits of Forecasting

In the hotel industry, reservation forecasting is very useful in the following ways.

1. It helps the reservation manager to project the future volume of business and the revenue that would be generated by the hotel.
2. The volume of the hotel reservation will help the FOM and the management to plan the following things-
   - Staff required in each department for the smooth functioning of the hotel
   - Minimum inventory of items required by each department to carry out their *tasks effectively*
   - Allocation of resources to serve the guests in the hotel in the best possible way.

C. Forecasting Room Availability

The most important short-term planning that front office managers do is **forecasting** the number of rooms available for future reservations. *Room availability forecasts* are used to help manage the reservations process and guide front office staff in effective rooms management. Forecasting may be especially important on nights when a full house (100 percent occupancy) is possible.

A room availability forecast can also be used as occupancy *forecast*. Since there is a fixed number of rooms in the hotel, forecasting the number of rooms available for sale and the number of rooms expected to be occupied forecasts the occupancy percentage expected on a given date. The forecasted availability and occupancy numbers are very important to the daily operations of the hotel. Occupancy forecasts are the foundation for making room pricing decisions. They also influence when rooms are to be placed on out-of-order status for maintenance or deep cleaning. Without an accurate forecast, rooms may go unsold or be sold at inappropriate rates. Room occupancy forecasts can be useful to the front office manager attempting to schedule the necessary number of employees for an expected volume of business. These forecasts may be helpful to other hotel department managers as well. For example, the housekeeping department manager needs to know how many rooms the front office expects to be occupied to properly schedule room attendants. Restaurant managers must know the same information to better schedule service staff. The chef requires this figure to determine how much food to purchase for the restaurants.

Obviously, a forecast is only as reliable as the information on which it is based. Since forecasts can serve as a guide in determining operating costs, every effort should be made to ensure forecasting accuracy.

Forecasting is a difficult skill to develop. The skill is acquired through experience, effective recordkeeping, and accurate counting methods. Experienced front office managers have found that several types of information can be helpful in room availability forecasting:

- A thorough knowledge of the hotel and its surrounding area
- Market profiles of the constituencies the hotel serves
- Occupancy data for the past several months and for the same period of the previous year
- Reservation trends and a history of reservation lead times (how far in advance reservations are made)
- A listing of special events scheduled in the surrounding geographic area
- Business and historical profiles of specific groups booked for the forecast dates
- The number of non-guaranteed and guaranteed reservations and an estimate of the number of expected no-shows
- The percentage of rooms already reserved and the cut-off date for group room blocks held for the forecast dates
- The room availability of the most important competing hotels for the forecast dates (as discovered through blind calls)
- The impact of citywide or multi-hotel groups and their potential influence on the forecast dates
- Plans for remodeling or renovating the hotel that would change the number of available rooms
- Construction or renovating plans for competitive hotels in the area

Forecasting Data

The process of forecasting room availability generally relies on historical occupancy data as well as business already committed. Historical data is used to take some of the guesswork out of forecasting. To facilitate forecasting, the following daily occupancy data should be collected:

- Number of expected room arrivals: based on existing reservations and historical trends for new reservations and on cancellations prior to the arrival date.

- Number of expected room walk-ins: based on historical records.
- Number of expected room stayovers (rooms occupied on previous nights that will continue to be occupied for the night in question): based on existing reservations.
- Number of expected room no-shows: based on historical records.
- Number of expected room under-stays (check-outs occurring before expected departure date): based on historical data.
- Number of expected room check-outs: based on existing reservations.
- Number of expected room overstays (check-outs occurring after the originally reserved departure date): based on historical records.

Some hotels with a very high double occupancy percentage may be as concerned with guest counts as room counts. For example, an all-inclusive resort with a large amount of business from vacationing couples may want to forecast guest as well as room count activity. Convention hotels may often have the same concerns. Chances are good that much of this information is available in reports, documents, and other data sources at the property. The hotel's daily reports will likely be invaluable in this research. These reports should be summarized and stored in a way that is easily accessible.

Occupancy History First Week of March						
Day	**Date**	**Guests**	**Room Arrivals**	**Room Walk-Ins**	**Room Reservations**	**Room No-Shows**
Mon	3/1	118	70	13	63	6
Tues	3/2	145	55	15	48	8
Wed	3/3	176	68	16	56	4
Thurs	3/4	117	53	22	48	17
Fri	3/5	75	35	8	35	8
Sat	3/6	86	28	6	26	4
Sun	3/7	49	17	10	12	5
Total		766	326	90	288	52
Occupied Rooms		**Overstay Rooms**		**Understay Rooms**		**Room Check-Outs**
90		6		0		30
115		10		3		30

120	12	6	63
95	3	18	78
50	7	0	80
58	6	3	20
30	3	3	45
558	47	33	346

Overall, these data are important to room availability forecasting, since they are used in calculating various daily operating ratios that help determine the number of available rooms for sale. Ratios are a mathematical expression of a relationship between two numbers that is determined by dividing one by the other. Most statistical ratios that apply to front office operations are expressed as percentages. The ratios examined in the following sections are percentages of no-shows, walk-ins, overstays, and under stays. Occupancy history data from the fictitious property shown in Exhibit 7 (the Holly Hotel) are used to illustrate the calculation of each front office ratio. Managers should look for consistency in ratios. Consistency may be roughly the same ratio every day or identifiable patterns. Without consistency, forecasting ratios and projecting operating performance may be very difficult.

1. Percentage of No-Shows. The percentage of no-shows indicates the proportion of reserved rooms that the expected guests did not arrive to occupy (and did not cancel) on the expected arrival date. This ratio helps the front office manager decide when (and if) to sell already-committed rooms to walk-in guests.

The percentage of no-shows is calculated by dividing the number of room no-shows for a specific period of time (day, week, month, or year) by the total number of room reservations for the same period. Using figures from Exhibit 7, the percentage of no-shows for the Holly Hotel during the first week of March can be calculated as follows:

2. Percentage of No-Shows

$$\text{Percentage of No-Shows} = \frac{\text{Number of Room No-Shows}}{\text{Number of Room Reservations}}$$

$$= \frac{52}{288}$$

$$= .1806 \text{ or } 18.06\% \text{ of Reserved Rooms}$$

Some properties track no-show statistics in relation to guaranteed and non-guaranteed reservations. Non-guaranteed reservations typically have a higher no-show percentage than guaranteed reservations, since the potential guest has no obligation to pay for the accommodations if he or she does not register at the property. Properly incorporating no-show allowances into room availability forecasts also depends on the hotel's mix of business; for example, corporate groups generally have a much lower no-show percentage than do other types of groups or individual guests. A hotel that works with a large corporate meetings market will most likely have a low no-show percentage. Conversely, a hotel with very little corporate group business, such as a hotel located in a suburban area alongside an interstate highway, is likely to have a much higher percentage of no-show reservations since guests desire flexibility in their travel plans. Hotels and resorts strive to control no-shows through a number of policies and procedures, such as requiring a cash or credit card deposit in advance of the stay and/or contacting the guest before arrival to confirm travel and room arrangements.

3. Percentage of Walk-Ins. The percentage of walk-ins is calculated by dividing the number of rooms occupied by walk-ins for a period by the total number of room arrivals for the same period. Using figures from Exhibit 7, the percentage of walk-ins for the Holly Hotel during the first week of March can be calculated as follows:

$$\text{Percentage of Walk-Ins} = \frac{\text{Number of Room Walk-Ins}}{\text{Number of Room Walk-Ins}}$$

$$= \frac{90}{326}$$

$$= .2761 \text{ or } 27.61\% \text{ of Room Arrivals}$$

Walk-in guests occupy available rooms that are not held for guests with reservations. Often, hotels can sell rooms to walk-in guests at a higher rate, since these guests may have less opportunity to consider alternate properties. Front desk agents are sometimes asked to show a guestroom to a walk-in guest—which tends to be much more effective than trying to sell rooms over the telephone or through a website. Walk-in guest sales help improve both occupancy and room revenues. However, from a planning perspective, it is generally better to have reservations in advance than to count on walk-in traffic.

Note that other ratios can dramatically affect the walk-in ratio. For example, if a hotel has ten no-shows beyond forecast, it may accept more walk-ins than usual to make up for the lost business. When this information is tracked for historical purposes, it is essential that the other ratios also be tracked to show how they affect one another. One effective way to predict walk-ins is to know what is going on in the marketplace. There will be a better opportunity for walk-ins (and a higher rate) if nearby hotels are experiencing high demand.

4. Percentage of Overstays. Overstays represent rooms occupied by guests who stay beyond their originally scheduled departure dates. Overstay guests may have arrived with guaranteed or non-guaranteed reservations or as walk-ins. Overstays should not be confused with **stayovers**. Stayover rooms are rooms occupied by guests who arrived to occupy a room before the day in question and whose *scheduled* departure date isn't until after the day in question.

Using historical data, the percentage of overstays is calculated by dividing the actual number of overstay rooms for a day or a period by the total number of *expected* room check-outs for the same day or period. The number of expected room check-outs is the number of rooms shown by the front office system or the manual count of occupied rooms as due for departure. Stated another way, the number of expected room check-outs can be calculated from historical data as the number of actual departures on the books minus under-stays plus overstays. Note that in this case, the term *under-stays* refers to people checking out early on the day in question, *not* to those guests who were *originally scheduled* to leave on the day in question but who chose to check out one or more days early. For purposes of this equation, those latter guests would be considered under-stays on the day they checked out.

Overstays and under-stays can be determined for periods beyond one day by summing the actual overstay and under-stay counts calculated separately for each day within the longer period. Using figures from Exhibit 7, the percentage of overstays for the Holly Hotel during the first week of March can be calculated as follows:

$$\text{Percentage of Overstays} = \frac{\text{Number of Overstay Room}}{\text{Number of expected check-outs}}$$

$$= \frac{47}{346 - 33 + 47}$$

$$= 1306 \text{ or } 13.06\% \text{ of Expected Check-Outs}$$

To help regulate room overstays, front office agents are trained to verify an arriving guest's departure date at check-in. Such verification can be critical, especially when the hotel is at or near full occupancy and there are no provisions for overstay guests. Overstays may also prove problematic when specific rooms have been blocked for arriving guests. This is especially important for suites or other rooms that may have special importance to an incoming guest.

5. Percentage of Under-stays. Under-stays represent rooms occupied by guests who check out before their originally scheduled departure dates. Under-stay guests may have arrived at the hotel with guaranteed or non-guaranteed reservations or as walk-ins.

The percentage of under-stays is calculated by dividing the number of under-stay rooms for a day or period by the total number of expected room check-outs for the same day or period. Using the same approach as that just described for determining the percentage of overstays, the under-stays are counted as under-stays only on the day of their early check-out, and under-stay counts should be determined separately and summed for each day in a multi-day period. Using figures from Exhibit 7, the percentage of under-stays for the Holly Hotel during the first week of March can be calculated as follows:

$$\text{Percentage of Under-stay Rooms} = \frac{\text{Number of Under-stay Rooms}}{\text{Number of expected check-outs}}$$

$$= \frac{33}{346 - 33 + 47}$$

$$= .0917 \text{ or } 9.17\% \text{ of Expected Check-Outs}$$

Guests leaving before their stated departure date create empty rooms that typically are difficult to fill. Thus, under-stay rooms may represent permanently lost room revenue. Overstays, on the other hand, are guests staying beyond their stated departure date and may boost room revenues. When the hotel is not operating at full capacity, overstays result in additional, unexpected room revenues. In an attempt to regulate under-stay and overstay rooms, front office staff should:

- Confirm or reconfirm each guest's departure date at registration. Some guests may already know of a change in plans, or a mistake may have been made in the original processing of the reservation. The sooner erroneous data are corrected, the greater the chance for improved planning.
- Present an alternate guestroom reservation form to a registered guest, explaining that an arriving guest holds a reservation for his or her

assigned room. A note card may be placed in the guest's room the day before or the morning of the scheduled day of the registered guest's departure.

- Review group history. Many groups, especially associations, hold large closing events for the entire group on the last day of the meeting. Guests may make reservations to include attending the final event. However, changes in plans or other priorities may require guests to leave early. While it is difficult for the hotel to hold guests to the number of nights they reserved, managers may be better able to plan for early departures, based on the group's departure history. Some hotels that have a lot of association business or a history of transient guests departing before their scheduled date may apply the reservation deposit to the last night of the stay, not the first night.
- Contact potential overstay guests about their scheduled departure date to confirm their intention to check out. Room occupancy data should be examined each day; rooms with guests expected to check out should be flagged. Guests who have not left by check-out time should be contacted and asked about their departure intentions. This procedure permits an early revised count of overstays and allows sufficient time to modify previous front office planning, if necessary.

7. Room Occupancy and Percentage

Total no. of room sold on a particular day is called room occupancy and percentage in relation to the total no. of rooms available for sale is termed as Room Occupancy Percentage. It is compared with budgeted room occupancy percentage and with the previous years to know the financial health of the hotel

$$\textbf{Room Occupancy and Percentage} = \frac{\text{No. of Rooms sold} \times 100}{\text{Total no. of lettable Rooms}}$$

8. House Count and Percentage

Total number of guests staying for the night is termed as House Count. The percentage of the house count is calculated in relation to the maximum number of guests who stay in the lettable rooms.

$$\textbf{House Count Percentage} = \frac{\text{Total number of guests staying} \times 100}{\text{Guests who can stay in the total lettable rooms}}$$

9. Multiple Occupancy and Percentage

The rooms sold to more than one person are termed as multiple occupancy. To know the multiple occupancy rooms the total rooms occupied are deducted from the total number of guests staying in the hotel.

$$\textbf{Multiple Occupancy Percentage} = \frac{\text{Multiple occupancy} \times 100}{\text{Total rooms occupied}}$$

10. Average Room Rate

Total room sale divided by total rooms sold is the average room rate. It is the room tariff earned per day per occupied room. It can be for a day, a month, season, off season, a year etc.

$$\textbf{Average Room Rate} = \frac{\text{Total Room Revenue}}{\text{Total no. of rooms sold}}$$

11. Revenue Per Available Room (Rev Par)

Total revenue earned is divided with the total number of lettable rooms to know the revenue per available room. Revenue per available room will be less than average room revenue unless cent percent occupancy is attained.

$$\textbf{Revenue Per Available Room (Rev Par)} = \frac{\text{Total revenue}}{\text{Total lettable rooms}}$$

12. Average Sale Per Guest

It is the average room income received per guest stay in the hotel.

$$\textbf{Average Sale Per Guest} = \frac{\text{Total room revenue}}{\text{Total guests stayed}}$$

13. Foreigners in the House and Percentage

Number of foreigners staying in the hotel is totaled and are compared with the budgeted foreigners and also compared with the previous year's foreigner's occupancy. The foreigner's occupancy and growth helps sales dept. to plan for the future marketing strategy.

$$\textbf{Foreigners Occupancy Percentage} = \frac{\text{Total foreigner's in the house} \times 100}{\text{Total guests staying}}$$

14. Cancellation Percentage

Rooms can be cancelled by giving a sufficient notice. The rules regarding cancellation differ from resort hotel to city hotel and for FIT's to groups and a even a size of group may require a different period of cancellation.

$$\textbf{Cancellation Percentage} = \frac{\text{Total no of cancellation} \times 100}{\text{Total number of guaranteed and confirmed reservations}}$$

15. Average Stay Per Guests

It is important for the hotel to know how many days on an average guest spend in the hotel. In case average stay per guest in your hotel is less than average stay of other similar other hotel and more over if you find that guests shift from the hotel to other than find out the reason for shifting of guests.

$$\textbf{Average Stay Per Guests} = \frac{\text{Total night spend}}{\text{Number of check out guests}}$$

Forecast Formula

Once relevant occupancy statistics have been gathered, the number of rooms available for sale on any given date can be determined by the following formula:

Total Number of Guestrooms

– Number of Out-of-Order Rooms

– Number of Room Stay-over

– Number of Room Reservations

– Number of Room Over-stays

+ Number of Room reservations × Percentage of No-Shows

+ Number of Room Under stay

Number of Rooms Available for sale

Note that this formula does not include walk-ins. They are not included because the number of walk-ins a hotel can accept is determined by the number of rooms that remain available for sale. If a hotel is full due to existing reservations, stay over's, and other factors, it cannot accept walk-ins.

As an example, consider the Holly House, a 120-room property, where on April 1 there are 3 out-of-order rooms and 55 stay over's. On that day, there are 42 guests with reservations scheduled to arrive. Since the percentage of no-shows has been recently calculated at 18.06 percent, the front office manager calculates that as many as 8 guests with reservations may not arrive (42 × .1806 = 7.59, rounded to 8). Based on historical data, 6 under-stays and 15 overstays are also expected. The number of rooms projected to be available for sale on April 1 can be determined as follows:

Total Number of Guestrooms	120
- Number of Out-of-Order Rooms	– 3
- Number of Room Stay-over	– 55
- Number of Room Reservations	– 42
- Number of Room Over-stays	– 15
+ Number of Room reservations × Percentage of No-Shows	+ 8
+ Number of Room Under stay	+ 6
Number of Rooms Available for sale	19

Therefore, the Holly House is considered to have 19 rooms available for sale on April 1. Once this figure is determined, front office management can decide whether to accept more reservations and can determine its level of staffing. Front office planning decisions must remain flexible; they are subject to change as the front office learns of reservation cancellations and modifications. Note also that room availability forecasts are based on assumptions whose validity may vary on any given day.

Sample Forecast Forms

The front office may prepare several different forecasts, depending on its needs. Occupancy forecasts are typically developed on a monthly basis and reviewed by food and beverage and rooms division management to forecast revenues, project expenses, and develop labor schedules. A ten-day forecast, for example, may be used to update labor scheduling and cost projections and may later be supplemented by a more current three-day forecast. Together, these forecasts help many hotel departments maintain appropriate staff levels for expected business volumes and thereby help contain costs.

Ten-Day Occupancy Forecast

Location ____________ # ____________ Week Ending ____________

Date Prepared: ____________ Prepared By: ____________

To be submitted to all department heads at least one week before the first day listed on forecast.

1. Date and Day (start week and end week the same as the payroll schedule)	Fri.	Sat.	Sun.	Mon.	Tues.	Wed.	Thur.	Fri.	Sat.	Sun.
2. Estimated Departures										
3. Reservation Arrivals—Group (taken from log book)										
4. Reservation Arrivals—Individual (taken from log book)										
5. Future Reservations (estimated reservations received after forecast is completed)										
6. Expected Walk-ins (% of walk-ins based on reservations received and actual occupancy for past two weeks)										
7. Total Arrivals										
8. Stayovers										
9. TOTAL FORECASTED ROOMS										
10. Occupancy Multiplier (based on number of guests per occupied room for average of the same day for last three weeks)										
11. FORECASTED NUMBER OF GUESTS										
12. Actual Rooms Occupied (taken from daily report for actual date to be completed by front office supervisor)										
13. Forecasted Variance (difference between forecast and rooms occupied on daily report)										

14. Explanation (to be completed by front office supervisor and submitted to general manager; attach additional memo if necessary)

APPROVED: ____________ DATE: ____________

General Manager's Signature

Ten-Day Forecast: At most lodging properties, the ten-day forecast is developed jointly by the front office manager and the reservations manager, possibly in conjunction with a forecast committee. Many properties develop their ten-day forecast from their yearly forecast. A ten-day forecast usually consists of:

- Daily forecasted occupancy figures, including room arrivals, room departures, rooms sold, and number of guests
- The number of group commitments, with a listing of each group's name, arrival and departure dates, number of rooms reserved, number of guests, and perhaps quoted room rates. A comparison of the previous period's forecasted and actual room counts and occupancy percentages

A special ten-day forecast may also be prepared for food and beverage, banquet, and catering operations. This forecast usually includes the expected number of guests, which is often referred to as the **house count**. Sometimes the house count is divided into group and non-group categories so that the hotel's dining room managers can better understand the nature of their business and their staffing needs.

First, the current number of occupied rooms is reviewed. The estimated numbers of overstays and expected departures are noted. Next, relevant reservation information is evaluated for each room (and guest) by date of arrival, length of stay, and date of departure. These counts are then reconciled with reservation control data. Then, the actual counts are adjusted to reflect the projected percentage of no-shows, anticipated under-stays, and expected walk-ins. These projections are based on the hotel's recent history, the seasonality of its business, and the known history of specific groups scheduled to arrive. Finally, conventions and other groups are listed on the forecast to alert various department managers to possible periods of heavy, or light, check-ins and check-outs. The number of rooms assigned each day to each group may also be noted on the sheet.

Most automated systems provide a summary of recorded data in a report format for the front office manager to use. However, only revenue management systems are programmed to "forecast" business. Programming hotel property management systems to successfully analyze historical trends and market conditions has been attempted in the past with little success.

Revenue management systems are much more sophisticated, with special trend analysis and regression analysis programming built in. Even with revenue management system forecasting, it is the front office manager's knowledge and skill that ultimately determines the accuracy of the forecast. Exhibit 9 presents a checklist that some revenue managers use when revising forecasts.

A yearly forecast provides an excellent starting point for developing shorter-term, more accurate forecasts. Managers can better assess business by reviewing current reservations and booking pace. The closer the forecast is, the more accurate it will be.

Here is a checklist for revising forecasts:

- List all group bookings and transient reservations on the books.
- Examine arrivals, departures, and group information for the given period.
- Determine if demand for this particular period of time is high or low.
- Chart the peaks and valleys on a graph to better identify high/low demand.
- Have sales agents call competing properties for rates and consider adjusting your rates.
- Make decisions to maximize revenue during each time period.

Three-Day Forecast: A three-day forecast is an updated report that reflects a more current estimate of room availability. It details any significant changes from the ten-day forecast. The three-day forecast is intended to guide management in fine-tuning labor schedules and adjusting room availability information. Exhibit 10 shows a sample three-day forecast form. In some hotels, a brief daily revenue meeting is held to focus on occupancy and rate changes for the next few days. The results of this meeting are often included in the three-day forecast

Room Count Considerations: Control books, charts, software applications, projections, ratios, and formulas can be essential in short- and long-range room count planning. Each day, the front office performs several physical counts of rooms occupied, vacant, reserved, and due to check out, to complete the occupancy statistics for that day. An automated system may reduce the need for most final counts, since the system can be programmed to continually update room availability information.

Three-Day Forecast

Date of Forecast: ______________________ **Forecast Completed By:** ______________________

Total Rooms in Hotel: ______________________

	Tonight	Tomorrow	3rd Night
Day			
Date			

	Tonight	Tomorrow	3rd Night
Previous Night Occupied Rooms[1]			
− **Expected Departures**			
− **Early Departures**			
+ **Unexpected Stayovers**			
+ **Unoccupied Rooms**[2]			
= **Rooms Available For Sale**			
+ **Expected Arrivals**			
+ **Walk-ins & Same Day Reservations**			
− **No-Shows**			
= **Occupied Rooms**			
= **Occupancy %**			
= **Expected House Count**[3]			

1. Previous night occupied rooms is determined from either the actual number of rooms occupied last night or the forecasted number of rooms from the previous night.
2. Unoccupied rooms equals the total number of rooms in the hotel less the number of rooms occupied.
3. Expected house count equals the forecasted occupied rooms times the multiple occupancy percentage for the day (found on the computer report).

Distribution: General Manager, Front Desk, Housekeeping, All Food and Beverage, Accounting, Sales, Banquets, Security

- Make counts of the rack and reservations. On tight days, a count should be made at 7:00 A.M., noon, 3:00 P.M., and 6:00 P.M. On normal days, a 7:00 A.M. and 6:00 P.M. count will suffice.
- Check room rack against the folio bucket to catch sleepers and skippers.
- Check housekeeping reports against the room rack to catch sleepers and skippers.
- Check for rooms that are due out, but still have balances on their folios, especially where credit cards are the indicated source of payment.
- Check reservations for any duplications.
- Call the reservations system to make sure all cancellations were transmitted.
- Check the switchboard, telephone rack, and/or alphabetical room rack to make sure that the guest is not already registered.
- Call the local airport for a report on canceled flights.
- Check the weather reports for cities from which a number of guests are expected.
- Check reservations against convention blocks to catch duplications.
- Check with other hotels for duplicate reservations if a housing or convention bureau indicated the reservation was a second choice.
- Check arrival dates on all reservation forms to be sure none were misfiled.
- Check the rooms cancellation list.
- If a reservation was made through the reservations manager, sales manager, or someone in the executive office and the property is close to full, call that staff person. Often, such guests are personal friends and are willing to help out by staying somewhere else.
- Close to the property's cut-off time, consider placing a person-to-person phone call to any guest with a nonguaranteed reservation who hasn't arrived. If the person accepts the call, confirm whether or not he or she will arrive yet that night.
- After the property's cut-off time, if it becomes necessary, pull any reservations that were not guaranteed or prepaid.
- If any rooms are out-of-order or not presently in use, check to see if they can be made up. Let housekeeping know when a tight day is expected, so that all possible rooms are made up.
- Before leaving work, convey in writing all pertinent information to the oncoming staff. Good communication is essential.

It is important for front desk agents to know *exactly* how many rooms are available, especially if the hotel expects to operate at nearly 100 percent occupancy. Once procedures for gathering room count information are established, planning procedures can be extended to longer periods of time to form a more reliable basis for revenue, expense, and labor forecasting. The checklist in Exhibit 11 may be applicable to non-automated and semi-automated operations alike.

Illustration 1:

Hotel Taj has 280 rooms. Five rooms are out of order and three are occupied by the executives. The confirmed and guaranteed reservations for 80 rooms have been received. The expected no shows are 5%. It is expected that eight rooms will be under stay and ten over stay. The total stayovers will be 110 rooms. Expected walk- in are five. The total expected departures will be 30. Calculate the number of rooms to be reserved in order to have cent percent occupancy.

Solution

Total rooms	280
-out of order rooms	5
-rooms occupied by executives	3
-total stayovers	110
-confirmed and guaranteed reservations	80
+ no show (5% of 80)	4
+ total under-stay	8
- overstays	10
+ total expected departures	30
Rooms to be reserved to have cent percent occupancy	114

Illustration 2:

Hotel Park View has 350 rooms. On 1st July 2007, there are 15 out of order rooms and 120 stayovers. There are 100 guests with reservations expected to arrive and the no-show percentage has been calculated at 10%. It forecasted that ten understays and 15 overstays are to be expected that day.

(a) Give the room available forecast formula.

(b) Using that formula, calculate the number of rooms still to be sold for 100% occupancy on 1st July 2008 using the above given information showing each step.

Solution: Note

There is a reservation for 100 guests, it is assumed that they will be occupying 100 rooms.

Total no. of rooms

-out of order rooms

-stayovers

-expected arrivals (reservations)

+ no shows

-overstays

+understays

No shows = 10% of reservations

$10\% \times 100 = 10$ rooms

Total no shows available	350
-out of order rooms	15
-stayovers	120
-reservations	100
+ No-shows 10% × 100	10
+ understays	10
-overstays	15
Rooms to be sold to have 100% occupancy on 1 July 2008	120

Illustration 3

Hotel lake palace has 300 rooms. On 12th may, there are 6 Out of Order rooms and 10 rooms are occupied by hotel executives.90 stay over and 65 rooms are expected to check-in. The No-show percentage has been calculated at 20%. It is forecasted that 7 under stay and 8 overstays are to expected that day. 40 rooms are expected to check out. Calculate the number of rooms still to be sold for 100% Occupancy on 13th May using the above given information.

Solution:

Calculation: No-shows = 20% of total reservation are expected to check-in

Total No-shows = $20\% \times 65 = 13$ rooms

Total Rooms 300

LESS

Stay over	90
Reservation	65
Out-of-Order	06
Room Occupied by hotel Executives	10
Total Expected overstay	08
	179
	121

ADD

Expected Departure	40
Total No-shows	13
Total under stay	07
	60
Total Rooms available for sale on 13th may	61

Section Keywords

Forecasting—*The process of predicting events and trends in business; typical forecasting for the rooms division includes room availability and occupancy.*

Overstays—*Guests who stay after their stated departure date.*

Stayovers—*A room status term indicating that the guest is not checking out today and will remain at least one more night; a guest who continues to occupy a room from the time of arrival to the stated date of departure.*

Under-stays—*Guests who check out before their stated departure date.*

House count—*The forecasted or expected number of guests for a particular period, sometimes broken down into group and non-group business.*

QUESTIONNAIRE

1. Define Forecasting?
2. Explaining what are the benefits of Forecasting?
3. What are the key factors required for Forecasting?
4. Forecasting, as a front office function is very useful to the entire hotel's operations? Explain in detail.
5. What do you mean by forecast? Explain with example ten days forecast and three days forecast technique.
6. What data is useful for forecasting room's availability? Give various formulas for their calculation.
7. State the forecast formula.
8. In a 200room hotel, 60 rooms have confirmed reservations with a 5% no show factor. There are 100 guaranteed reservations with a history of no shows at 2%. The predicted member of stay-over is 5rooms and predicted under stays are 6 the predicted member of walk-ins for this period is 10.

Calculate the number of additional rooms reservations needed to achieve 100% occupancy.

9. Prepare the format of ten day forecast and three forecasts.
10. In order to carry out effective or realistic forecasting at the Front Office, what are the necessary inputs or information? Explain.

23
BUDGETING

- BUDGETING DEFINITION
- NEED OF PREPARING A BUDGET
- OBJECTIVES OF BUDGETARY CONTROL
- CLASSIFICATION
- ADVANTAGES OF BUDGETING
- LIMITATION OF BUDGETING
- LIMITATIONS OF BUDGETARY CONTROL
- GOALS OF BUDGETING PROCESS
- BUDGETING INCOME STATEMENT

BUDGETING

A **budget** is a quantitative expression of a plan for a defined period of time. It may include planned sales volumes and revenues, resource quantities, costs and expenses, assets, liabilities and cash flows. It expresses strategic plans of business units, organizations, activities or events in measurable terms

A budget is a predetermined statement of managerial policy during the given period which provides a standard for comparison with the results actually achieved."

Preparing a budget is a professional task and includes coordination and efforts of management personnel all the managers are responsible for revenue forecasting (budgeting).the accounting division is responsible coordinating the budget plans of all departments

Need of a Preparing a Budget

Budget helps to aid the planning of actual operations by forcing managers to consider how the conditions might change and what steps should be taken now and by encouraging managers to consider problems before they arise. It also helps co-ordinate the activities of the organization by compelling managers to examine relationships between their own operation and those of other departments. Other essentials of budget include:

- To control resources
- To communicate plans to various responsibility centre managers.
- To motivate managers to strive to achieve budget goals.
- To evaluate the performance of managers
- To provide visibility into the company's performance
- For accountability

In summary, the purpose of budgeting tools:

1. Tools provide a forecast of revenues and expenditures, that is, construct a model of how a business might perform financially if certain strategies, events and plans are carried out.
2. Tools enable the actual financial operation of the business to be measured against the forecast.
3. Lastly, tools establish the cost constraint for a project, program, or operations

Control and Review of Budget

It is the process of determining various budgeted figures for the enterprises for the enterprises for the future period and then comparing the budget figures with actual performance for calculating variances. First of all, budgets are prepared and then actual results are recorded. The comparison of actual result and budgeted figures will enable the management to find out discrepancies and take adequate measures at proper times budget estimates are also reviewed and modified periodically depending upon various factors. The budget goals should be achievable but not achievable very easily. A budgetary control is a continuous process which helps in planning and coordination

Objectives of Budgetary Control

I. To insure the perfect planning for future by setting up various budgets
II. To increase the revenue
III. To reduce the cost
IV. To have proper coordination among different departments
V. To maximise the profit to minimise the capital investment
VI. To operate departments with efficiency and economy
VII. To anticipate capital expenditure for future
VIII. Eliminate the wastes and increase in profitability
IX. Fixation of responsibility of various individuals in the organisation
X. To minimize the capital investment
XI. Budgetary control is exercised by putting budgets and actual side by side. Variances are not normally revealed in the accounts. Standard costing variances are revealed through accounts

Budgetary Control is planned to assist the management for policy formulation, planning controlling and co-ordinating the general objectives of budgetary control and it can be stated in the following ways:

1) Planning: A budget is a plan of action. Budgeting ensures a detailed plan of action for a business over a period of time.
2) Co-ordination: Budgetary control co-ordinates the various activities of the entity or organization and secure co-operation of all concerned towards the common goal.

3) Control: Control is necessary to ensure that plans and objectives are being achieved. Control follows planning and co-ordination. No control in performance is possible without predetermined standards. Thus, budgetary control makes control possible by continuous measures against predetermined targets. If there is any variation between the budgeted performance and the actual performance, the same is subject to analysis and corrective action.

As budgets serve different purpose, different types of budgets have been developed. The following are the different classification of budgets developed on the basis of time, functions, finance, flexible and other types of budgets.

(A) Classification on the basis of Time

1. Long-Term Budgets
2. Medium term budgeting
3. Short-Term Budgets
4. Current Budgets

(B) Classification according to Functions:

1. Operating budget
2. Flexibility
3. Fixed budget

(C) Classification on the basis of finance

1. Capital budgets
2. Revenue budget

(D) Classification on the basis of flexible

(E) Other types of budgets

1. Standard budget
2. Zero budget

Classification on the Basis of Time

1. Long-Term Budgets: Long-term budgets are prepared for a longer period that varies between five to ten years. It is usually developed by the top level management. These budgets summaries the general plan of operations and its expected consequences. Long-Term Budgets are prepared for important activities like composition of its capital expenditure, new product development and research, long-term finance etc.

2. Short-Term Budgets: These budgets are usually prepared for a period of one year. Sometimes they may be prepared for even a shorter period as for quarterly or half yearly. The scope of budgeting activity may vary considerably among different organizations.
3. Current Budgets: Current budgets are prepared for the current operations of the business. The planning period of a budget is generally for months or weeks. As per ICMA London, "current budget is a budget which is established for use over a short period of time and related to current conditions."
4. Medium term budgeting : these budgets are generally for two to five years and can be for revenge targets, cost targets. etc,

Classification on the Basis of Function

1. Functional Budget: The functional budget is one which relates to any of the functions of an organization. The number of functional budgets depends upon the size and nature of business. The following are the commonly used functional budgets:
   1) Sales Budget
   2) Purchase Budget
   3) Production Budget
   4) Selling and Distribution Cost Budget
   5) Labour Cost budget
   6) Cash Budget
   7) Capital Expenditure Budget
2. Master budget: The master Budget is a summary budget. This budget encompasses all the functional activities into one harmonious unit. The ICMA England defines a Master Budget as the "summary budget incorporating its functional budgets, which is finally approved, adopted and employed".

When the functional budgets have been completed, the budget committee will prepare a master Budget for the target of the concern. Accordingly, a budget is prepared incorporating the summaries of all functional budgets. It comprises budgeted profit and loss account, budgeted balance sheet, budgeted production, sales and costs. The ICMA, England, defines a Master Budget as "the summary budget incorporating its functional budgets, which are finally approved, adopted and employed." The master Budget represents the activities of a business during a profit plan.

Operating Budget

The sales budget, production budget or sale expected revenue, cost control budget, labour cost control budget, plant utilization budget, operational expenses budget, manufacturing expenses budget, sales expenses budget, marketing expenses budget, etc are commonly used operating budgets there can be separate operational budgets for all the above mentioned activities. These can be separated operational budgets for all the above mention activities. These budgets relate to the different activities or operations of a business house. The operating budget for a business house may be constructed in terms of programs or responsibility areas

The increase in units of production or sale, expected revenue, cost of various products, etc is major program of business house and is termed As program budget. These budgets are, thus useful, in locating areas where efforts may be required to reduce cost, increase revenue, increase turnover, etc.

The budgets which are concerned with cash receipts and disbursements, operational expenses, capital expenditure, operating profit, gross profit, net profit, etc are termed as financial budgets. Commonly used financial budget are cash budget, income statement, operational cost budget, capital expenditure budget, etc various functional budget are integrated into master budget. This budget is prepared by the ultimate integrated into master budget. This budget is prepared by ultimate integrations of separate functional budget and is used to coordinate the activities of various functional departments and also help as control device

Flexibility

There are some budgets which are fixed in nature and for a specific period and others are flexible in nature.

Fixed Budgets

A fixed budget is designed to remain unchanged irrespective of the level of activity actually attained.

A budget drawn for a particular level of activity is called fixed budget. According to ICWA London "fixed budget is a budget which is designed to remain unchanged irrespective of the level of activity actually attained." Fixed budget is usually prepared before the beginning of the financial year. This type of budget is not going to highlight the cost variances due to the difference in the levels of activity. Fixed Budgets are suitable under static conditions.

Classification on the Basis of Finance

Capital Budget

Capital budget are usually long term or medium term budgets and involve a large amount of money. For purchasing the assets like machinery, building, new business house, goodwill, etc. the amount spend is called capital expenditure. Whenever capital budget is prepared it is always kept in mind the utility of the capital expenditure can also be prepared for the capital gain especially in case of stock market investment by stock brokers and investors in equity market

Revenue Budget

Revenue budgets are forecasts of a company's sales revenues and expenditures, including capital-related expenditures. It is essential that you establish whether you possess enough financial means to conduct operations, grow your business and ultimately make a profit. Without this planning, your company's future may be uncertain as you may not know how much money you're taking in or spending. Revenue budgets ensure that businesses efficiently allocate resources -- and in doing so they save time, effort and money.

Flexible Budget

Flexible Budget: A flexible budget is a budget which is designed to change in accordance with the various levels of activity actually attained. The flexible budget which is also called Variable Budget or Sliding Scale Budget takes both fixed, variable and Semi fixed manufacturing costs into account.

Flexible Budget is also called variable or sliding Scale budget. "It takes both the fixed and manufacturing costs into account. Flexible budget is the opposite of static budget showing the expected cost at a single level of activity. According to ICMA, England defined Flexible Budget is a budget which is designed to change in accordance with the level of activity actually attained."

According to the principles that guide the preparation of the flexible budget a series of fixed budgets are drawn for different levels of activity. A flexible budget often shows the budgeted expenses against each item of cost corresponding to the different levels of activity. This budget has come into the use for solving the problems caused by the application of the fixed budget.

Advantages of Flexible Budget

1) In flexible budget, all possible volume of output or level of activity can be covered.

2) Overhead costs are analysed into fixed variable and semi-variable costs.
3) Expenditure can be forecasted at different levels of activity.
4) It facilitates at all times related factor, it can be compared, which are essential for intelligent decision making.
5) A flexible budget can be prepared with standard costing or without depending upon what the Company opts for.
6) Flexible budget facilitates ascertainment of costs at different levels of activity, price fixation, placing tenders and Quotations.
7) It helps in assessing the performance of all departmental heads as the same can be judged by terms of the level of activity attained by the business.

Distinction Between Fixed Budget and Flexible Budget

Fixed Budget

1. Fixed budget is inflexible and does not change with the actual volume of output achieved.
2. Fixed budget assumes that conditions would remain static.
3. Costs are not classified according to their variability i.e. fixed, variable and semi variable.
4. Comparison of actual and budgeted performance cannot be done correctly if the volume of output differs.
5. It is difficult of forecast accurately the results in it.
6. Only one budget at a fixed level of activity is prepared due to an unrealistic expectation on the part of the management
7. Fixed budget has a limited application and is inefficient as a tool for cost control.
8. If the budgeted and actual activity levels vary, the correct ascertainment so coasts and fixation of prices becomes difficult.

Flexible budget

1. Flexible budget can be suitably recanted quickly according to level of activity attained.
2. Flexible budget is design to change according to changed conditions.
3. Coasts are classified according to the nature of their variability.

4. Comparisons are realistic as the changed plan figures are placed against actual ones.
5. Flexible budget clearly shows the impact of various expenses on the operational aspects of the business.
6. Series of budgets are prepared at different level of activities.
7. Flexible budget has more application and can be used as a tool for cost control.
8. Flexible budget helps in fixation of prices and submission of tenders due to correct ascertainment of coasts.

Other Types of Budget

Standard budget

A *Standard Budget* is a vehicle for variance. It is commonly derived from estimates on future costs that have **Fixed and Variable cost components.**

Standard budgets present information at only one level of activity and does not provide information on how the variable portion of the costs would affect the budget. When used in Variance Analysis this can lead to unfavourable variances being falsely identified.

A "standard budget" is a list of goods and services that a family of a specified size and composition would need to live at a designated level of well-being, together with the costs of those goods and services. Considerable work on standard budgets has been done in the United States and other countries in recent years, mostly by non-government analysts. Budgets have not been used to develop official poverty lines, and in most cases have not been used to calculate the size of a nation's low-income population.

Zero budget

A budgeting system where all existing activities are assessed and cost justified in the same way as new proposals. The system removes the implied right of existing activities for the continued allocation of resources. The new companies which have no budgets to support make a budget which does not refer to previous figures. Even old companies sometime make zero budgets that mean they do not refer to previous budget. In zero budgets all future expenses have to be estimated and totalled to know the budget cost of the production for making sale budget, the management anticipates that how many units of products can be sold and what will be the selling price of each product. After multiplying and totalling the management will be able to know the sales budget.

Advantages of Budgeting

The advantages of budgetary control may be summarized as follows:

1. It facilitates reduction of cost.
2. Budgetary control guides the management in planning and formulation of policies.
3. Budgetary control facilitates effective co-ordination of activities of the various departments and Functions by setting their limits and goals.
4. It ensures maximization of profits through cost control and optimum utilization of resources.
5. It evaluates for the continuous review of performance of different budget centres.
6. It helps to the management efficient and economic production control.
7. It facilitates corrective actions, whenever there is inefficiencies and weaknesses comparing Actual performance with budget.
8. It guides management in research and development.
9. It ensures economy in working.
10. It helps to adopt the principles of standard costing

- *Planning orientation.* The process of creating a budget takes management away from its short-term, day-to-day management of the business and forces it to think longer-term. This is the chief goal of budgeting, even if management does not succeed in meeting its goals as outlined in the budget - at least it is thinking about the company's competitive and financial position and how to improve it.
- *Profitability review.* It is easy to lose sight of where a company is making most of its money, during the scramble of day-to-day management. A properly structured budget points out what aspects of the business produce money and which ones use it, which forces management to consider whether it should drop some parts of the business, or expand in others.
- *Assumptions review.* The budgeting process forces management to think about why the company is in business, as well as its key assumptions about its business environment. A periodic re-evaluation of these issues

may result in altered assumptions, which may in turn alter the way in which managements decides to operate the business.

- *Performance evaluations.* You can work with employees to set up their goals for a budgeting period, and possibly also tie bonuses or other incentives to how they perform. You can then create budget versus actual reports to give employees feedback regarding how they are progressing toward their goals. This approach is most common with financial goals, though operational goals (such as reducing the product rework rate) can also be added to the budget for performance appraisal purposes. This system of evaluation is called responsible accounting
- *Funding planning.* A properly structured budget should derive the amount of cash that will be spun off or which will be needed to support operations. This information is used by the treasurer to plan for the company's funding needs.
- *Cash allocation.* There is only a limited amount of cash available to invest in fixed assets and working capital, and the budgeting process forces management to decide which assets are most worth investing in.
- *Bottleneck analysis.* Nearly every company has a bottleneck somewhere, and the budgeting process can be used to concentrate on what can be done to either expand the capacity of that bottleneck or to shift work around it.

Limitations of Budgeting

1. Uncertain budget
2. Budgetary revision requirement
3. Budgets too easy to achieve
4. Non-achievable budgets discourage the concerned employees
5. Discourage efficient people
6. Difficulty in coordination
7. Differences among different department of achievement or failure
8. Depends upon support of top management

Check List for Accurate Room Count

1. During the busy season the reception should make the room report at least thrice a day that is at 7 am, 2 pm, and 9 pm. Even in between these timings

the receptionist can check on phone with housekeeping cashier, bell desk to know the latest room status. The room status board on chart is kept updated at all moments. Room status gives the information regarding the let table rooms that weather it is occupied or not, if occupied then how many guest are staying under repair, if room is under repair check with maintenance department and try to get it cleared as early as possible.

2. Compare room rack with room rack with bill folios to ensure that rooms shown as occupied by reception have an appropriate bill folio. In case there is no then find out that the room has been checked out or shifted to other room
3. Housekeeping also prepares room report thrice a day
4. Compare the reception room with housekeeping report and In case of any discrepancy then find out the reasons for discrepancy
5. Check expected arrival list and ensure there is no duplication. Sometimes a guest may make his booking directly as well along with the seminar conference, etc booked through some company or agency.
6. Ensure all cancelation received by reservation department have been updated
7. Check with airports with cancellation of any flights and with railway station for cancellation of any train. Check if guest is expected to arrive through cancelled flight or train.
8. Check others hotels for duplication for reservation, some guest reserve themselves with more than one hotel
9. Compare the expected arrival list with the mail and form to ensure that there is no mistake made by room reservation department
10. In case of over booking find out the reservations made through hotel staff as it might be possible to shift them to other hotels as they might be personnel friends of hotels staff
11. Non guaranteed reservation can be cancelled after the cut off timely usually6 pm, if the guest hand not given the expected arrival time
12. Book or hold room in the similar types of hotels as due to over flow of guests they can be shifted to the other similar hotels
13. The receptionist must write his observation and remarks in the reception log book for the next shift receptionist

14. At late night check the wakeup call register. If there are quite a few people who have asked for every morning wakeup then it can be expected they might be checking out. Also check out the check out time for all expected departures.

Limitations of Budgetary Control

Budgetary Control is an effective tool for management control. However, it has certain important limitations which are identified below:

1. The budget plan is based on estimates and forecasting. Forecasting cannot be considered to be an exact science. If the budget plans are made on the basis of inaccurate forecasts then the budget programme may not be accurate and ineffective.
2. For reasons of uncertainty about future, and changing circumstances which may develop later on, budget may prove short or excess of actual requirements.
3. Effective implementation of budgetary control depends upon willingness, co-operation and understanding among people reasonable for execution. Lack of co-operation leads to inefficient performance.
4. The system does not substitute for management. It is mere like a management tool.
5. Budgeting may be cumbersome and time consuming process.

Goals for the Budgeting Process

1. Maximise revenues
2. Minimise expenses
3. Minimise investment
4. Maximise profit

The front office manager efficiency depends on that how much revenue of his department he can increase and how many expenses he can reduce to maximise the profits. He also tries to minimise the investment and have maximum revenue. The revenue earned per rupee invested should be higher to prove front office managers efficiency

An organisation in divided into various department and sub department and that are so structured that managers are responsible for groups of related activities for which they can be held responsible. There are known as responsibility centres

Responsibility Centres Falls into Four Categories

1. Revenue centre's managers are responsible for maximising revenue. The room revenue can be increased by increasing the room sale even if some discount or package tours are offered specially during off season.
2. Cost centre's managers effort is to reduce the cost but not at the cost of services. Usually revenue earners blame cost control department that due to control and unnecessary cost control the quality of services are getting affected and hence the sale is reducing.
3. Profit centre's managers are responsible for maximising profit (maximum revenue and minimum cost). Both revenue centres and cost centre's executives coordinate to maximise profit.
4. Investment centre for any business the investment control is very important. Any project which over runs the cost can easily become sick. Increase in investment will increase and interest burden. Underutilised assets can always increase the cost of production per unit and hence reduction in profit.

In budget there are three basis categories

Budgeted income statement: these are budget used to plan for maximising sales, minimizing costs, and maximizing profits.

Budgeted cash flows: budgeted cash flow are budgeted used to plan for maximizing sales, minimizing investment, as it is necessary to know how much cash is available for investment; what the planned expenditure are and what financing will be needed. This information is available from the cash flow budgets for operations and capital budget and the financial budget- all of which are cash flow budgets.

Budgeted balance sheet: budgeted balance sheet shows the impact on the assets, liability and equity accounts produced by the transaction recorded on both the income statement and cash flows the budgets. There are preparing at the higher management level.

Budgeted Income Statement (BIS)

The room division is a profit centre, so the room division budget is concerned with planned to maximize revenues and minimize expenses. This statement specifies the desired sales goals that are the basis for planning expenses .this statement specifies the desired sales goals that are the basis for planning expenses and capital expenditures refurbishing, increasing supplies inventory, etc.

Budgeted Cash Flows (BCF)

Budgeted cash flows are very helpful in planning day to day activities of a business

Difference Between BCF & BIS

Budgeted income statement is prepared on the basis of accrual accounting system and is composed of revenues and expenses. Revenues are recorded when a service is rendered, not when the hotel receives payment for it. Similarly, expenses are recorded when an asset or service is consumed, not when it is paid for. The amount of cash that a hotel receives on a given day and the amount of revenue earned will not be the same because some sale of services may be credit sales for which the hotel receives no cash in the current accounting period. Some expenses recorded on the current income statement are not paid for in current accounting period and therefore do not represent an out flow of cash

Budgeted cash flow's help managers to plan expected total cash receipt and expenditure and indicate the net cash flow difference between receipts and expenditure. For preparing an operating cash budget, estimates of when actual payments on sales will be received. In others words budgeted cash flow is a form of cash book which shows total receipts and payments

The Budget Cycle

1. Establishing attainable goals or objectives
2. Planning to achieve these goals or objectives
3. Evaluating results – comparing actual results with those planned and analysing the difference or variances
4. Taking corrective action, if required.
5. Improving the effectiveness of budgeting.

1. **Establishing attainable goals or objectives:** Top management must determine the communication the objective of the organisation to the lowest level. By preparing the budget, the subordinate tell the management how they can respond to the challenge set for them and what goals they can achieve. The budget should not be imposed from the top to down. Employees should be allowed to participate especially in the hospital industry, where most of them are the representative of the hotel for the guests and influence their impressions.

Specific objects need to be set for the organisation and department for example to have a 10% overall profit margin to attend an annual sales growth rate of 20%etc. realism must play a part in setting goals. And all limitations or constraints should be considered. For instance, very few hotels runs ay 100% occupancy the year around so it would be unwise to use 100% occupancy as the budgeted occupancy on an annual basis. Storage of capital could limit expansion plans. Management policy regarding the marketing which the hotel may operate may limit budgets. Customs demanding and completion must always be kept in mind. Adding more rooms does not automatically increase the demand for room in the area.

The right type of budget should be selected (fixed, flexible, or zero base) and proper incentive to meet or exceed budget goals should be established along with open communication channels with subordinates.

2. **Planning to achieve goals and objectives:** Once objective have been determined, plans must be made to achieve them. The room department is a profit centre and so the room manager is responsible for maximizing sales and minimizing expenses. A restaurant manager must select the skilled staff chef must purchase a raw material in the right quantities and quality required to cater to expected demand and so on. Over the long term, a budget expansion of facilities might require management to make plans for financing the project

3. **Evaluating results:** This is one of the most important steps in the budget cycle. Differences between the budgeted and actual performance should be identified and analysed. Although various do not themselves offer solution to possible problems, they do not point the fact that problem may exist.

4. **Taking corrective actions** the next stop requires taking corrective action, if required. The cause of the difference in performance could be the result of a circumstance that no one could foresee or predict. Conversely a difference could be cause by the fact that selling prices were not sufficient increase to compensate for an inflation rate of cost increases or that budgeted forecast in room occupancy was not sufficiently reduced to compensate for the construction for the construction of a new hotel nearby. Whatever the reason and irrespective of whatever the variance is negative or positive, it should be corrective if possible so that the future budgets can be more realistically planned operations

5. **Improving effectiveness of budgeting:** The final step of the budgeting cycle emphasizes the constant need to improve the budgeting process. The information provided from past budgeting cycles, especially the information

provided from analyzing variance between actual and budgeted figures, will be helpful.

Preparing the Budget

Since the room department is a profit centre, the room's division manager is responsible for maximising sales and minimising expenses. Therefore, the room division manager is only responsible for preparing a budgeted income statement and a budgeted operation cash flow.

Budgeted income statements are primary concern of day to day management of a hotel and the procedure for their preparation is as follows:

1. Estimate sales revenue levels by department
2. Deduct estimated departmental operating expenses for each department.
3. Combine estimated departmental operating income and deduct estimated undistributed expenses to arrive at net income.

Since sales are the basics of calculating expenses and cash needs, budgets should be prepared in the following order:

1. Sales budget
2. Expense budget
3. Operating cash flows

Sales budget: The process of preparing a sales budget for a new business will be different from that for an establishment business since the latter's past experiences services as a basis for its future plan.

Expense budget: once sales have been projected, expenses must be matched to them there are 3 types of expenses:

1. Variable
2. Semi variable
3. Fixed

Variable: They vary with proportion of sales .if sales increases then variable sales is also increases in same proportion and vice-versa

Semi variable: They vary with sales but not in same proportion.

Fixed: Theses expenses do not change with the sales but this remains fixed for short time

How a Budget is Prepared?

- Since, for the scope of this course, only a Rooms Division Department budget shall be prepared, the Rooms Division manager shall only estimate next period's room revenue, and direct expenses. Putting it in other words, the Rooms Division Manager shall not care about estimating capital expenses (i.e. Indirect Expenses) since in responsibility accounting; a manager is responsible and liable only for his department!
- The Rooms Division Manager shall first forecast demand for rooms for the next period in question, and then might use historical averages, industry average... to estimate Room Revenue and Room Direct Expenses

1. Estimating Room Revenue:

- By using an appropriate forecasting method, the Rooms Division Manager can forecast demand measured in room nights. Later, the Rooms Division Manager shall multiply the total room nights by the Average Room Rate (**ARR**), either using hotel historical or industry averages, to come up with the estimated Room Revenue.
- Later, according to hotel historical figures, the Rooms Division Manager shall estimate the room allowances figure and subtract it from the estimated total room revenue to come up with the net room revenue.

2. Estimating direct expenses:

- Direct Expenses (i.e. Variable Costs) in the Rooms Division Department can be divided into 4 categories:
  1. Wage Expenses (Hourly Wage * Estimated Total Labor Hours needed)
  2. Frills (i.e. Free of Charge Replenished Room Items)
  3. Material (i.e. Cleaning Supplies, Utensils...)
  4. Laundry & Linen Expenses (Cost of pressing, cleaning, pressing, storing...)
- The Rooms Division Manager might consider country averages, and or historical averages, along with current hotel / labor union collective bargaining contracts for the coming period, suppliers' price increase intentions, the relative change of local currency against some major foreign currencies, to estimate department direct expenses.

Rooms Division Department Item Budgeting (Illustration)

Expense Items	2002	%	2003	%	2004	%	2005	%
Wage / Benefits	$525,600	7.80%	$638,750	8.44%	$821,250	9.69%	$983,141	10.53%
Laundry / Linen	$257,975	3.83%	$264,044	3.49%	$277,594	3.27%	$277,208	2.97%
Materials	$44,224	0.66%	$45,265	0.60%	$46,599	0.55%	$46,046	0.49%
Frills	$773,924	11.48%	$784,410	10.36%	$791,980	9.34%	$770,335	8.25%
Total Expenses	$1,601,723	23.76%	$1,732,469	22.89%	$1,937,423	22.85%	$2,076,730	22.25%
Room Revenue	$6,740,020	100.00%	$7,569,331	100.00%	$8,477,890	100.00%	$9,333,617	100.00%

In this example, first we have forecasted the revenue for the budget year (i.e. 2005), which is $ 9,333,617. In order to estimate the item expenses, we should first establish a standard (i.e. Percentage of Total Revenue). The average of the historical percentage item expense is the best standard that we can use. The average can be simple, moving average, or weighted average. The last column in the above table indicates these standards. Now, in order to budget the item expenses for year 2005, we multiply the last year expenses by the percentage standards that we established. Here, the percentage standards become the company expenditure objectives.

Refining Budget

If the actual operating figures and budgeted figures are distant from each other, then this suggests a refining or revision of our budget (i.e. revision of room demand, estimated room revenue, and room's direct expenses).

Evaluating Front Office Operations

Evaluating the result of front office operations is an important management function. Without thoroughly evaluating the results of operations, managers will not know whether the front office is attaining planned goals. Successful front office managers evaluate the results of department activities on a daily, monthly, quarterly, and yearly basis. The following sections examine important tools that front office managers can use to evaluate the success of front office operations. These tools include.

The daily operations report:

1. Occupancy ratios
2. Rooms revenue analysis
3. The hotel income statement
4. The rooms schedule
5. Rooms division budget reports
6. Operating ratios
7. Ratio standards

THE DAILY OPERATIONS REPORT

The daily operations report, also known as the manager's report, the daily report, and the daily revenue report, summarizes the hotel's financial activities during a 24 hour period. The daily operations report provides a means of reconciling cash, bank accounts, revenue and accounts receivable. The report also serves as a posting reference for various accounting journals and provides important data that must be input to link front and back office automated functions. Daily operations reports are uniquely structured to meet the needs of individual hotel properties.

Room statistics and occupancy ratios from an entire section of a typically daily operations report. Enriched by commends and observations from the accounting staff, statistics shown on the daily operations report may take on the more meaning. For example, statistics about the number of guests using the hotel's valet parking services take on added significance when remarks indicate that valet sales are down while occupancy is up. The front office manager may assume that the front office is not properly promoting available guest valet parking services.

The information provided by the daily operations report is not restricted to the front office manager or hotel general manager. Copies of the daily operations report are generally distributed to all department and division managers in the hotel.

S. no.	Room division entry	Source documents
1.	Salaries and wages	Time. cards payrolls records
2.	Commission	Travel agency billing
3.	Employee benefit	Payroll record
4.	Contract cleaning	Suppliers invoice

5.	Guest transportation	Invoice
6.	Laundry and dry cleaning	Housekeeping and outside laundry charges for employees uniform
7.	Linen	Suppliers invoices
8.	Operating supplies	Suppliers invoices
9.	Reservation expenses	Reservation system invoices
10.	Other operating expenses	Suppliers invoices

QUESTIONNAIRE

1. Why there is need of preparing a budget
2. What is budgeting
3. Explain the advantages of budgeting
4. Explain the disadvantages/limitations of budgeting
5. Explain Difference between BCF & BIS
6. Define budget cycle
7. Why there is need of preparing a budget in an hotel industry
8. What are the goals of budgeting process
9. Classify budgets
10. Difference between standard budget and zero budget

24

YIELD MANAGEMENT

- COMPONENTS OF YIELD MANAGEMENT
- IMPORTANCE
- USES IN DIFFERENT INDUSTRY
  - AIRLINES
  - HOTELS
  - RETAILS
- COMPONENTS OF YIELD MANAGEMENT
  - CAPACITY MANAGEMENT
  - DISCOUNT ALLOCATION
  - DURATION CONTROL
- MEASURING YIELD
- BREAK-EVEN ANALYSIS
- ELEMENTS OF YIELD MANAGEMENT
- POTENTIAL HIGH AND LOW DEMAND TACTICS
- QUESTIONS

Yield management is a variable pricing strategy, based on understanding, anticipating and influencing consumer behavior in order to maximize revenue or profits from a fixed, perishable resource (such as airline seats or hotel room reservations or advertising inventory). As a specific, inventory-focused branch of revenue management, yield management involves strategic control of inventory to sell it to the right customer at the right time for the right price. This process can result in price discrimination, where a firm charges customers consuming otherwise identical goods or services a different price for doing so.

Revenue management presents a more precise measure of performance because it combines occupancy% and ADR into a single statistics the yield statistic. Simply stated, revenue management is a technique used to maximize room revenues. Revenue management also called yield management takes into account as many of the factors influencing business trends as possible. It is also an evaluative tool that allows the front office manager to use potential revenue as the standard against wish actual revenue can be compared.

There are various approaches to revenue management. Often, each approach is modeled to meet the needs of an individual hotel. Although revenue management analysis can be performed manually, this approach is cumbersome, time consuming and error prone. With the use of computer and appropriate application software, revenue management calculations can be automatically performed very quickly and accurately.

CONCEPT OF YIELD MANAGEMENT

The concept of yield management originated in the airlines industry most travelers know that passengers on the same flight often pay different fares. Super saver discounts, three day advance purchase plans, stay over Saturday night packages, and so forth have become the norms for airlines pricing. What is not as widely known is the potential application of revenue management to other service industries.

Yield Management has proven successful in the lodging, car rental, cruise lines, rail road's and touring industries-basically, in situations where reservations are taken for a perishable commodity. The key to successful implementation appears to be an ability to monitor reservations and to develop reliable forecast.

Revenue management is based on supply and demand. Prices tend to rise when demand exceed supply, conversely, prices tend to fall when supply exceed demand. Proper pricing adjustments, which take existing.

IMPORTANCE

There are three essential conditions for yield management to be applicable:

- That there is a fixed amount of resources available for sale.
- That the resources sold are perishable (there is a time limit to selling the resources, after which they cease to be of value).
- Those different customers are willing to pay a different price for using the same amount of resources.

If the resources available are not fixed or not perishable, the problem is limited to logistics, i.e. inventory or production management. If all customers would pay the same price for using the same amount of resources, the challenge would perhaps be limited to selling as quickly as possible, e.g. if there are costs for holding inventory.

Yield management is of especially high relevance in cases where the constant costs are relatively high compared to the variable costs. The less variable cost there is, the more the additional revenue earned will contribute to the overall profit. This is because it focuses on maximizing expected marginal revenue for a given operation and planning. It optimizes resource utilization by ensuring inventory availability to customers with the highest expected revenue contribution and extracting the greatest level of 'willingness to pay' from the entire customer base.

USES IN DIFFERENT INDUSTRY

Airlines

In the passenger **airline** case, capacity is regarded as fixed because changing what aircraft flies a certain service based on the demand is the exception rather than the rule. When the aircraft departs, the unsold seats cannot generate any revenue and thus can be said to have perished, or have spoiled. Airlines use specialized software to monitor how seats are reserved and react accordingly. There are various inventory controls such as a nested inventory system. For example, airlines can offer discounts on low-demand flights, where the flight will likely not sell-out. The converse, selling more-expensive seats when there is excess demand, managing off demand.

Hotels

Hotels use this system in largely the same way, to calculate the rates, rooms and restrictions on sales in order to best maximize their return. These systems measure constrained and unconstrained demand along with pace to gauge which restrictions to implement, e.g. length of stay, non-refundable rate, or close to arrival. Yield management teams in the hotel industry have evolved tremendously over the last 10 years and in this global economy targeting the right distribution channels, controlling costs, and having the right market mix plays an important role in yield management. Yield management in hotels is selling rooms and services at the right price, at the right time, to the right people.

Retails

In the rental car industry, yield management deals with the sale of optional insurance, damage waivers and vehicle upgrades. It accounts for a major portion of the rental company's profitability, and is monitored on a daily basis. In the equipment rental industry, yield management is a method to manage rental rates against capacity (available fleet) and demand.

Some of the other industries are intercity buses, multifamily housing, Insurance, Telecommunications ETC

COMPONENTS OF YIELD MANAGEMENT

To Maximise Revenue 3 Ways Are Used In Yield Management:

1. Capacity management
2. Discount allocation
3. Duration control

CAPACITY MANAGEMENT

Capacity management is a process used to manage information technology (IT). Its primary goal is to ensure that IT capacity meets current and future business requirements in a cost-effective manner. One common interpretation of capacity management is described in the ITIL framework. ITIL version 3 views capacity management as comprising three sub-processes: business capacity management, service capacity management, and component capacity management.

IN HOTEL: Cancellation at last moments and no show can never be eliminated. Capacity management basically means overbooking. Capacity management includes "determining how many walk-ins should be accepted on the day of arrival based on expected cancellations, no show, late arrival, and early morning departure."

Capacity management involves various methods of controlling and limiting rooms supply. **For example:-** hotels will typically accept statistically supported number of reservations in excess of actual number of rooms available in an attempt to offset the potential impact of early checkouts, cancellations, and no shows. Capacity management (also called selective over booking) balances the risk of over selling guest rooms against the potential loss of revenue arising from room spoilage (rooms going unoccupied after the hotel stopped taking reservations for the given date).

DISCOUNT ALLOCATION

Discounting involves restricting the time period and producing minimum rooms available at reduced or discounted rate. For each discounted room type, reservations are requested at various available rates. The theory is that the sole of a perishable item at a reduced room rate is often better than no sale at all.

The primary objective of discount allocation is to protect enough remaining rooms at a higher rate to satisfy the projected demand for rooms at that rate, while at the same time filling rooms that would otherwise have remained unsold. This process is repeated for each rate level from rack rate on down. Implementing such as scheme requires a reliable mechanism for demand forecasting.

The second objective of limiting discount by room type is to encourage up selling. In an upwelling situation a reservation agent, or front desk agent, attempts to place a guest in a higher rated room. This technique requires a reliable estimate of price elasticity and the probability of upgrading. (Elasticity refers to the relationship between price and demand. If a small increase in price reduces a dramatic drop in demand, the market is said to be price elastic. If a small increase in price produces little or no effect on demand, the market is said to be price inelastic.)

DURATION CONTROL

Duration control places time constraints on accepting reservations in order to protect sufficient place for multiday request representing higher level of revenue which means that under yield management a reservation for a one night stay may be rejected even though it is available for the night.

For example:- if Wednesday is closed to selling out but adjacent nights are not, a hotel may want to optimized its revenue potential for last few remaining rooms on Wednesday by requiring multiday stays, even at discounted rate, rather than accepting reservations for Wednesday only. Similarly, if the hotel is projected to be close to capacity Tuesday, Wednesday and Thursday, then accepting a 1 night stay during any of those days may be detrimental to the hotels overall room revenue since it may block occupancy on the others day. Hotels facing such situations may require that reservations for projected full occupancy periods must be for more than 1 night.

These strategies may be combining for example:- duration control may be combined with discount allocation .A three night stay may be available for discount, while a one night stay may require the rack rate. It must be cautioned, though, that using these strategies must not be apparent to the guest. It would be difficult to explain to a guest why he/she must stay 3 nights to get a Discounts Rate if he/she wants to stay only 1 night. Proper use of revenue management relies on Selling; it never divulges the revenue management strategy being used.

Measuring Yield

Yield management is designated to measure revenue achievement. One of the principal computations involved in yield management is the hotels yield statistic. The yield statistics is a ratio of actual room revenue generated by the potential room revenue. Potential room revenue is the amount of money that would be received if all the rooms are sold at their respective rack rates.

Potential revenue can be determined in more than 1 way. Some properties calculate their potentials revenue as the amount that would be earned if all rooms were sold at the double occupancy rate. Other properties calculate their potential revenue by taking into account the %age mix of rooms normally sold at both single and double occupancy. The second method results in lower total potential revenue figure, since single rooms are assumed to be sold at less than double rooms. In fact while it is unlikely that a hotel will attain potential that is based on 100% double occupancy (1st method), a hotel using the second method may actually be able to exceed its potential if demand for double rooms exceeds sales mix projections.

Since the hotel yield statistic will vary with the method used, once a preferred method has been chosen, it should be used consistently. The second method (using both single and double occupancy) is illustrated in the formulas that follow. For hotels using the 1st method (based on 100% double occupancy), formulas 1,3,4 and 5 are not applicable, for such hotel, the potential average double rate (formula 2) will be the same as the potential average rate(formula 5).

The mathematical competition required:

FORMULA 1

It means that all rooms both single as well as double are sold for single occupancy or to one person.

$$\text{Potential average single rate} = \frac{\text{Single room revenue}}{\text{Number of rooms}}$$

FORMULA 2

It means all rooms both single as well as double are sold for double occupancy. An extra bed is added in each single room to be occupied by two persons.

$$\text{Potential average double rate} = \frac{\text{Double room revenue}}{\text{Number of rooms}}$$

FORMULA 3

The rooms occupied by more than one person are termed as Multiple Occupancy. It is important to know about multiple occupancy because it indicates sales mix and helps balance rates with future occupancy demand.

$$\text{Multiple occupancy percentage} = \frac{\text{Rooms occupied with multiple occupancy} \times 100}{\text{Total occupied rooms}}$$

FORMULA 4

As it has been discussed that hotel can sell a room with single occupancy and the same room can be sold with double occupancy irrespective whether the room is a single room or a double room.

$$\text{Rate Spread} = \frac{\text{Potential average double rate}}{\text{Potential average single rate}}$$

FORMULA 5

Potential average rate is the rate which is derived keeping in view the multiple occupancy percentage, rate spread and potential average single rate.

$$\text{Potential average rate} = \frac{(\text{Multiple occupancy percentage} \times \text{Rate spread})}{(\text{Potential average single rate})}$$

FORMULA 6

The percentage of actual rate and potential average rate is termed as Rate Achievement Factor (AF). It is also termed as rate potential. The actual average rate is divided by potential average rate and multiplies by 100.

$$\text{Rate achievement factor} = \frac{\text{Average room rent} \times 100}{\text{Potential average rate}}$$

FORMULA 7

An important element in Yield management is the maximum return or maximum profits or yield.

$$\text{Yield} = \frac{\text{Rooms nights sold} \times \text{Actual room rate} \times 100}{\text{Rooms nights available} \times \text{Potential average rate}}$$

FORMULA 8

The same yield can be achieved by either by increasing the tariff and the percentage of occupancy can go down or by increasing the percentage of occupancy and then the average tariff can come down.

$$\text{Identical yield occupancy} = \frac{\text{Current occupancy percentage} \times \text{ARR} \times 100}{\text{Proposed average room rent}}$$

FORMULA 9

The equivalent yield can be used when management wants to know what other combinations of room rate and occupancy percentage provides equivalent net revenue.

$$\text{Equivalent Yield} = \frac{\text{Current contribution margin} \times 100}{\text{Revised contribution Margin}}$$

NUMERICAL

Hotel XYZ has 500 rooms and average room rent earned is Rs.3000 per room. It is operating at 70% occupancy. The hotel has 250 single rooms with one bed only and 350 double rooms with two beds. The room tariff is as follows:

Single room tariff sold to one person = Rs 4000

Single room sold to two persons = Rs. 5000

Double room tariff sold to two persons = Rs.6000

Double room tariff sold to one person = Rs.4500

Solve It.

Breakeven Analysis

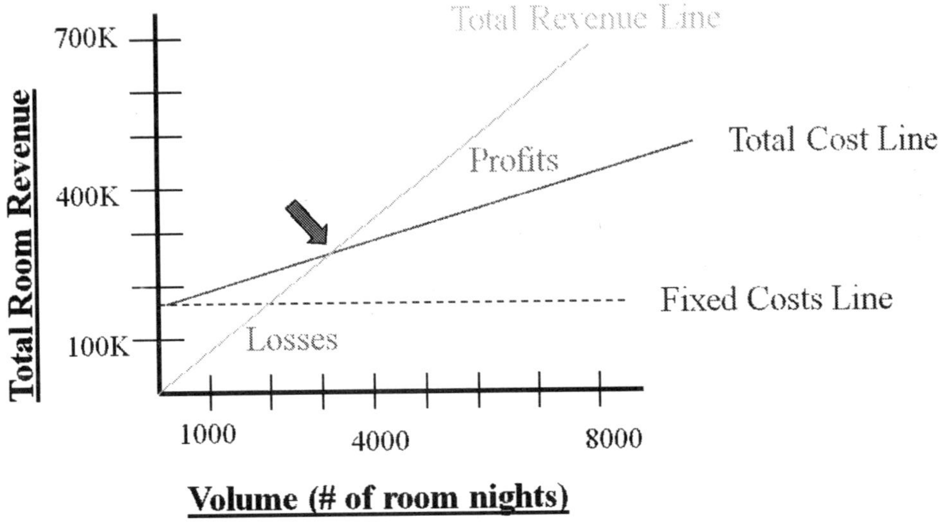

The analysis is done by the management to see that the loss in revenue earned from the room division is offset by the revenue earned from non room revenue earning departments or not.

Total Fixed Costs

To calculate the breakeven point for a given time period, a manager must first be able to calculate the total fixed costs that the hotel will incur. Total fixed costs are the sum of all the expenses that a hotel must pay for during a time period that will no fluctuate because of occupancy.

Typical fixed costs may include mortgage and insurance expenses, managers' salaries and benefits, property taxes, the payroll and benefits expenses of the least number of employees that must work even if the hotel has no guests, and the expenses of the utilities that must be maintained even if the hotel has zero occupancy (e.g., such as maintaining a minimum amount of heat to keep water pipes from freezing in the Winter).

With each of these aforementioned expenses, the amount of the expense will not deviate regardless of how many or how few guestrooms are sold.

Variable Costs

The next step is that a hotel manager must calculate the variable costs associated with selling each unit, in this case a guestroom. Variable expenses are deemed "variable" because they are only incurred if a room is sold or used.

If the guestroom remains vacant for the night, there are no variable costs that the hotel must pay for; any required costs associated with maintaining a non-used guestroom would be considered a fixed cost.

Variable costs for guestrooms will typically include the expense of labor and supplies to service the room after use (e.g., room attendant labor, chemicals, amenities, and utility expense), the labor, chemical and utility expense associated with servicing the guestroom's linens, the expense of the utilities associated with the guest's occupancy (e.g., electricity, water, heat, etc.), and

The guestroom's fare share contribution towards a capital budget for replacing furniture, fixture, and equipment in the guestroom every 3-7 years as part of a regularly scheduled refurbishment.

Selling Price

It is no surprise that hotels set the minimum selling price for each guestroom at or above the variable expenses for each guestroom. Failure to do so would be foolish and lead to assured deeper financial loss with every room sold.

But the room price must also reflect its contribution towards supporting the hotel's total fixed costs. Knowing the total fixed costs for the entire hotel and the variable costs associated with each sold guestroom, when coupled with the average selling price,

A hotel manager can easily calculate the breakeven point for the hotel, both in terms of number of guestrooms that must be sold but also in guestroom revenue that must be generated, in order for the hotel to realize a point of profitability.

ELEMENTS OF YIELD MANAGEMENT

There are 5 elements of yield management:

1. Group reservations
2. FIT (Free Individual Travelers) reservations

3. Food and beverage sale
4. Convention and conference business
5. Special events

1. **Group reservations:** Group form the nucleus of room revenue and understanding group booking trends and requirement is critical to yield management. When a request comes for a group reservation the following point need to be desired.
   - Does the group request fit into the hotels strategy for the period?
   - Are there other groups who are interested in the same period?
   - What meetings space will the group require?
   - What impact will this group have on booking additional group business for the same dates?
   - Do the fib functions include catered events or will the group use the hotel restaurants?
   - What revenue can the hotel plan to earn for rooms, f&b, and others sources?

2. **FIT (Free Individual Travelers) reservations:** Transient rooms are those sold to free individual travelers. Transient business is usually booked closer to date of arrival than group business. A commercial hotel may book a majority of its group business 3-6 months before arrival but booked transient business only 1-3 weeks before arrival.

   At a resort hotel group booking may be established 1-2 years in advance, while transient business may be booked 3 months or so in advance. Here also, management needs to track the booking pace and lead time of transient business in order to how current reservations compare with historical and anticipated trends. This leads to more complex subject of transient room pricing.

   In order to maximize room revenue, front office managers may decide to classify rooms by their locations, desirability, or size and charge more for better rooms. Rooms those are small, near noisy corridors, unrenovated or that offer poor views may be consider less desirable and be classified as standard rooms to be assigned the lowest rates. More desirable rooms may be classified as deluxe and have higher rates.

3. **Food and beverage sale:** Food and beverage activities, especially catering for functions, receptionsetc. Generate revenue independently such groups normally do not take up rooms in the hotel.

The hotel should book such groups who also need catering services such as breakfast, lunch and dinner service etc. along with conference rooms and other function facilities so as to get revenue from accommodation as well as food and beverage.

Special packages can be made for and offered to such groups. Cooperation and coordination between departments is necessary to maximize revenue from all revenue centres also, certain market segment have a tendency to purchase more food and beverage than others and this factor must be considered to determine which is the most profitable customer to offer the reservation is .for e.g.:-groups are usually on an inclusive tariff, whereas business guest may use in house food and beverage outlets.

4. **Convention and conference business:** These can have a drastic effect on yield management strategies of the hotel. Even if the hotel is not in the immediate of the convention, transient guest and smaller groups displayed by the convention may book at the hotel due to room availability.

   When this is the case, the front office manager should be aware of the convention and demand for guestrooms it is creating in the area. If the demand is substantial, transient and group rate should reflect this fact to take full advantage of the opportunity.

   Conventions may also make the trend analysis of group and transient room sales invalid. If the booking pace of either group or transient room sale alters significantly the FOM should immediately investigate the matter. An increase in demand could indicate the convention in the area or a large booking at a competitor. A decrease could indicate a major cancellation at a competitor, which is now reducing its regular pricing to fill guestrooms.

5. **Special events:** Special events such as concerts, festivals and sporting events are held in or near the hotel. The hotel may be able to take advantage of this by controlling discounts or requiring a minimum length of stay – say during Christmas etc. guests wishing to stay over Christmas may be require guaranteeing 4-5 day minimum stay.

   Similarly, rooms discount will be eliminated during this high demand period. Also, prepaid or nonrefundable packages may be put in place to guarantee the anticipated revenues. Both discounts and minimum lengths of stay should be managed carefully so the hotel does not loose frequent guests.

Low Demand Tactics

During periods of low demand, don't just sell the room based on price, sell the value and benefits associated with the hotel, its amenities, location, and relationships.

1. Offer more packages that bundle ancillary services and amenities with the guestroom. These may include free movies, discounts to local attractions, shopping coupons to nearby stores, welcome gifts, or food and beverage offerings. The goal is to create greater perceived value for the price paid.
2. Keep discounted rate plans open, even if at a higher rate in peak seasons. Encourage upgrades and offer stay-sensitive price incentives.
3. Don't require minimum-night stay restrictions unless you are certain the hotel will sell out well before the arrival date. A minimum-night stay restriction is a tactic used to shift demand onto lower demand shoulder nights immediately before or after nights that will assuredly sell out.
4. Involve your front desk staff in generating business by offering them incentives for selling upgrades that generate higher room rates or for converting walk-in inquiries into reservations.

   Encourage front desk staff to occasionally participate in sales calls with experienced sales managers to learn what it takes to overcome resistance and close the deal.
5. Establish relationships with competitors for overflow referrals. Offer to accommodate their guests when they are sold out and offer to send them your overflow when you are overbooked.
6. Cross-market with other properties to sell "the location" instead of the brand. Remember that some locales are not necessarily perceived as destination locations; hence, when market occupancy increases for a geographic location, all hotels tend to benefit from this increased demand.
7. Establish a "don't let them leave practice", meaning give front desk personnel the rate ranges they need to ensure that a guest is not put off by rate hesitancy. This does not mean excessive discounting, but providing training that provides sensitivity and common sense.
8. Know the lowest rate acceptable at that given moment in the hotel based on variable costs. This means that Management must know the break-even point in its hotel. To calculate the breakeven point a manager

must know both the variable costs and fixed costs associated with each hotel room. Please see the associated article in this issue of TRC that thoroughly explains how to calculate the breakeven point.

High Demand Tactics

What should you do when there is high demand for guestrooms in order to maximize revenue? Here are ten steps to consider implementing when projected occupancy is expected to be 85% or higher.

1. Close deep discounts off of rack rate but continue to honor mandatory discounts such as AAA, AARP, and government/military rates. But recognize a Manager's Special at a 20% discount could be a good business decision to fill those last 5 rooms.
2. Use minimum length of stay restrictions carefully.
3. Reduce group allocations immediately at the cut-off date if not picked up according to room block agreements. The cutoff date is typically 14 or 21 days prior to a group's scheduled arrival.
4. Stop accepting 4 p.m. or 6 p.m. non-guaranteed reservations.
5. Apply stricter guarantee/cancellation policies. Consider accepting only direct billing guarantees and credit card guaranteed reservations with 24-hour or 48-hour cancellation requirements.
6. Raise rates to be consistent with your competition. This of course means you must know and track what your nearest competitors are selling their guestrooms for. Smith Travel Research STAR reports on your "campest" (competitive set) will be invaluable in this regard.
7. Evaluate and possibly raise rates for all packages, or limit their availability on certain days.
8. Save suites/executive room types for guests who pay non-discounted rates or who are highest tier members of your brand's loyalty reward program.
9. Don't automatically eliminate sell-through reservations, as a multi-night stay that coincides with a high demand night could net a week-long stay. Look carefully at the recent history of no-shows and cancellations to determine this.
10. Double check all corporate and credit card guarantees so you can be certain to fill all those rooms and will experience minimal slippage.

QUESTIONNAIRE

1. What are the goals of yield management?
2. Why is communication between the various revenue centers important to the successful implementation of revenue management?
3. What are the importance and limitations of using historical data when planning revenue management strategies?
4. What might be the impacts of closing discount rates when business is down?
5. What role does booking pace plays in yield management?
6. What is a wash factor and how does it affect revenue management?
7. Why is transient displacement analysis so important to determine whether to accept a group reservation?
8. What is difference between marginal cost and fixed cost?
9. What does the equivalent occupancy equation considered that the identical yield equation does not?
10. Should a group reservation be accepted or rejected solely on the basis of its effect on room revenue, why or why not?
11. What are the several tactics that may be appropriate to take when room demand is low?
12. What are the several tactics that may be appropriate to take when room demand is high?
13. What is the hurdle rate? How it is used in revenue management
14. What avail-ability strategies are there to work with yield management?
15. Front office manager of XYZ hotel has the following information:

    Total no of rooms: 500

    Occupancy:80%

    Rack rate: Rs.3500

    175 rooms sold@Rs.3000

    125 rooms sold @ Rs.2700

    100 rooms sold @ Rs.2500

    Calculate Yield Percentage.

25

TIMESHARE AND VACATION OWNERSHIP

- INTRODUCTION
- USES OF TIMESHARE
- TYPES OF TIMESHARE
- ADVANTAGES AND DISADVANTAGES
- RESORT CONDOMINIUM INTERNATIONAL
  - _ RCI POINTS
  - _ RCI WEEKS
- HOW TO IMPROVE TIMESHARE CONCEPT IN INDIAN GOVERNMENT

INTRODUCTION

A time share is a property with a particular form of ownership or use rights. These properties are typically resort condominium units, in which multiple parties hold rights to use the property, and each sharer is allotted a period of time (typically one week and almost always the same time every year) in which they may use the property. Units may be on a partial ownership, lease, or "right to use" basis, in which the sharer holds no claim to ownership of the property. A timeshare is a property or the right to use a property, typically a resort condominium unit, in which multiple parties have rights, such as the right-to-use. The notion of a timeshare was originally created in Europe in the 1960s. A ski resort developer in the French Alps marketed his resort by encouraging guests to "stop renting a room" and instead "buy the hotel". The timeshare concept was quickly embraced by developers' worldwide, boosting sales of surplus condominium units at a time when the resort industry was depressed. Due to the promise of timeshares for exchange, timeshares or "vacation ownership" often sell regardless of their deeded resort (most timeshares are deeded into a certain resort site). What is not often disclosed is that all timeshares differ in trading power. If a timeshare is in Hawaii or Southern California it will exchange extremely well, however, those areas are some of the most expensive in the world. The vast majority of timeshares trade through two international exchange companies; Interval international and RCI. Critics contend timeshares are often overpriced, especially in places such as Mexico and Florida where almost every resort offers timeshare. As such, timeshares are unique among real estate assets in that buyers are almost certain to save significant money if the owners travel annually.

The timeshare concept has in recent years been embraced by many lodging companies, including category leaders Starwood, Hyatt, Hilton, Marriott, and Disney. Timeshares are an extremely profitable segment for such companies. The timeshare segment is expected to provide continued revenue and profit growth through 2030, despite an expected slowdown in traditional hotel operations. Being once known as the travel vehicle of the future timeshares will now only become more expensive as they enter the American mainstream.

The first hotel timeshare in the US was the Hilton Hale Kaanapali on the Island of Maui in Hawaii. Time share ownership is not the same as real estate ownership, and real estate brokers do not typically handle timeshares. There are many companies and websites which specialize in reselling time-shares. Be sure to research the company to be sure they can do the job.

USES OF TIME SHARE

Time share is business model whereby a company owning property, typically resort condominiums, sells small time slices of property to customers. Time share buyers:

- Use their usage time
- Rent out their owned usage
- Give it as a gift
- Exchange internally within the same resort or resort group
- Exchange externally into thousands of other timeshare resorts
- Assign their usage time to the point system to be exchanged for airline tickets, hotels, travel packages, cruises, amusement park tickets,
- Instead of renting all their actual usage time, rent part of their points without actually getting any usage time and use the rest of the points,
- Rent more points from either the internal exchange entity or another owner to get a larger unit or more vacation time or at a better location,
- Save or move points from one year to another.

Some developers, however, may limit which of these options are available at their properties.

Timeshare owners can elect to stay at their resort during the prescribed period, which varies depending on the nature of their ownership. In many resorts, they can rent out their week or give it as a gift to friends and family.

Timeshares offer owners the possibility of exchanging their week, either independently or through several exchange agencies, to stay at one of the thousands of other resorts worldwide. There are many exchange agencies, of which the two largest are Resort Condominiums International and Interval International. They have resort affiliate programs and members can only exchange to affiliate resorts. It is most common for a resort to be affiliated with only one of the larger exchange agencies, but it isn't rare to find a dual affiliate resort. Together they have over 7,000 resorts. The timeshare resort one purchases determines which of the major exchange companies can be used to make exchanges. RCI and II charge a yearly membership fee and fees for when they find an exchange. They also bar members from renting weeks for which they already have exchanged.

Timeshare owners can also exchange their timeshare through independent timeshare exchange companies. Dial an Exchange, Trading Places, Hawaii

Timeshare Exchange; Platinum Interchange, The San Francisco Exchange, Timex and Redweek.com are the main independent exchange companies. Owners can exchange with these independent exchange without needing the resort to have a formal affiliation agreement with the companies.

Timeshare owners may also arrange a direct exchange. This requires locating a timeshare owner with the location and weeks both mutually desire. This form of exchange is rare but since it can save in exchange fees it is often sought after. Several bulletin boards have been created to help timeshare owners meet others and swap.

Timeshares take different forms depending on the seller. The vast majority consist of one week of ownership, i.e. 1/52 year, but some developers sell point based systems that are a different form of vacation currency that allow hotel stays, car rentals, and stays at large networks of resorts.

TYPES OF TIME SHARE

Deeded vs. Right to Use

A major difference in types of timeshare ownership is that between deeded and right to use contracts.

With deeded contracts the use of the timeshare resort is usually divided into week long increments and these are sold as fractional ownership and are real property. As with any other piece of real estate the owner may use his or her week, rent his or her week, give it away, leave it to his or her heirs or sell the week to another prospective buyer. While this form of ownership can offer additional security to the owner as a form of physical ownership, deeded timeshare ownership can be as complex as outright property ownership in that the structure of deeds varies according to local property laws. Leasehold deeds are common and offer ownership for a fixed period of time after which the ownership reverts to the Freeholder. Occasionally, leasehold deeds are offered in perpetuity however many do not convey ownership of the land but merely the apartment or 'unit' of accommodation.

With right to use, the timeshare purchaser has the right to use the property in accordance with the contract but at some point the contract ends and all rights revert to the property owner. In other words, the right to use contract grants the right to use the resort for a specific number of years. In many countries there are severe limits on foreign property ownership, so this is a common method for developing timeshare resorts in countries such as Mexico. Disney Vacation Club is also sold as a right to use. Care should be taken with this form of ownership as the right to use often takes the form of 'club membership' or right to use the reservation system. Where the reservation system is owned by a Company not in the control of the owners, the right of use may be lost with the demise of the controlling Company.

Fixed Week Ownership

The most basic unit is a fixed week; the resort will have a calendar enumerating the weeks roughly starting with the first calendar week of the year. An owner may own a deed to use a unit for a single specified week. For example, week 26 normally includes the fourth of July holiday's week 51, Christmas and so on. If an owner owned Week 26 at a resort he or she could use that week every year.

Floating Week Ownership

Sometimes units are sold as floating weeks. The ownership will be specific on how many weeks the owner owns and from which weeks the owner may select for the owner's stay. An example of this may be a floating summer week where the owner may request any week during the summer season, generally weeks 22 through 36. In this example there would be competition for prime holidays such as the weeks of Memorial Day, Fourth of July, and Labor Day. The weeks when schools may still be in session would not be so high in demand. Some floating contracts exclude major holidays so they may be sold as fixed weeks.

Rotating/Flex Week Ownership

Some are sold as rotating weeks, commonly referred to as *flex* weeks. In an attempt to give all owners a chance for the best weeks, the weeks are rotated forward or backward through the calendar, so in year 1 the owner may have use of week 25, then week 26 in year 2, and then week 27 in year 3. This method give each owner a fair opportunity for prime weeks, but it is not flexible.

Vacation Clubs

Major international hotel chains such as Hilton, Accor, and Marriott have introduced their own Vacation Ownership Programs, which are based on point systems. The share of membership sold is either deeded or with right to use the club's services for a certain number of years.

There are also Vacation Clubs that may own units in multiple resorts in different locations, offering services to a private customer base for a sense of "exclusivity". Some clubs consist only of individual weeks at other developer's resorts. Vacation clubs cater to a wide range of economic backgrounds and income levels.

Points Programs

Resort based points programs are also sold as deeded and as right to use. Points programs annually give the owner an amount of points equal to the level of ownership. The owner in a points program can then use these points to make travel arrangements within the resort group. Many points programs are affiliated with large resort groups offering a large selection of options for destination. Many resort point programs provide flexibility from the traditional week stay. Resort point program members, such as world mark by whydham may request from the entire available inventory of the resort group.

A point's program member may often request fractional weeks as well as full or multiple weeks' stays. The number of points required to stay at the resort will vary based on a points chart. The points chart will allow for factors such as:

- The popularity of the resort;
- The size of the accommodations;
- The number of nights;
- The popularity of the season;
- And the specific nights requested.

SIZES OF TIMESHARE UNITS

Timeshare properties tend to be apartment-style units ranging in size from studio units (with room for two) to three and four-bedroom units. These larger units can comfortably house large families. Timeshare units normally include fully equipped kitchens with a dining area, dishwasher, televisions, VCRs and more. It is not uncommon to have washers, and dryers either in the unit or easily accessible on the resort. Kitchens are equipped to the size of the unit, so that a unit that sleeps four should have at least four glasses, plates, forks, knives, spoons, and bowls so that all four guests can sit and eat at once.

Timeshare units are usually listed by how many the unit will sleep and how many the unit will sleep privately.

- Sleeps 2/2 would normally be a one bedroom or studio
- Sleeps 6/4 would normally be a two bedroom with a sleeper sofa

Sleep privately refers to the number of guests who will not have to walk through another guest's sleeping area to use a restroom. Timeshare resorts tend to be strict on the number of guests per unit. Unit size can affect demand at a given resort where a two-bedroom unit may be in higher demand than a one-bedroom unit at the same resort. The same does not hold true comparing resorts in different locations. A one bedroom with a great location may still be in higher demand than a resort with less demand. An example of this may be a one bedroom at a great beach resort compared to a two bedroom unit at a resort located inland from the same beach.

MONETORY ADVANTAGES AND DISADVANTAGES

Bid adieu to pricey hotels when vacationing and lock in predictable payments by buying a timeshare. Even if the cost of lodgings and amenities go up, your timeshare payment won't budge. Save additional money by making your timeshare a headquarters for meals and entertaining. Such are the advantages of timeshare ownership.

On the other hand, sinking your cash into a timeshare locks you in for the duration of your contract. Over time, maintenance costs could rise in direct proportion to the rate at which the property is aging. Lose your job or your home or experience catastrophic financial or health problems and you could find yourself stuck in a market that's glutted with timeshare for sale. The number of foreclosed timeshares on the market tends to follow the same trend as foreclosed residential properties.

CONVENIENCE ADVANTAGES AND DISADVANTAGES

Timeshare properties tend to be located in places that are most desirable for vacationers, so you probably won't experience inconveniences if you decide to buy a timeshare. Make your plans, pack up and fly off to a retreat that's located in close proximity to the shopping, recreational and entertainment facilities you prefer.

You can't be expected to check out every property listed in the timeshare catalog, so if you like switching destinations, you may not find out about an ill-managed property until you're there. You might get a credit for another stay if you find yourself at a less-than-desirable property, but you can't get back lost time, nor can some people easily dismiss the memories of a vacation gone badly.

OWNERSHIP ADVANTAGES AND DISADVANTAGES

Some folks love amassing property, but ownership has some disadvantages. On the plus side, you can rent out your timeshare and even turn a profit if you've a mind to do so. You may even be able to take advantage of the marketing skills of your property's holding company. You can also bequeath a timeshare to your heirs. But if forking over $10,000 for the right to pick only one or two dates during the calendar year when your family can occupy the residence doesn't sound like a great advantage to you, you might wish to rethink the idea of owning a timeshare. If your timeshare holding company experiences financial errors, efforts to maintain the property you own could go by the wayside.

SOCIAL ADVANTAGES AND DISADVANTAGES

The average timeshare owner is 49 years old, married, well educated and earning $70,000 a year, so social advantages for the 50-something demographic are promising. Hang out with like-minded people, hit the golf links or beach with contemporaries and cement friendships while on vacation at your timeshare. But if you're a vacationer longing for quirky, new or unusual vacation experiences and challenges and you adore meeting new people from all walks of life, the staid, predictable social environment of a timeshare could quickly become boring.

INVESTMENT ADVANTAGES AND DISADVANTAGES

You decide to invest $10,000 in return for the use of a timeshare one week each year for life. How much sense does that make? You put down a cash deposit and pay off your investment in seven years, on average, while you kick in a monthly assessment fee on top of the mortgage obligation. Sure, you can deduct the interest on your loan, but asking a broker to show you a comparable investment with a greater yield could open your eyes to other options. Take a tip from the Better Business Bureau, and separate the idea of real estate investments from timeshare ownership. The first truly is an investment. The second is a pre-paid vacation accommodation.

GENERAL DISADVANTAGES

While buying a timeshare has its advantages, there are many, many disadvantages to doing so. However, we have noticed that we would have probably been better off not buying it at all. Here are some reasons why:

1. **Timeshares are not very good for spontaneous traveling, especially in high season**. Let's say you are feeling like you really need a vacation and go to your timeshare and want to find out what's available. Sure, there might be a couple of places here and there but you won't have much selection. You might have to end up renting a regular hotel at the place you

really want to go to instead of going through the hassle of going to wherever is available through the timeshare.

2. **There aren't as many resorts available as they made you think**. When you buy a timeshare they dazzle you with the possibility of traveling all over the world, telling you a huge amount of resorts. You think, "Wow, so many? Surely I will be able to just go anywhere!" Not so fast. While some timeshare purchasers might be world travelers, most of us aren't. Most of us will never go to Africa or Asia and we have to simply stay local most years. Do not let them impress you with tales of world travel unless you are already doing it.
3. **Hidden Fees**. When they tell you how much you are going to pay a month, you aren't counting in all the other fees. Sure, they might tell you in passing but they are obviously going to highlight the advantages. You have to pay a maintenance fee every year or every two years ranging from $300-$600. If you belong to RCI, you must pay a $99 yearly fee. Every time you go to a resort you must pay a fee depending on your stay. If you are staying for less than a week most likely you will have to pay a housekeeping fee and they don't even clean your room every day. Some resorts charge you to park your car and for the use of a safe deposit, even if you didn't use it. If you want to give your reservation as a gift to someone else, you must pay $50 for a "guest certificate". All of these fees you will continue to incur in even after you finish buying your timeshare and even if you barely use it.
4. **Resell Values are horrible**. You buy your timeshare and you think, "Well, if it doesn't work, I can always sell it." Wrong. Yes, you can sell it but the resell values are awfully low. If you haven't finished paying chances are you will not get enough to pay off your debt and if you have finished paying it, you will not get your investment back. There are many websites that claim to help you resell your timeshare but they either want money up-front or a huge commission or both!
5. **They are too expensive**. If you purchase a timeshare from a specific resort, chances are you are paying too much for it. If you absolutely need to buy a timeshare do it from one of those reselling websites or from eBay.
6. **They will send you to collections too quickly**. My husband and I moved twice after purchasing the timeshare and we changed our address with RCI but not with the actual timeshare. We didn't know when we were supposed to pay the maintenance fee so it was past due since they sent us a letter to our old address. All of sudden I receive a collections letter and I called my timeshare. I asked them why I hadn't received a phone call from them and I was informed that that is why they hired a collection agency, so they wouldn't have to make phone calls. I understand I made a mistake, but come on, I am paying for an expensive time share here, and shouldn't their customer service be a little bit more cooperative? The bank where I

am paying off my car has called me a couple of times, but my timeshare can't.

7. **The interest rates are up to the roof**. I have pretty decent credit and I got approved for the loan immediately. However, they are charging me a 16% interest rate. When we purchased it we were so excited we believed them when they told us that if we sent extra payments through the years we would finish paying it quicker. It seemed to me we were not the only ones that had to pay such a high interest rate.
8. **They won't let you cancel your reservation after 24 hours**. Once you reserve your room and 24 hours go by you can forget about getting your money or points back if you have to cancel. Your only hope is to transfer your reservation to someone else and that will cost you $50.
9. Many of these places are still "under construction". It doesn't happen all the time but many of these resorts aren't complete yet so they don't have everything that their webpage boasts. They don't let you know if the pool or Jacuzzi isn't working either.
10. **Even if you have "points" they aren't enough most of the time**. If you purchase a timeshare that includes a point system, they never end up being enough and they are always trying to sell you more. This is especially true if you are trying to vacation in high season.

If I had known a bit more about what timeshares entitle, I would have definitely not have purchased. Be careful and investigate before you make the same mistake.

GENERAL ADVANTAGES

If you are locking in a specific week every year, you know that you are getting away. By doing so, you know in advance when and where your vacation will take place. Everything is very certain. Most people rarely get away. It is far from being healthy. By paying in advance for your vacation and assuming you value your money, you will not let that time go to waste and you will actually get away.

Some plans allow you to exchange locations. Therefore, one year you can vacation in one destination and next year on a different continent. It is a nice way to see the world. You do not have to research hotels. It is all done for you.

By owning a timeshare, you more or less know your vacation costs. You have your fixed costs and an annual maintenance cost. By knowing your costs upfront, it removes a lot of the unknown and it makes it easier to budget your other expenses

You can use the week yourself or you can share it with your family and friends. If you see that you do not have the time to take vacation during a specific year, you can give the timeshare to your relatives and friends. How cool is that? By doing so you definitely become Mr. Popular.

Some timeshares from time to time will give you a bonus. An extra few days here or there can really make a big difference.

RESORT CONOMINIUM INTERNATIONAL (RCI)

Resort condominium international (RCI) is the registered international organization and is registered in 42 countries and has 325 timeshare companies as its member with 37,922 rooms worldwide. It has 140 resorts in north and south pacific and serves more than 7,50,000 owners worldwide. RCI is the global leader in leisure accommodation with access to about 4,00,000 leisure accommodation units in more than 100 countries. It has 30 vacation accommodation brands including vacation ownership condominiums, villas and cottages, fractional interest and private residence clubs etc. and worldwide offices.

RCI Provides Following Services

- Exchange services
- Rental programs
- Sales table programs
- Club servicing
- Global advisory services

RCI Weeks

- Owner buys seven days period to a specific home resort.
- Owner buys a fixed week or floating week booked within certain season based on the resort.
- Owner deposits time with RCI each year.
- Week exchanged for comparable week at another resort.

RCI Points

- World's first global based exchange offering for the timeshare industry, launched in 2000.
- Owner buys a fixed week or floating week booked with certain season based on resort, and cedes that inventory to RCI for the term of their membership for their points.
- Points allocated based on various factors (size of condominium, resort location, quality, season, duration, etc.).

- Flexibility to use points as desired (length of stay, season, resort).
- Use points for airline tickets, cruises, car rental, hotel rooms, etc.

Government and Industries Role to Improve the Timeshare Business in India:

It is the responsibility of both industry and government to insure growth in timeshare business through new investment and strong consumer safe guards. The industry must ensure self regulation, code of ethics in business conduct and overall excellence in product and services.

Government must take the following steps in order to have a manifolds growth in timeshare business and this can pay rich dividends keeping in view that it is the largest labor intensive industry in the world.

- Industry recognition
- Project and operation incentives
- Regulatory framework
- Selective infrastructural support
- Utilize industry potential to drive domestic tourism.

GLOSSARY OF COMMON TIMESHARE TERMS

Acceleration

The ability to use your vacation program more quickly (travel more) while shortening the length of the original program.

Appraisal

The estimated worth of a timeshare, expressed in terms of market value. Timeshare appraisals are not necessary for buying or selling a timeshare on the resale market and are often considered unreliable. Market value of a timeshare can be estimated by market value survey or the comparing of prices of similar timeshare listings on the resale market.

Arda (American Resort Development Association)

The leading organization based in the U.S. upholding professionalism and establishing Code of Ethics within the timeshare industry

Banking

The ability to save unused timeshare weeks to use later. Banked timeshare weeks can be exchanged for other locations and different timeshare weeks. Banking is sometimes called "space banking".

Biennial or EOY (Every Other Year)

Allows owners to travel every second year as opposed to every year

Check-in Date

Typically in the timeshare world check in days are Friday, Saturday and Sunday depending on the resort.

Closing Costs

Expenses at closing on a timeshare property including deed preparation for deeded timeshares, recording fees, administrative fees, escrow costs, and equity transfer for right-to-use timeshares

CRDA (Canadian Resort Development Association)

The leading organization based in Canada upholding professionalism and establishing Code of Ethics within the timeshare industry

Deed

This legal document demonstrates ownership rights with title to a timeshare property. Once a timeshare property is deeded the owner can bequeath, rent, or sell the timeshare just as an owner can do with traditional real estate properties.

Exchange

The ability to deposit your week into an exchange company (commonly referred to as "space-banking") and extract a week in another resort somewhere other than your home property.

Exchange Company

A company that coordinates the trading of timeshare weeks that timeshare owners deposit. There are two main timeshare exchange companies. These are Resort Condominiums International (RCI) and Interval International (II). RCI and II are affiliated with more than 5,000 resorts globally and enable a timeshare owner to trade his or her vacation week at a specific resort with another owner's vacation week at a different resort. This process gives timeshare owners worldwide travel possibilities.

Fee Simple

Owners can will their timeshare to anyone they choose

Fixed Unit

The timeshare owner has the same exact unit every year in the same timeshare resort.

Fixed Week

The timeshare owner has the timeshare during a specific numbered week of the calendar year, every year. Timeshare weeks are numbered sequentially from the first week of the calendar year to the last.

Floating Week

Depending on the timeshare resorts availability, the timeshare owner can use the timeshare during any week of the season purchased. If a timeshare week is in high-season, the owner can reserve any comparable week in the high-season that is available.

Fractional Ownership

Typically purchasing multiple weeks (often five) in a resort or condominium style of property. Often, but not always receiving one week per season with one for trading through an exchange company

Gold Crown Resort

The highest rating given by RCI for a timeshare resort which includes the highest of standards and meets all site requirements including available amenities.

Internal Exchange

A timeshare owner can exchange a timeshare week in the same timeshare resort or in another resort within a resort network under the same company ownership.

Interval

In timeshare ownership an interval is a measure of time representing one seven-day week in sequentially numbered weeks from 1 to 52 or 53.

Lease

These programs typically range from 20 to 99 years and eventually expire. They are often purchased in countries such as Mexico where deeds do not exist

Lockout

Normally a studio unit and a one bedroom unit (make up a two bedroom to sleep eight people) but can be separated to receive more travel but smaller units.

Maintenance Fee/ Dues

The yearly fee a timeshare owner pays the timeshare resort Management Company or homeowners association for timeshare property upkeep, insurance, utilities, and taxes.

Management Company

A company that manages daily operations of the timeshare resort for a yearly fee to timeshare owners or with funds received by the homeowners association.

Points/Credits

A numeric form of currency utilized in the timeshare world- Factors considered are unit size, seasons, location, amenities, etc. Points also offer flexibility in terms of shorter stays including nightly travel and various checks in dates.

RCI

Resort Condominiums International is one of the two main timeshare exchange companies.

Resale

A timeshare or vacation club being sold by the owner(s) after it was originally purchased from a developer.

Right-to-Use

A timeshare lease that generally expires after a said period of time-normally (RTU) programs range from about 20 -99 years and whatever is left can be willed, sold, or donated to whomever the owner chooses.

Season

Typically there are three colors for different travel times around the world. These seasons are harmonious with demand in each area. To travel high time is indicated by (red) to travel mid-season is (white) and to travel low season is (blue). With other travel clubs there can be other colored seasons as well.

Special Assessment

An additional fee over the yearly maintenance fee levied for special circumstances such as a major timeshare resort refurbishment.

Timeshare

The purchase or lease of a resort for an interval of time with the option to exchange for other time intervals at the same or a different resort. Timeshare ownership allows for affordable vacationing in that the timeshare owner only pays for an increment of time in contrast to full ownership of a vacation property.

Vacation Club

Also known as a holiday club, this is an organization which is unregulated by laws covering the sale of timeshares. Buyers need to be aware of companies that are less than reputable. A vacation club offers timeshare weeks to its members.

Vacation Ownership

A recent term as of late synonymous with the word timeshare. Often used by multi-destination clubs that is aligned with flexible points systems.

QUESTIONNAIRE

Q.1 Write detailed note on RCI & RCI Points.

Q.2 What are the issues and challenges which Time Share Hotels are facing in India ?

Q.3 Write a detailed note on role of government in promotions of time share hotel in India.

Q.4 What is the role of RCI in Timeshare hotels & resorts?

Q.5 How the Timeshare hotels business is different from other Hotels business?

Q6 What do you understand by timeshare hotels?

Q7 What are the different uses of timeshare?

Q8 How is timeshare different from hotel business?

Q9 Classify various types of timeshare in detail?

Q10.What are the type of accommodation offered by timeshare hotels?

26

FRENCH USED IN FRONT OFFICE OPERATION ADVANCE FRENCH

- COMMON SENTENCES
- COMMON SENTENCES & TERMS USED IN FRONT OFFICE DEPARTMENT

COMMON SENTENCES

Do you speak English?	*Parlez-vous anglais ?*	*Par - lay vooz ah(n)-glay?*
I speak a little French	*Je parle un peu français*	*Zhuh parl uhn peh frahn-say*
I'm here on vacation ... for work	*Je suis là pour les vacances* *... pour le travail*	*Zhuh swee lah poor vac-kahwnse* *... poor trav-eye*
I don't understand	*Je ne comprends pas*	*Zhuh nuh comp-rond pah*
Please speak slowly	*Parlez lentement, s'il vous plaît*	*Par-lay lawn-teh-mont, seal voo play*
How do you say ____ in French?	*Comment dit-on ____ en français?*	*Come-ahn deet-on ____ ahn frahn-say?*
Yes Yeah (informal)	Oui Ouais	*Wee* *Way*
No	*Non*	*No*
Where are the restrooms? Where is ______? ... the hotel? ... the hospital? ... the beach? ... the airport? ... the bank?	*Où sont les toilettes ?* *Où est _____ ?* *... l'hôtel?* *... l'hôpital?* *...la plage?* *... l'aéroport?* *... la banque?*	*Oo soh(n) lay twa-let?* *Oo ay _____ ?* *... low-tell?* *... low-pea-tahl?* *... lah plah-sheh?* *... lare-oh-pour?* *... lah bahn-kh*
Sorry to bother you...	*Excusez-moi de vous déranger...*	*Ek-sku-zay mwa duh voo day-rah(n)-zhay...*
...but I have a problem.	*...mais j'ai un problème*	*...may zhay uh(n) proh-blem.*
Can you help me?	*Pouvez-vous m'aider ?*	*Poo-vay voo meh - day?*
Would you take our/ my picture, please?	*Est-ce que vous prendriez notre/ma photo, s'il vous plaît?* *Prendriez-vous notre/ma photo, s'il vous plaît?*	*Esk-kuh voo pren-dray noh-tra/mah foh-toh, seal voo play?* *Pren-dray voo noh-tra/mah foh-toh, seal voo play?*
I would like . . .	*Je voudrais . . .*	*Zhuh voo dray . . .*
How much?	*Combien?*	*Cohm bee-e(n)?*
Do you take foreign [credit] cards?	*Est-ce que vous acceptez les cartes étrangères ?*	*Es-kuh vooz ack-sep-tay lay cartz ay-trahn-jer-ay?*

It's too expensive!	*C'est trop cher!*	*Say trohp reesh!*
I am looking for . . .	*Je cherche . . .*	*Zhuh shairsh . . .*
Here. It's here! *(there it is!)*	Ici. C'est là!	*Ee-see.* *Say lah!*
Let's go!	*Allez vous-en*	*Ah-lay vooz- ahn*
It's great! ... good ... bad ... terrible	*C'est chouette!* *... bon* *... mal* *... terrible*	*Say shwet!* *... bohn* *... mahl* *... tare-ee-bleh*
I have a headache ... stomach ache	*J'ai mal à la tête* *... au ventre/ au coeur*	*Zhay mahl deh teht* *... oh vahn-trah/ oh couhr*
Goodbye *(until we see each other again)(3)* Goodbye *(see you later/ see you at another hour/ later on the same day)* Goodbye *(forever/ I'm never going to see you again)*	*Au revoir* *À tout à l'heure* *Adieu*	*Ah reh-vwarh* *Ah toot ah luhr* *Ah-dyooh*

COMMON SENTENCES & TERMS USED IN FRONT OFFICE DEPARTMENT

- I'd like to reserve a room for three nights - Je voudrais réserver une chambre pour trois nuits.
- Is breakfast included in the price? - Est-ce que le petit déjeuner est compris dans le prix?
- We'd like to have a view of the mountains - On aimerait avoir une vue sur les montagnes.
- Do you have a room on the ground floor? - Vous avez une chambre au rez-de-chaussée?
- The shower is not working - La douche ne marche pas
- There is no hot water - Il n'y a pas d'eau chaude.
- Is the hotel far from the beach? - Est-ce que l'hotel est loin de la plage?
- Could you call me a taxi? - Pourriez-vous m'appeler un taxi?
- Could you recommend a good restaurant? - Pourriez-vous nous conseiller un bon restaurant?

- We're leaving at six tomorrow morning - Nous partons à six heures demain matin.
- Animals are accepted/allowed - Les animaux sont acceptés/animaux domestiques admis.
- We have Wifi access - On a un accès Wifi
- You can look up flight arrival and departure times on the television in the room - Vous pouvez consulter sur la télé de la chambre les tableaux des arrivées et des départs d'avions.
- Cancellations must be made one day before your expected date of arrival- Les réservations doivent être annulées 1 jour avant votre date d'arrivée prévue.
- There is a safe in the room or at reception - Il
- y a un coffre fort dans la chambre ou à la reception.
- Fast check-in and payment (procedure) - Enregistrement et règlement rapides
- Situated close to ... - Situé à deux pas de/situé proche de ...
- Situated in the heart of Paris - Situé dans le coeur de Paris
- Situated in a pedestrian precinct - Situé dans une rue pietonne
- Within easy walking distance of the Louvre Museum - possibilité de se rendre facilement à pied au Musee du Louvre
- Room service - service en chambre
- A soundproof room - une chambre insonorisée
- An air-conditioned room - une chambre climatisée
- Maintenance (cleaning) - l'entretien
- The lift - l'ascenseur
- Luggage - les bagages
- The bathroom - la salle de bains
- Towels - les serviettes
- The key to the room - la clé de la chambre
- An iron - un fer à repasser
- A hairdryer - un sèche cheveux
- A trouser press - une presse à pantaloon